T0301555

Environmental Regulation and Food Safety

Environmental Regulation and Food Safety

Studies of Protection and Protectionism

Edited by

Veena Jha

Edward Elgar
Cheltenham, UK • Northampton, MA, USA

International Development Research Centre
Ottawa • Cairo • Dakar • Montevideo • Nairobi • New Delhi • Singapore

Copublished by

Published by
Edward Elgar Publishing Limited
The Lypiatts
15 Lansdown Road
Cheltenham
Glos GL50 2JA
UK

Edward Elgar Publishing, Inc.
William Pratt House
9 Dewey Court
Northampton
Massachusetts 01060
USA

International Development Research Centre
PO Box 8500
Ottawa, ON K1G 3H9
Canada
www.idrc.ca / info@idrc.ca
ISBN 1-55250-185-X (ebook)

This book has been printed on demand to keep the title in print.

A catalogue record for this book
is available from the British Library

ISBN 978 1 84542 512 8

Typeset by Cambrian Typesetters, Camberley, Surrey

Contents

Acknowledgements

All consultants who have worked on this project are gratefully acknowledged for their contributions. Overall guidance to the project was provided by Mr René Vossenaar, Chief, Trade, Environment and Development, International Trade Division, UNCTAD. The project was coordinated by Dr Veena Jha. Administrative assistance to the project was provided by Ms Angela Thompson and Ms Jayashri Mahesh. Dr Jha also gratefully acknowledges the contribution of other UNCTAD staff members, especially Ms María Pérez-Esteve and Ms Eugenia Nunez for their valuable comments, indicating the sources of information, correcting factual inaccuracies and pointing out inconsistent arguments. Ms María Pérez-Esteve also coordinated the Central American section of the project. Dr Jha especially thanks IDRC for providing the financial assistance without which this project could never have been undertaken. Sandhya Pandey copy edited the book. All the errors that remain are, of course, the editor's own.

The views expressed in this book should not be attributed to UNCTAD or to its member states.

Contributors

Cerina Banu Issufo Mussa
Ministry of Industry, Trade (and Tourism), Mozambique

María Pérez-Esteve
Economic Affairs Officer, Agriculture and Commodities Division of the World Trade Organization (WTO)

Sophia Twarog
United Nations Conference on Trade and Development (UNCTAD)

Veena Jha
India programme coordinator of UNCTAD in New Delhi, affiliated to the International Trade Division of UNCTAD, Geneva

René Vossenaar
UNCTAD, Head, Trade, Environment and Development Branch, Division on Trade in Goods and Services and Commodities

Max Valverde
Professor of Law, National University of Costa Rica

Nimrod Nakisisa Waniala
Director, Private Sector Foundation, Trade Policy Capacity Building Project, Kampala, Uganda

The late **Eduardo Gitli**
Formerly a Coordinator, International Center on Economic Policy for Sustainable Development, National University of Costa Rica

Abbreviations

ACP	African, Caribbean and Pacific
AoA	Agreement on Agriculture
APEDA	Agricultural and Processed Food Products Export Development Authority (India)
APHIS	Animal and Plant Health Inspection Service (United States)
CAC	Codex Alimentarius Commission
CBTF	UNEP–UNCTAD Capacity Building Task Force on Trade, Environment and Development
CITES	Convention on International Trade in Endangered Species
COMESA	Common Market for Eastern and Southern Africa
CTE	Committee on Trade and Environment (WTO)
FAO	Food and Agriculture Organization
FDA	Food and Drug Administration (United States)
EC	European Community
EDB	Environmental Database (WTO)
GAP	Good Agricultural Practice
GATS	General Agreement on Trade in Services
GATT	General Agreement on Tariffs and Trade
GMP	Good Manufacturing Practices
HACCP	Hazard Analysis Critical Control Point
ICCAT	International Commission for the Conservation of Atlantic Tunas
IDRC	International Development Research Centre (Canada)
IPM	Integrated Pest Management
IPPC	International Plant Protection Convention
ISO	International Organization for Standardization
ITC	International Trade Centre
JITAP	Joint Integrated Technical Assistance Programme (ITC, UNCTAD and WTO)
KEPHIS	Kenya Plant Health Inspectorate Service
LDC	Least Developed Country
MAG	Ministry of Agriculture and Livestock (Costa Rica)
MRL	Maximum Residue Level
MTS	Multilateral Trading System
NEP	National Enquiry Point
NTB	Non-Tariff Barrier

OIE	Office International des Epizooties (International Office of Epizootics)
PPM	Process and Production Method
ppm	parts per million
R&D	Research and Development
SADC	Southern African Development Community
SCM	Subsidies and Countervailing Measures
SMEs	Small and Medium-sized Enterprises
SPS	Sanitary and Phytosanitary
TBT	Technical Barriers to Trade
TED	Turtle Excluder Device
TRIPS	Trade-Related Aspects of Intellectual Property Rights
UNBS	Uganda National Bureau of Standards
UNCTAD	United Nations Conference on Trade and Development
UNDP	United Nations Development Programme
UNEP	United Nations Environment Programme
UNIDO	United Nations Industrial Development Organization
USFDA	United States Food and Drug Administration
WHO	World Health Organization
WTO	World Trade Organization

Preface

The United Nations Conference on Trade and Development (UNCTAD), with the support of the International Development Research Centre (IDRC) in Canada, has implemented a technical cooperation project to help identify policies that can address constraints faced by developing countries, especially the least developed countries (LDCs), in responding to sanitary and phytosanitary (SPS) measures and environmental requirements in international markets. Studies were undertaken in three developing regions: South Asia, Eastern and Southern Africa and Central America. Sub-regional or national workshops were held in New Delhi, India (11–13 January 2001), San José, Costa Rica (20 August 2001) and Kampala, Uganda (13 September). These resulted in five scoping papers. The first paper discusses the main results of the project and some ideas for follow-up activities. The other four papers deal with three different regions and with organic agriculture and include three case studies. They are as follows:

Paper 2: regional scoping paper on South Asia (Bangladesh, India, Nepal and Sri Lanka)
Paper 3: regional scoping paper on Central America (Costa Rica in particular)
Paper 4: regional scoping paper on Eastern and Southern Africa (experiences of Kenya, Mozambique, the United Republic of Tanzania and Uganda)
Paper 5: scoping paper on organic agriculture (Costa Rica, India and Uganda).

This project was coordinated with similar activities by other intergovernmental organizations. For example, the New Delhi workshop was organized in cooperation with the World Bank. Similarly, the UNCTAD and the OECD secretariats coordinated activities under this project and the OECD project on 'The Development Dimension of Trade and Environment: Strengthening OECD and developing country co-operation to help developing country exporters meet environmental standards'.

UNCTAD's work in this area is in accordance with the Bangkok Plan of Action, which called upon UNCTAD to promote analysis and consensus building in full cooperation with other relevant organizations, so that issues that could potentially yield benefits to developing countries could be identified. This included 'examining the potential trade and developmental effects and opportunities of environmental measures, taking into account the concerns of developing countries, particularly regarding the potential effects on small and medium-sized enterprises' (paragraph 147, fourth bullet).

The project and workshop were also relevant in the context of the UNCTAD programmes on (a) 'Capacity Building for Diversification and Commodity-based Development' and (b) 'Technical Assistance and Capacity Building for Developing Countries, especially LDCs, and Economies in Transition in support of their participation in the WTO post-Doha work programme' (UNCTAD/RMS/TCS/1). This programme contains a specific 'window' on environment, including environmental/SPS requirements and market access for developing countries, particularly the least developed countries (LDCs).

In this book, the five papers have been combined. The first chapter provides a background to the overall project, the need, regional scope, the main issues, methodology and the main conclusions. The issues include the effect of trade standards on developing countries, costs of compliance, responses and policy implications. The next chapter provides details of the two main conventions regulating standards and world trade, the Agreement on Technical Barriers to Trade (TBT) and the Agreement on the Application of Sanitary and Phytosanitary Measures (SPS). In subsequent chapters, the trade conditions for several products in various developing countries are analysed according to the effects, cost and responses in those countries. These experiences are then summarized under the different issues, and general conclusions are drawn regarding their effects and the lessons that can be learned from them.

1. Introduction

Veena Jha

BACKGROUND

Environmental, health and sanitary standards required by developed countries are sometimes perceived as new non-tariff barriers to trade by developing countries. Environment-related trade measures can take several forms, such as technical standards and regulations, certain sanitary and phytosanitary (SPS) measures, packaging regulations, labelling requirements, non-automatic licences, quantitative restrictions, taxes and charges, as well as informal (non-government) requirements.

The WTO secretariat has compiled a database of environment-related notifications. The complexity of the concept of environmental standards is evident from the ambiguity in the categories of these notifications. The WTO secretariat notes that environment-related notifications can broadly be grouped in two categories. The first consists of those notifications that list environmental or related factors as the principal objective for notifying. The provisions of the GATT 1994 and the WTO Agreements that refer explicitly or are generally regarded as related to environmental objectives include the following:[1]

Annex 2 paragraph 12 of the Agreement on Agriculture (AoA);
Article 5 paragraph 2 of the Agreement on the Application of Sanitary and Phytosanitary Measures (SPS);
Articles 2 and 5 of the Agreement on Technical Barriers to Trade (TBT);
Article XIV (b) of the General Agreement on Trade in Services (GATS);
Article 27.2 of the Agreement on Trade-Related Aspects of Intellectual Property Rights (TRIPS);
Article XX (b) and (g) of the GATT 1994.

The second category includes notifications 'that are not primarily environment-related, but include reference to environment-related aspects'. For instance, notifications containing the text of regional trade agreements may include a clause for a specific environmental provision. In such cases, reference is made only to the environmental objective or criteria. The notifications might comprise, and usually do contain, broader objectives or other criteria.

The difficulties of defining environmental standards are illustrated by this classification procedure which includes several kinds of standards which may be environment-related. Obviously, if another researcher were to look at these notifications, environment-related standards could be defined more broadly or more narrowly. (For further reference to the WTO Environmental Database and the notification procedure please see Chapter 8, Annex 1.)

Most case studies carried out under the project refer to SPS measures. It is difficult to draw a clear distinction between SPS measures for environmental objectives and SPS measures for food safety purposes. In a broad sense, since all SPS measures are taken for the safety and protection of human, animal and plant health, they can be considered environmental measures. In practice, however, only part of the SPS measures are directly related to the environment. A large part of the measures examined in the case studies refer to food safety issues. However, in many cases, SPS measures taken for food safety objectives by the importing country are the result of environmental problems in the exporting countries. The African case studies on fishery products provide several examples (such as fish poisoning being a result of pesticide residues in Lake Victoria).

Whatever the classification of such measures, the studies clearly indicate that they may add to the difficulties many producers and exporters already face in maintaining existing export markets or penetrating new ones. Experience shows that large producers, particularly in the more advanced developing countries, are generally more likely to be able to cope with environmental requirements. However, UNCTAD research has indicated that small and medium-sized enterprises (SMEs) and producers, particularly in the least developed countries (LDCs), may face significant problems.[2]

Food standards, restrictions on the use of certain substances, and other SPS measures can have significant effects on market access for developing countries. A recent World Bank study predicts that the implementation of a new aflatoxin standard in the European Union will have a negative impact on African exports of cereals, dried fruits and nuts. On the basis of an econometric model, it is estimated that the EU standard, which will reduce health risk by approximately 1.4 deaths per billion a year, will decrease African exports of these products to the EU by 64 per cent or US$670 million, compared with the exports likely when an international standard is used.[3] UNCTAD's Least Developed Countries Report, 1998, provides a series of examples of LDCs, such as Bangladesh, Madagascar, Mozambique, Nepal and Uganda, which have already suffered significant export losses on account of the problems they face in responding to environmental, health and sanitary requirements in developed country markets.

The European Union's measures and regulations concerning fish and fishery products provide an example of the complexity of environmental, health and sanitary requirements being applied simultaneously. These consist of both specific legislation concerning fishery products (such as health conditions for the production and placing on the market of fishery products, restrictions on veterinary medicines, etc.) and the obligation to introduce a system based on the principles of Hazard Analysis Critical Control Point (HACCP) in fish processing companies,[4] as well as other relevant legislation.

The case of aflatoxin standards is another illustration of the increasing stringency of SPS measures and the complexity of testing methods.[5] Risk assessment methodologies are complex and many developing countries lack the knowledge as well as the physical infrastructure (laboratory facilities, equipment) to carry out such assessments.

In several cases, exporters feel that sanitary and phytosanitary measures as well as other requirements in developed country markets are unjustified and used for protectionist purposes. The following examples have been quoted:

- Scientific data for specific thresholds or limit values sometimes appear to be questionable. The fact that such threshold values vary widely between countries would seem to strengthen this point;[6]
- In some cases products which have first been refused have subsequently been allowed access to the domestic market, but at a lower price (for example, peanuts);
- Imports have been banned because they contain certain substances, whereas the importing country itself exports such substances.[7]

THE PROJECT

Reasons

There is concern in many developing countries that gains in market access that could be obtained in WTO (World Trade Organization) negotiations on agriculture may be eroded by non-tariff measures such as standards, regulations and other such requirements. Therefore, many developing countries feel that in agriculture and related sectors, and in standards and regulations, SPS measures are an issue of key concern, along with the traditional WTO issues such as tariffs and quantitative restrictions. It is to be noted that to counter this concern both the AoA and the Agreement on SPS Measures were negotiated as part of an 'agricultural package' which aimed to ensure that the benefits of liberalized agricultural trade were not reduced by disguised restrictions or other non-tariff barriers to trade.[8]

Recent work, including that by UNCTAD, the World Bank, UNIDO, FAO, ITC, WTO, Codex and other organizations, has contributed to the identification of a range of policies and measures that have been successfully applied in several developing countries and/or at the international level to overcome constraints in complying with environmental requirements and SPS measures in international markets.[9] However, in the process of globalization and with increasingly stringent environment and health-related requirements, identifying policies to strengthen the capacities of developing countries to respond to such requirements is essential.

This work therefore addressed the following common policy issues:

- How can governments and business communities in developing countries mitigate the possibly adverse effects of SPS measures and environmental requirements on trade and competitiveness?
- How can developing countries be proactive in developing mechanisms that set standards for products that they wish to export?
- How can developed countries, in their standard setting processes, best take account of the implications of their SPS measures and environmental standards on the exports of developing countries?
- How can bilateral and multilateral aid agencies assist developing countries in maintaining export competitiveness and responding to environmental and SPS requirements?
- What recommendations could be made in the context of the WTO?

Main Activities

To assist in this process, UNCTAD, with the support of the International Development Research Centre (IDRC) in Canada, implemented a technical cooperation project. The research carried out under this project examined the effect of environmental and SPS standards, both positive and negative, on trade from developing countries. For the surveyed developing countries, the issues addressed were:

- compliance costs;
- opportunity costs of trade lost and the time taken to regain market shares;
- responses to the standards;
- perception of the protectionist nature of standards;
- recommendations to strengthen the capacities of developing countries to respond to such standards at the national, bilateral, and multilateral levels.

The research focus of this project was in three geographical areas: South Asia, Central America, East Africa and Mozambique.

Product Selection

Consultants were encouraged to select products such as fishery products, marine products or horticultural products in order to encourage either inter-regional or intra-regional comparisons. Case studies carried out under the project are set out in Table 1.1.

Methodology

The studies were conducted on the basis of a list of research questions, interviews, secondary literature and validation seminars or peer review processes in the country or the region concerned. Several papers were commissioned in each region. The researchers were encouraged to answer as many of the questions as they could and to add any other information that they thought would be relevant to the project. A lead researcher was then requested to collect all the evidence from a particular region and to put together a scoping paper that reflected the major concerns of that region. This report has been prepared on the basis of the papers written for this project.

While specific figures on costs are not available from other countries, indications of trade losses have been quoted by a number of them. Strictly speaking, trade losses should also be included in the calculation of compliance costs, as they indicate the losses a country has to incur if it does not meet the standard.

These regions were chosen because they share common climatic and other geographical characteristics that make them similar enough for their experiences to be compared. Two LDCs in South Asia and three LDCs in Africa reported their experience of the implementation of and compliance with SPS-related standards.

Issues to be addressed

The experts carrying out research under the project examined which (external and/or domestic) factors cause (potentially) adverse trade effects of SPS measures and/or environmental requirements. They proposed policies and measures that could prevent such effects, especially the strengthening of national and regional capacities to respond to such standards and SPS measures. Recommendations were made for:

- action at the national level;
- action at the international (bilateral or multilateral level); and/or
- measures in the context of the MTS, particularly the SPS and TBT Agreements.

Table 1.1   Cases examined under the project

South Asia	Fishery products	*India* (and other South Asian countries): HACCP standards: implications on trade and competitiveness. *Bangladesh* (August 1997) and *India* (May 1997, August 1997): effects of, and experiences in dealing with, EU bans on exports of fishery products.
	Peanuts	*India*: responding to aflatoxin standards by setting national standards and promoting indigenous development of technology.
	Rice	*India*: standards for pesticide residues and exports to the EU, the USA and Japan.
	Spices	*India* and *Sri Lanka*: experiences in dealing with aflatoxin standards and other SPS measures.
	Tea	*India*: meeting standards on pesticide residues.
	Organic food products	*India*: experience in standard setting, certification, exports and institutional support to the organic sector.
Costa Rica/ Central America	Poultry	*Costa Rica* (and other Central American countries): effects of (a) the application of the US SPS regulations concerning specific avian diseases (Newcastle disease) and (b) HACCP requirements on exports to the USA and intra-Central American trade. Policy responses.
	Fishery products	*Costa Rica*: experience in dealing with (a) US measures concerning imports of shrimp (turtle excluder devices), and (b) HACCP requirements in the USA and Europe for shrimp and fish.
Eastern Africa and Mozambique	Fishery products	*Kenya, Mozambique, United Republic of Tanzania* and *Uganda*: experiences with regulation 91/493/EEC, policies and measures required to be authorized to export to the EU market; experiences in dealing with environmental/health issues and related EU measures. *Kenya, United Republic of Tanzania* and *Uganda* (1997): presence of salmonellae in Nile perch from Lake Victoria. *Kenya, Mozambique, United Republic of Tanzania* and *Uganda* (1997): outbreak of cholera. *Kenya, United Republic of Tanzania* and *Uganda* (1999): fish poisoning in Lake Victoria as a result of pesticide residues.
	Horticulture	*Kenya*: EU regulation on pesticide application (Maximum Residue Levels, MRL)
	Organic food	*Uganda*: organic standards, certification, institutional support.

Methodology
The analysis carried out under the project is based on:

- interviews with producers/exporters, industry associations, government officials and others;
- use of primary and secondary information. Where possible, compliance costs were estimated.

Questions
The following questions provided guidance for the analysis carried out under the project.

Have there been adverse trade effects? Adverse trade effects may include:

- loss of export markets, either because producers cannot comply technically or because compliance costs are prohibitive
- diversion of exports to markets where requirements are less stringent
- price reductions

Factors causing (potentially) adverse trade effects may include:

- lack of transparency in the design and implementation of the measure in the importing country
- stringency of the measure (which may be perceived as unreasonable), inadequate use of science and risk assessment
- lack of awareness of or access to information on the part of the exporter (and/or of the importing firm or retailer)
- compliance costs
- firm size (problems which are typical for small sized enterprises)
- insufficient domestic infrastructure (for example, lack of testing and certification facilities)
- legal factors (no comparable domestic standards or lack of enforcement of domestic legislation)
- insufficient access to technology
- insufficient supply of environment-friendly inputs, prescribed chemicals
- cost of imported inputs.

Avoiding unnecessary adverse impacts on exports from developing countries and strengthening their capacities to respond to SPS measures and environmental requirements are to be found in the following:

- the area of trade rules (WTO)
- more transparent and participatory preparation of standards in the importing country

- implementation by the importing country aimed at avoiding unnecessary adverse effects on developing countries
- bilateral and/or multilateral cooperation, transfer of technology, technical assistance
- at the national level: trade promotion (dissemination of information, building infrastructure, etc.)
- effective implementation of comparable standards in the domestic market or on a regional basis
- promoting a process of innovation, enterprise development, etc.
- regional cooperation
- specific measures for SMEs
- branding and umbrella certification.

With regard to trade rules, possible recommendations in the context of the WTO could focus on areas such as:

- use of provisions for technical assistance
- assessment of the risk of non-fulfilment
- regional standards and their possible use
- equivalence
- special and differential treatment
- transparency.

Questions for the food processing industry in the brainstorming session at the Federation of Indian Chambers of Commerce and Industry (FICCI):

- What are the major constraints that you face in expanding processed food exports?
- Have you been given any subsidies? If so, what and by whom?
- What are the major problems that you have with food standards?
- Do you have any tie-ups with multinationals and have those helped standards?
- How?
- Are there adequate testing facilities available in India and have you received any technical assistance from within the WTO framework?

Countries Included

South Asia
A seminar was organized jointly with the World Bank in New Delhi, India, 11–13 January 2001. The papers presented at this seminar included the following:

- Bangladesh: Mr Sahadad Hussain, 'SPS Measures and Environmental Management in Bangladesh'.
- India: Mr Charles Kittu, 'Issues on SPS and Environmental Standards for India – the case of spices', and Mr Basu, 'Issues on SPS and Environmental Standards for India – the case of aflatoxin in peanuts'.
- Nepal: Mr Tika Karki, 'Issues on SPS and Environmental Standards for Nepal'.
- Sri Lanka: Mr S.L. Ginige, 'Issues on SPS and Environmental Standards in Sri Lanka'.

The project also benefited from the presentation of papers prepared in the context of a World Bank project. These were:

- Mr Sarfraz Khan Qureshi, Pakistan Institute for Development Economics, Islamabad, 'Agriculture and the New Trade Agenda in the Next WTO Round: Evaluation of Issues, Interests, Options and Strategies for Pakistan'.
- A.K.M. Abu Bakar Siddique, 'An Overview of Agriculture, Agricultural Trade in Bangladesh in the Context of Technical Barriers, SPS and Environmental Standards'.
- Saman Kelegama, 'An Overview of Agriculture, Agricultural Trade in Sri Lanka'.

The seminar served to test the main propositions set out by the authors of the various papers. The participants included researchers, officials from the Ministry of Commerce, agricultural export agencies, the Ministry of Health, the private sector, NGOs, diplomats, and representatives of international organizations such as the FAO, our co-sponsors the World Bank, and UNDP. Veena Jha was the lead researcher.

Central America
A meeting on Standards and Trade took place in San José on 20 August 2001. Three papers were presented and discussed on the following sectors: poultry, organic agriculture, and fisheries. Forty-four participants attended the meeting, including experts from the private sector and technical institutions, government officials, trade negotiators, NGOs and academics. The names of the authors and papers presented are as follows:

- Max Valverde: 'Sanitary and Environmental Barriers to Trade in Fisheries from Central America'
- Eduardo Gitli: 'International Trade of Poultry Products'.

Eduardo Gitli was the lead researcher.

East Africa and Mozambique
A regional meeting took place in Kampala, Uganda, on 13 September 2001. The meeting was attended by several people from the Ministry of Fisheries, agricultural export agencies, the Ministry of Commerce, the Ministry of Agriculture, the codex focal point, a number of exporters and the FAO. A total of seven papers were presented and discussed. World Bank consultants who are embarking on a similar project also attended the meeting. The authors and the papers they presented are:

- Rachel Ntoyai: 'SPS in Kenya' including an overall picture of rejections, expenditure on meeting standards as well as institutional changes that had to be brought about to establish SPS standards
- Halima Noor: 'SPS Measures and their Impact on Kenya: horticulture and fisheries'
- Nimrod Waniala: 'Impact of SPS Measures on Uganda's Fish Exports'
- Margaret Ndaba: 'Impact of SPS on Fish and Horticultural Products from EAC'
- Fish Inspection Department, 'Mozambique HACCP Experience'
- Mchallo, 'The Impact of Timber on the Environment'
- Cerina Mussa, 'Trade and Environment: Sanitary and Phytosanitary Measures'.

Mr Nimrod Waniala was the lead researcher.

LESSONS LEARNED

While all the questions were not answered in equal detail by the researchers, they made a number of important observations, which have been categorized below:

Importance of the Standards in the Market Place

The most convincing evidence of the importance of standards for exports by developing countries was illustrated by the case of East Africa and Mozambique. Although these countries have preferential trading arrangements with the European Union, the ACP agreement in particular, they have faced difficulties in exporting fishery products to the EU on account of SPS and other such measures.

Compliance Costs and Trade Effects

The second question addressed was whether these standards really entail trade displacements and whether the cost of compliance is high. On both these counts it was found that most countries surveyed by the project suffered trade losses and that the cost of compliance was high. One exception that deserves mention is the case of Costa Rica which was able to improve its share in the US markets due to the restrictions on Thailand and other Asian countries, because they did not use TEDs. However, this advantage was temporary as Costa Rica's general competitiveness in shrimp exports is rather low. The project also showed that large producers are at less disadvantage than smaller ones.

Protection versus Protectionism

The third question was whether producers in the developing countries concerned perceive certain standards as protectionist. The project showed that in several cases exporters perceive that SPS and similar measures applied in developed country markets are unjustified and are used for protectionist purposes. The following reasons were advanced:

- The severity of certain controls increases when prices in the domestic market of the importing country are low, and consequently imports are discouraged as they would further drag down the price. For example, controls are perceived to be more stringent during the domestic production season or when inventories are high. This was the case, for instance, for horticultural products and for mango pulp.
- Scientific data for specific thresholds or limit values sometimes appear to be questionable. The fact that such threshold values vary widely between countries would seem to strengthen this point. This was the case for fisheries in Costa Rica and for aflatoxins and honey.
- It is alleged that in some cases products that had earlier been refused were subsequently allowed into the domestic market at a lower price. Thus standards are perceived to be a mechanism for bidding down the export price. This was shown particularly in the case of peanuts free of aflatoxin, which could not be sold at the higher price. Instead, importers preferred to buy peanuts containing aflatoxin at a lower price.
- Countries in the same region that share the same water or climatic conditions may be subject to differential degrees of SPS measures. This happened in the case of poultry exports from Guatemala and the export of fishery products from Kenya.

Regional Strategies

The fourth issue was to examine whether the coping strategies of different countries and regions tend to be different. One factor that stood out was that, notwithstanding doubts about the validity of the claims made about certain

SPS measures, non-compliance with SPS or TBT standards is not a reasonable option; in fact, capacity building is required for assistance in complying with these standards. However, there appears to be a difference in the perceptions of the three regions. In Central America, SPS standards are considered a condition for doing business. Thus, the coping strategy for a country like Costa Rica is to engage proactively in standard setting processes and to anticipate standards, if possible. However, other countries in Central America, such as Guatemala, appear to feel that in the case of poultry exports their long-term interest is better served by focusing on regional markets rather than elusive developed-country markets. In the African countries surveyed by this project, except in the case of products which may be banned, the exporters are willing to accept lower prices for their relatively low quality products and continue exporting to the European Union. However, their long-term strategy is based on better implementation of standards as well as better price realization. In South Asia, a two-pronged strategy can be observed – one is market diversification and the other is to establish a leadership role in standard setting for products in which they have a dominant market position. This region also shows a greater tendency to question the validity of standards as well as to establish regional and national capacities to challenge the standards.

Market Premiums

The fifth question was: does meeting standards yield market premiums? It is often stated that if these standards are a challenge, complying with them can provide a useful opportunity for accessing these markets. Or alternatively, if the products are deemed environment-friendly and conducive to health, there should be market premiums and additional market opportunities. The evidence from this project shows that this is more of an exception than a rule. The truth is that consumers want the best possible food for the lowest possible cost. Market premiums, if any, arise at the retail end: the producer rarely benefits.

NOTES

1. The Agreement on Subsidies and Countervailing Measures (SCM) originally contained a category of 'non-actionable' subsidies (Article 8.2(c)). This category applied provisionally for five years ending 31 December 1999 and, pursuant to Article 31 of the Agreement, could have been extended by consensus of the SCM Committee. No consensus was reached. There have been no notifications invoking this Article.
2. See Jha, Markandeya and Vossenaar, *Reconciling Trade and the Environment: Lessons from Case Studies in Developing Countries*, Edward Elgar, 1999.
3. Tsunehiro Otsukti, John S. Wilson and Mirvat Sewadeh, *Saving Two in a Billion: A case study to quantify the trade effect of European food safety standards on African exports*: Development Research Group (DECRG), The World Bank (2002).

4. HACCP (Hazard Analysis Critical Control Point) is a systematic approach to the identification of hazards and the development of control systems to reduce the risks associated with these hazards. The methodology is used extensively in the food industry (including storage and distribution) to target and reduce harmful biological, chemical or physical contaminants, and verify that control systems are working as intended to minimize or eliminate them. HACCP is not confined to food production, however, but is also used in many other industries such as healthcare.
5. See Tsunehiro Otsukti et al., op. cit. See also Veena Jha, paper presented in the second workshop organized under the project Strengthening Research and Policy Capacities in Trade and Environment in Developing Countries, Havana, May 2000.
6. For example, a study on Zimbabwe points out that in peanut butter processing Zimbabwe had adopted an aflatoxin limit of 20 parts per billion, but the Nordic countries were proposing to adopt a standard of 4 to 5 parts per billion. The study reports that the Zimbabwean industry asked whether there was scientific justification for this stricter standard and whether investments should be made in Zimbabwe to adapt to the proposed new Nordic standards. It also questioned the extent to which technological implications for producers were considered when setting strict requirements in importing countries, especially if there was no domestic production. See Jabavu Clifford Nkomo, Benson Mutongi Zwizwai and Davison Gumbo, 'Zimbabwe', in Veena Jha, Anil Markandya and René Vossenaar, *Reconciling Trade and the Environment: Lessons from Case Studies in Developing Countries*, Edward Elgar (1999, Ch. 14).
7. The USA, for example, exports sodium bi-sulphide to Costa Rica when it has banned its usage in the USA and banned imports of shrimp cleaned with sodium bi-sulphide to the USA. See Jha, Markandeya and Vossenaar, op. cit.
8. The package also includes the concessions and commitments that WTO members have to undertake on market access, domestic support and export subsidies, along with the Ministerial Declaration concerning Least Developed and Net Food-Importing Developing Countries.
9. 'Development Dimensions of Trade and Environment Case Studies', dated 3 Oct 2002, No. COM/ENV/TD (2002) 86, OECD, Paris.

2. Environmental and Health Regulations

Veena Jha

INTRODUCTION

The Agreement on Technical Barriers to Trade (TBT) aims to ensure that technical regulations, standards and conformity assessment procedures do not create unnecessary obstacles to trade. However, it recognizes that each Member should not be prevented from taking measures necessary to protect human, animal and plant life or health, or the environment, and that each country has the right to define the level of protection that it deems appropriate in these areas. The Agreement encourages Members to use international standards where these are available, but it does not require them to harmonize their domestic regulations and standards upwards or downwards as a result of international standardization activities. This Agreement is subject to the same principles as the GATT, that is, Articles I and III are its cornerstone, and exceptions, in Article XX, also apply to it.[1] This Agreement incorporates a Code of Good Practices that has been developed for voluntary standards on the basis of 'best endeavour'.

The Agreement on the Application of Sanitary and Phytosanitary Measures (SPS) addresses a variety of measures used by governments to ensure that human and animal food is safe from contaminants, toxins, disease-causing organisms and additives. It also provides measures to protect human health from pests or diseases carried by plants and animals. The TBT Agreement does not cover these measures. The SPS Agreement explicitly recognizes the right of governments to take measures to protect human, animal and plant health in their countries; but where trade restrictions result, these measures should be taken only to the extent necessary for health protection, on the basis of scientific principles and evidence. If there is insufficient scientific evidence, governments may temporarily impose precautionary restrictions while they seek further information. Governments are to determine the level of health protection they consider to be appropriate on the basis of an evaluation of the risks involved. SPS measures are to be applied in a non-discriminatory manner. Furthermore, if there are a number of measures which could be used to ensure the determined level of health protection, governments are to use those which are no more trade restrictive than necessary to achieve the appropriate level, provided they are technically and economically feasible.

SOME DETAILS ON TBT AND SPS

TBT

The GATT rules governing the use of product standards are contained in the Agreement on Technical Barriers to Trade. The 1979 Agreement was revised in the Uruguay Round. The Agreement makes a distinction between standards for which compliance is mandatory and those for which compliance is voluntary. The term 'technical regulation' is used for mandatory standards, and the term 'standard' is used to denote voluntary standards.

Technical regulations adopted for environmental objectives are explicitly within the scope of the TBT Agreement. The preamble to the Agreement states 'that no country should be prevented from taking measures necessary' *inter alia* 'for the protection of human, animal or plant life or health' or 'for the protection of the environment', 'at levels it considers appropriate, subject to requirements' that:

- 'They do not constitute a means of arbitrary or unjustifiable discrimination between countries where the same conditions prevail'
- They are not 'a disguised restriction on international trade'
- They are 'otherwise in accordance with the provisions of the Agreement'

The 1979 Agreement did not cover process and production methods (PPMs). The revised Uruguay Round Agreement now defines technical regulations as rules which refer to 'product characteristics and their related production methods'. However, this wording is understood to limit PPMs to processes and production methods that have an effect on the characteristics of the product itself. For example, the revised text would allow the prohibition of pharmaceutical imports which do not meet the specified requirements of good manufacturing practices and cleanliness of the plant, because that would affect the quality of the product.

The Agreement requires that standards are applied on a 'most favoured nation' (MFN) basis to imports from all sources (that is, all WTO members have the right to be treated like the 'most favoured nation'), and that the imported product should not be treated less favourably than the 'like product' of national origin (national treatment rule) (Article 2.1).

Whenever a relevant international standard does not exist, or the technical content of a proposed regulation is not in accordance with that of an international standard, and if such a technical regulation is likely to have a significant effect on trade, it must be notified to the GATT Secretariat in the form of a draft. The TBT text has a provision for the establishment of National Enquiry Points (Article 10); they receive the notifications from the GATT Secretariat and facilitate access to information on national standards. These notification system obligations will reduce the possibility of standards becoming barriers to trade.

The Agreement encourages countries to use international standards. Where technical regulations are required and relevant international standards or their formulation is imminent, countries shall use them as a basis, except when such international standards would be an ineffective or inappropriate means for the fulfilment of legitimate objectives (Article 2.4).

When international standards are found to be an ineffective or inappropriate means for the fulfilment of the legitimate objectives, countries may deviate from them; for instance, because of fundamental climatic or geographical factors or fundamental technological problems. The TBT Agreement explicitly recognizes that environmental protection constitutes such a legitimate objective.

The revised TBT Agreement takes into account the risks non-fulfilment would create and requires that technical regulations shall not be more restrictive than necessary to fulfil a legitimate objective.[2] In assessing such risks, relevant elements of consideration are, *inter alia*, available scientific evidence and technical information, related processing technology and intended end use of the products (Article 2.2).

The importance which the Agreement places on the use of scientific evidence is further emphasized by the provisions for dispute settlement, particularly regarding the possible establishment 'of a technical expert group to assist in questions of a technical nature, requiring detailed consideration by experts' (Article 14.2). Specific procedures for the expert groups are included in an Annex to the Agreement.

Further, in order to ensure that trade is not affected because of the differences in standards, the Agreement requests countries 'to accept as equivalent' technical regulations of the trading partner which are different from their own, provided that they fulfil the objectives of their own regulations (Article 2.7).

The reason for the special and differential treatment of developing countries is to give them more time to comply with the obligations of the TBT, that is, with the notification of their domestic regulations. It does not give them a differential schedule to meet standards in OECD countries. Further, while there are provisions for harmonizing measures or accepting the rules of other countries as equivalent, it is possible that establishing equivalence may be a slow process. The regulators also realize that such measures will inevitably have trade limiting effects – the important issue will be to learn how to establish equivalence at the earliest.

SPS

SPS measures include any measure that an importing country may take to protect human or animal life or health within its territory, from risks that may arise from additives, contaminants, toxins, or disease-causing organisms in foods, beverages and feedstuffs, as well as to prevent the establishment or spread of pests. The Agreement calls on countries to base their SPS measures on international standards and to help in the development of such international standards by participating in the activities of organizations like the Codex Alimentarius Commission and the International Office of Epizootics.

The SPS provisions differ from those of the TBT Agreement in three important aspects. First, the TBT Agreement requires that product regulations be applied on an MFN basis, while the SPS permits members to impose different sanitary and phytosanitary requirements on food, animal or plant products sourced from different countries, provided that they 'do not arbitrarily or unjustifiably discriminate between countries where identical or similar conditions prevail'. The rationale for this is that differences in climate, pests or diseases and food safety conditions are considered.

Secondly, the provisions of the SPS Agreement explicitly permit governments to choose not to use international standards. If national standards are higher than international standards, they may be used, and, should they result in a greater restriction of trade, the government may be asked to show scientific justification for the measures or to demonstrate that the international standard would not result in the level of health protection it considers appropriate.

The third aspect is that the SPS Agreement introduces the Precautionary Principle which permits member countries to adopt SPS measures on a 'provisional basis' in cases where 'relevant scientific evidence is insufficient'. This principle takes into account 'pertinent information' that a member country may have or which other members or the relevant international organizations may have. The Rio Declaration stipulates that the precautionary approach should be adopted only where nonadoption of the measure, because of the lack of full scientific certainty, could lead to 'threats of serious or irreversible damage'. Since there is the risk of irreversible damage due to the spread of pests and diseases in the case of trade in animals, plants and their products, the SPS Agreement incorporates this precautionary principle.

The procedure for adaptation to regional conditions under SPS Article 6 is burdensome. Thus it should be made clear in this Article that scientific and administrative support shall be provided by international organizations and developed countries to facilitate the implementation of these provisions. Moreover, if a country or an area is found to be disease free, all trading partners should accept this without demanding additional evidence.

The SPS agreement, like the TBT, reflects a concern that rules which are identical may be trade distorting in their application, and may not provide imported products 'equivalent competitive opportunities' to those of like domestic products. However, Article 9 does provide for technical assistance for developing countries, and Article 6 allows exporters to adapt to regional pest and disease free conditions. Article 10.2 recognizes that it may take developing countries longer to comply with new regulations. It remains to be seen how this concern will be translated into the national legislation of importing countries. Under Article 10.3, there are exceptions to obligations that must be met within time limits and these may be of some help to developing countries. However, invoking this Article will not be in the interest of their trade.

The SPS Agreement can also be used by a country to prevent or limit the risk of damage from the entry, establishment or spread of pests. SPS measures include relevant laws, decrees, regulations, requirements and procedures, including end product criteria, processing and production methods, and packaging and labelling requirements directly related to food safety. The formulation of these measures is to be based upon standards, guidelines and recommendations developed by international organizations. However, each government may determine its own level of acceptable risk and is explicitly permitted to impose more stringent measures than international standards require. A country that selects a standard that exceeds international guidelines must justify its use in case of a trade dispute.

Panels hardly ever tested GATT rules on sanitary and phytosanitary measures. A GATT standards Code written in 1979 proved inadequate to provide the level of health protection that the members desired. Efforts to draft the SPS Agreement began in the late 1980s. SPS has more stringent rules than GATT. There is no provision like the exception to health protection standards in GATT Article XX (b) that a government can use as defence in a lawsuit under SPS.

Some specific SPS requirements
SPS pertains to laws or regulations that protect against exposure to pests, microorganisms, additives, contaminants and toxins in foods. It provides for protection against insecticide in fruit, but protection against bioengineering in food might not be covered. In addition, a measure governed by SPS is excluded from the TBT (WTO) Agreement. In all SPS cases, panels consult experts (a provision under SPS), but the burden of proof lies with the government lodging the complaint.

The science requirement SPS Article 2.2 requires that SPS measures, based on scientific principles and maintained with sufficient scientific evidence, are to be applied only to the extent necessary to protect health. In the case of Agricultural Products Panel of Japan versus Canada, the Appellate Body interpreted this provision to mean that 'a national or objective relationship between the SPS measure and the scientific evidence' is required. The panel and the Appellate Body concluded that Article 2.2 was being violated because Japan could not show that the quarantine and fumigation used for one variety of fruit or nut would be inadequate for other varieties. While the SPS Agreement requires the use of 'sound science', this term does not appear in the Agreement. Other scientists can challenge a scientific study for an SPS measure. The Agreement has no provision for dealing with conflicts of science; however, future panels will, no doubt, throw some light on this issue.

Risk assessment requirement Article 5.1 requires SPS measures to be based on the assessment of risk to life or health, as appropriate to the circumstances. However, according to panel interpretations both 'mainstream' and 'divergent' views on risk assessment would be admitted. Further, the agreement does not require any quantitative conclusions, but does mandate that the complainant must find evidence of an 'ascertainable' risk. In the Salmon case of Australia versus Canada, 'unknown and uncertain elements' made for improper risk assessment. In the Beef Hormones case, evidence on record showed that the use of hormones as a growth promoter was safe, yet the EU argued that the evidence on risk assumed 'good veterinary practice', which may not have been the case. The EU was faulted for not conducting a risk assessment of this prospect – a violation of Article 5.1.

SPS disciplines can disallow health regulations aimed at genuinely unsafe practices by insisting that a health measure in dispute should be 'based on' the risk assessment. In the Beef Hormones case, the panel asked for reliable risk assessment and undertook an analysis of the EU's decision-making process. In this case it rejected the EU's attempt to incorporate minimum procedural obligations into SPS. It brought into play terms such as 'sufficiently warrant', 'sufficiently support', 'reasonably warrant', 'reasonably support', or 'rationally support' the use of the health measure, and 'objective relationship' or 'national relationship' between the risk and the measure.

In the Beef Hormones case, this test found that the EU risk assessment did not support the ban. One expert testified that one in a million women would get breast cancer from eating the meat produced with growth hormones. It is unclear whether the expert was deemed speculative or the risk unimportant.

It is to be noted that violation of Article 5.1 is also a violation of the science requirement in Article 2.2. This conclusion was upheld in the Salmon Panel.

However, there is no instruction in the SPS Agreement to apply cost–benefit analysis in determining risk assessment.

The requirement for national regulatory consistency   Article 5.5 states that, 'with the objective of achieving consistency', a government shall avoid arbitrary or unjustifiable distinctions if such distinctions result in discrimination or a disguised restriction on international trade. SPS Agreements call on the WTO Committee on SPS Measures to develop guidelines for the implementation of this provision. Neither of the first two SPS panels was willing to await those guidelines.

Three elements of violation of Article 5.5 should be noted:

- the defendant government must be seeking different levels of health protection in 'comparable' situations;
- the differences from the government's intended level of protection must be 'arbitrary or unjustifiable';
- the health measure embodying these differences must result in discrimination or a disguised restriction on international trade.

In the Salmon Panel, the Appellate Body offered five arguments. The first two point to the lack of risk assessment and the different levels of health protection being sought. The third argument says that there was a 'substantial' difference in the level of health protection being sought. The fourth argument is that an Australian government draft report in 1995, which would have been tolerant of salmon imports, was revised in the final report of 1996; and the fifth argument is that Australia lacks strict internal controls on salmon equivalent to those it imposes at the border against foreign diseases. According to the Appellate Body, whereas no single argument might be conclusive, together they add up to a trade law violation.

It is unclear why the Appellate Body did not realize that an island nation might need stricter health controls at its perimeter than within its borders. According to the Australian government, there are at least 20 diseases of salmon that are currently not found in Australia.

The requirement of least trade restrictiveness   Article 5.6 states that governments shall ensure that SPS measures are 'not more trade restrictive than required to achieve their appropriate level' of protection. To prove a violation there must be an alternative measure conveniently available that is significantly less restrictive to trade. In two cases, the parties were found to have violated this Article, but the charge of violation was withdrawn on appeal. However, in analysing an alternative measure, panels will consider whether it matches the intended level of protection and not the level of protection actually achieved by the SPS measure. The complainant must also show that such an alternative measure exists.

The requirement to use international standards   Article 3.1 states that governments 'shall base' their SPS measures on international standards (Codex Alimentarius, IOE, IPPC). When such standards do not exist, Article 3.1 is ineffective. Even when international standards exist, a member country may, nevertheless, use a higher or lower standard or conform to the international standard. It is not clear whether the use of international standards will provide a 'safe harbour'. Even if a country uses standards higher than the international ones, they must meet all SPS requirements, that is, 'sound science', risk assessment and regulatory consistency, and they must be the least trade restrictive. However, it is worth noting that by using an international standard a country signals an irrefutable presumption of non-discrimination. In the Beef Hormones case, the burden of proof shifted onto a government not using the international standard.

The recognition of equivalence   Article 4.1 requires an importing country (or a government refusing to import) to accept an SPS measure by an exporting country as equivalent to its own, if the exporting government can objectively demonstrate that its health measure achieves the level of protection chosen by the importing government.

The transparency requirement   Annex B requires governments imposing a regulation to notify the WTO and to allow time for affected governments to make comments and for the regulators to take such comments into account.

The Precautionary Principle   The Precautionary Principle is an emerging tenet in international environmental law. It implies that 'where there are threats of serious or irreversible damage, lack of full scientific certainty shall not be used as a reason for postponing cost-effective measures to prevent environmental degradation'. This definition has been set out in the 1990 Bergen Ministerial Declaration on Sustainable Development and reiterated in the Rio Declaration (principle 15).

The Precautionary Principle has recently been cited in several international legal instruments. Besides the Rio Declaration, it has been fixed in the Framework Convention on Climate Change (Article 3 para. 3), the World Charter for Nature (principle 11 lit. b) and the Treaty of Maastricht, which will amend Article 130 R para. 2 of the EEC Treaty by adding the Precautionary Principle to the guidelines for European environmental policy and legislation.

The principle could be implemented, for instance, by the application of the best available, and not excessively expensive, technology. Once it is an obligation in international law, the principle will influence State responsibility by becoming a primary obligation of the State, which when infringed could lead to payment of damages.

The nuances in the usage of the principle concern:

- the circumstances under which the principle can be applied (only when there is a serious threat perceived);
- the amount of scientific proof required (that is, some or none);
- how cost-effective the measures are (which could undermine the principle itself, since it implies that non-cost-effective measures should not be taken to prevent even serious or irreversible damage);
- the extent of cooperation required in implementing preventive measures;
- concessions for developing countries;
- the specificity of definitions (vague recommendations can effectively operate as legal loopholes);
- the legal status accorded to the principle.

In the SPS Agreement the language used in Article 5.7 is not inadequate. Proposals to tighten or loosen this Article, considering its usage as an internationally agreed principle in the environmental context, may be premature. Proposals to incorporate the Precautionary Principle into Article 5.7 are problematic, since outside the realm of environment this principle is not generally acceptable. Besides, cost-effectiveness is a consideration in justifying precautionary measures, since the Rio principles advocate that 'measures based on the Precautionary Principle must include a cost/benefit assessment'. On the other hand, the SPS Agreement does not mandate the use of cost–benefit analysis.

Some trade disputes concerning the SPS measures

EC measures concerning meat and hormones in meat products   In 1989 the EC banned imports of meat produced with hormones from the United States and Canada. The EC claimed that the hormones contained in the meat might be carcinogenic. In 1998, the WTO Appellate Body ruled against the EC. The EC was given 15 months to bring its law in conformity with SPS rules. Because the EC failed to remove the ban, the United States and Canada took retaliation measures. Various aspects of the panel findings are discussed below.

Australia – measures affecting the importation of salmon   In 1975 Australia banned imports of uncooked salmon from Canada to prevent the introduction of exotic pathogens into its environment. In October 1998 Australia was given eight months to bring its law into conformity with SPS. When Australia failed to remove the ban, Canada threatened trade retaliation.

Japan – measures affecting agricultural products In 1950 Japan banned imports of apples, cherries, nectarines and walnuts, because it deemed them potentially infested with coddling moth. In 1987 it agreed to lift this ban subject to the condition that certain quarantine and fumigation requirements be met. However, each variety of fruit was to be individually tested. This provoked the WTO dispute. The Appellate Body ruled against Japan in February 1999. At the end of 1999, Japan agreed to bring its regulation into conformity with SPS rules.

Developing countries' concerns with SPS
The SPS Agreement (Article 3.1) encourages members to use international standards in their regulations. If national regulations conform to international standards, there is an irrefutable assumption that they do not constitute unnecessary restrictions to trade. Currently, the international standards formulation procedures are not uniform; for example, for food, there are two major international standardizing organizations, the International Organization for Standardization (ISO) and the Codex Alimentarius Commission. Since these standards are increasingly arrived at by a majority vote rather than by consensus, in practice only a relatively small number of countries can set the standards for all.

Many developing countries find it difficult to effectively participate in the standardization process owing to lack of technical expertise and/or financial constraints. Even though 89 per cent of all countries are in the category of developing/least developed countries, most of them are unable to attend the meetings of the standardization committees; therefore the developed countries fix standards which are often difficult for developing countries to comply with.

Article 10 of the SPS Agreement provides for special and differential treatment (S&D) of developing countries. This Article enjoins upon members to take into account the special needs of developing countries as well as the LDCs. It seeks to do so by:

- allowing longer time frames for compliance with new SPS measures;
- granting, upon request, exceptions from time limits for fulfilling obligations under this Agreement;
- encouraging and facilitating the active participation of member developing countries in the relevant international organizations.

Since these provisions of Article 10 are not codified, they remain as 'best endeavour clauses' instead of being mandatory.

The Doha Declaration has further stressed the right of countries to impose their own standards:

> We recognize that under WTO rules no country should be prevented from taking measures for the protection of human, animal or plant life or health, or of the environment at the levels it considers appropriate, subject to the requirement that they are not applied in a manner which would constitute a means of arbitrary or unjustifiable discrimination between countries where the same conditions prevail, or a disguised restriction on international trade, and are otherwise in accordance with the provisions of the WTO Agreements.

This weakens the role of international standards or provides more leeway to countries to diverge from international standards. While the latter part of the sentence qualifies the earlier it does appear to uphold the current trend of setting national standards, especially on environmental issues.

Article 3.3 of the SPS Agreement permits members to introduce or maintain SPS measures that are of a higher level than those dictated by international standards, provided there is a scientific justification for adopting them. As a result of this clause, exporters from developing countries have to comply with varying standards set by different countries and quite often they do not know how to meet these higher standards. There have been many instances of the goalposts being moved by the developed countries as soon as the standards initially set by them are met; for example, the EU has frequently been raising the SPS standards for imports of animal or aquatic products. Sometimes different states of the same country, such as the USA, set different standards for the import of a particular agricultural product.

The cost of meeting these standards could be prohibitive. For example, a recent World Bank study predicts that the implementation of a new aflatoxin standard in the European Union will have a negative impact on African exports of cereals, dried fruits and nuts. On the basis of an econometric model it is estimated that the EU standard, which would reduce health risk by approximately 1.4 deaths per billion a year, will decrease African exports of these products to the EU by 64 per cent or US$670 million.[3] The balance between precaution (Article 5) and trade displacement has also been difficult to achieve, as is shown by this example. According to the EU Agriculture commissioner Fischler, the Doha Declaration has widened the cover for measures based on precaution. This has the potential to disrupt trade from developing countries. Another problem stems from the lack of correct understanding of Article 4 of the SPS Agreement, which stipulates that measures which are demonstrably equivalent should be acceptable. Some members of the WTO have interpreted equivalence to mean sameness in the use of technology to achieve the required level of SPS protection. The Doha Declaration on Implementation has urged members to move forward on this issue.

Another cause for concern is the recent trend of introducing 'production process' measures in SPS. In these cases, the emphasis is not on the quality of the exported product, but on how that product was produced; for example, management practices, manufacturing facilities, types of fishing nets. This includes considerations of 'animal welfare', that is, how the animals were kept, transported and slaughtered.

These are the general problems that developing countries have reported with respect to standards under the SPS Agreement. However, South Asian countries have some specific problems that are addressed in the next section.

Whereas tariffs and quantitative restrictions on food and agricultural products are being reduced as a result of agricultural negotiations in the World Trade Organization (WTO), the use of environmental standards and sanitary and phytosanitary (SPS) measures has increased. Changes in consumer preferences and increased competition in the food sector have contributed to this development. Food safety rules have emerged first at the national and regional levels, but a wide range of international standards on health and food safety have been developed and such standards are increasingly important in international trade. There is a consumer demand all the year round for products which, traditionally, were only available seasonally. There is also a demand for a variety of products that are not always locally available. Consumers benefit from the vast improvements in the quality and frequency of transport. Fresh products from anywhere can be delivered to consumers everywhere. As this increases the risk of pests and diseases being transmitted across borders, safeguards are needed to protect human health and the environment. However, an SPS measure that is implemented with a wider objective than simply the safeguarding of health can be a very effective protectionist tool that is especially difficult to challenge because of its technical nature.

Two instruments negotiated under the Uruguay Round address these problems. The WTO Agreement on the Application of Sanitary and Phytosanitary Measures (SPS Agreement) attempts to address the balance between food safety standards and trade interests. In other words, it attempts to address the resolution of conflicts between the right of exporting countries to market access and the right of importing countries to maintain certain health and safety standards. In cases where there is doubt about the appropriateness or proportionality of certain measures, the

SPS Agreement should provide clear indications to determine whether the measure is primarily a barrier to trade or really a measure to protect health. The other instrument is the Agreement on Technical Barriers to Trade (TBT). The TBT Agreement deals with technical standards and regulations, some of them non-mandatory, for industrial and agricultural products. The general philosophy of both agreements is to ensure that these measures do not create unnecessary obstacles to trade. The ultimate objective is to make it harder for WTO members to use such measures to protect domestic industry from foreign competitors.

There is no specific WTO agreement on environmental standards and regulations. Environmental requirements can be technical standards (TBT Agreement), SPS measures (SPS Agreement), exceptions under Article XX of GATT, or trade measures stemming from non-trade agreements negotiated in other forums, particularly multilateral environmental agreements (MEAs). The Committee on Trade and Environment (CTE) has been examining 'the effect of environmental measures on market access', especially on developing countries, and particularly, on the least developed among them' ('item 6'of its work programme). This issue has also been highlighted in paragraph 32(i) of the Doha Ministerial Declaration.

When obstacles to trade, under the guise of discriminatory rules or complex certification systems, get themselves projected onto trade they are more difficult to discuss and to negotiate than tariffs and quotas. While high tariffs may impede commerce, they do provide a starting point for discussion, because they are usually transparent. But it is impossible to reach an agreement when the importing country refuses to discuss health security issues. It will only report its decisions. The alternative is to take the subject to the WTO dispute settlement mechanism. However, for a small country such an intense 'lawyer consuming' event is a complicated matter. Besides, most cases are in the 'grey areas'.

Is There a Real Basis for Health and Environmental Concerns in Developing Countries?

More than 200 known diseases are transmitted through food.[4] The causes of food-borne illnesses include viruses, bacteria, parasites, toxins and metals. The symptoms range from mild gastro-enteritis to life-threatening neurological, hepatitic and renal syndromes.[5] The World Health Organization (WHO) has estimated that, in some countries, mortality due to food-borne and water-borne diseases could be responsible for between one third and half of the total number of deaths.[6] Thus standards and regulations to protect human and animal life are essential.

As trade grows exponentially, there is growing concern about its effect on the transmission of diseases across borders. Food safety standards have become more stringent, particularly in developed countries. Exporters from developing countries need to comply with all the requirements imposed by the national authorities of importing countries. Consumer and environmental groups, industry associations and other stakeholders often exert pressure for increasingly stringent standards.[7] Exporters from developing countries can perceive certain environmental and SPS measures as a means to exclude their products, avoid competition and protect the national industries of developed nations. Such a possibility cannot be ruled out.

Like food safety standards, environmental requirements usually respond to legitimate objectives, but may also be used as a means to protect domestic industry. Deterioration of the environment is quite visible throughout the world, mainly in the big cities. Global warming, depletion of the ozone layer and other environmental problems have significant economic and social impacts. In some cases, such as the loss of biodiversity, environmental damage may be irreversible. However, as there are different rates of return for future environment conditions, preferences for environmental measures may vary according to the levels of economic and cultural development. It is easier to agree about pesticide residuals than about the need to save turtles or crocodiles from extinction. In the first case, there is an immediate threat to human life or health. In the second case, poor countries may find that there is a short-term trade-off between conservation and feeding people. The distinction between what is 'right' and what is 'wrong' is blurred.

What is important to remember when judging a standard is the subjective intent behind it and the fact that measures must be proportionate to their intended objective so that they are the least trade restrictive. For example, under the SPS Agreement, WTO members remain free to set whatever human, plant and animal health and safety standards they consider appropriate to their domestic circumstances. These are the 'easy cases' which become more complex when we refer to levels of pollution nationally allowed, which depend on the physical features of the country and the habitants' preferences. Besides, the very idea of foreign trade is based, since Ricardo's early writings, on national differences 'in climate', which today we call the 'environment'.

Under current conditions, environmental restrictions may be related to Article XX of the GATT or to the TBT agreement, because environmental provisions are included in the WTO under somewhat indirect approaches.[8] In either case, standards may, willingly or unwillingly, serve as a restriction to trade. We may then have serious problems and it is necessary to draw a mixed strategy of domestic policies and international action that can prevail. In most cases, standards are not a protectionist device and it is important to have a flexible institutional framework to solve problems when they arise.

The SPS and TBT Agreements provide guidelines to determine whether an SPS or TBT measure is protectionist in nature or responds to a legitimate concern. Where SPS measures are concerned, WTO members have the right to adopt SPS measures that are necessary to protect health, provided that they are consistent with the provisions of the SPS agreement. This right is qualified in three ways:

- SPS measures should only be applied to the extent necessary;
- they should be based on scientific principles and not maintained without sufficient scientific evidence (except as provided for in Article 5.7);
- SPS measures may not be applied in a manner which would constitute a disguised restriction on international trade (Articles 2.2 and 2.3; Article 5.7 allows for temporary exceptions to this basic obligation, but only when the relevant science is unavailable or insufficient).

The TBT Agreement covers all technical regulations, voluntary standards and conformity assessment procedures except when these are SPS measures as defined by the SPS Agreement.

An additional rule of thumb can be proposed to judge whether measures fulfil legitimate environmental or health objectives or have been taken primarily for protectionist reasons. If the answer to any of the following questions is in the affirmative, SPS and/or environmental measures are more likely to be used as an instrument to restrict trade:

- Are there other visible pressures stemming from the private sector to protect the domestic industry of the importing country?
- What part of the domestic market in the importing country is provided by local supply? If such market shares are significant but declining, protectionist pressures are more likely to emerge.
- Are other trade measures (such as anti-dumping measures) already applied to the product concerned, including in other countries?

Generally, an environmental trade measure consists of a restriction on international trade with the purpose of promoting an environmental objective.[9] However, there are several types of environmental trade measures, or more correctly trade measures that can be used for promoting environmental purposes. Each of these is subject to different disciplines. Environmental trade measures can largely be divided into import prohibitions, export prohibitions, taxes and tariffs, standards (product–process), sanctions, subsidies and conditionalities.[10] In the case at hand, the measure taken by the USA is a process standard[11] distinguishing between products that are 'alike'.[12] Consequently, according to GATT case law such measures are considered to be quantitative restrictions disguised as domestic requirements. Such a regime will fall under GATT Article XI.[13] A process standard found to violate that rule could still be justified under Article XX, as the recent WTO case law has proved.[14] The non-compliance with this standard resulted in the denial of entry to the US market.

Environment and SPS

It is often very difficult to distinguish between environment and health and safety measures. For example, a standard on pesticide residue in food may address both consumer health and environmental concerns. Thus it could be considered both an environmental and a health standard. Consumer health concerns in the importing country may also be linked with an environmental issue in the country of production and export. For example, several restrictions on imports of fishery products that are analysed in the next section of this chapter have been imposed for consumer health reasons, but they are caused by environmental and sanitary problems. The lessons learned from the examination of potential trade barrier effects, their solutions, and the policies to address SPS measures may also help to further analyse environmental standards. Exporters face similar issues concerning the environment and SPS standards while evolving strategies to comply with quality standards.

Environment and health-related standards and regulations in international markets can potentially create barriers for exports from developing countries. Some African countries have had significant export losses because of difficulties in complying with such requirements.[15] Sanitary and phytosanitary (SPS) and environment-related measures are likely to become important factors for African exports in the future. First, standards in target markets are becoming more comprehensive and more stringent, in the food sector in particular. Secondly, when African countries seek to take advantage of trade liberalization and initiatives such as the African Growth Opportunity Act (AGOA) and Everything But Arms (EBA), they need to develop capacities to comply with a wide range of environmental requirements and SPS measures. This is partly because SPS measures play an increasingly important role in sectors where Eastern and Southern African countries have a comparative advantage, such as fisheries and horticulture. In fact, for many developing African countries non-compliance with SPS standards could be a major obstacle to the export of high-value agricultural and food products.

There is, therefore, a need to strengthen the capacities of African producers and exporters to respond to such requirements through appropriate policies

Table 2.1 Environmental measures, SPS and TBT in the post-Doha WTO work programme

Environment

Market access	The Doha decision instructs the CTE to give special attention, among other things, to the 'effect of environmental measures on market access, especially in developing countries, particularly in the least developed among them' (paragraph 32(i), first part).
	  Deadline: 1 January 2005.
	  Work on these issues should include the identification of any need to clarify relevant WTO rules. The Committee shall report to the Fifth Session of the Ministerial Conference, and make recommendations, where appropriate, for future action, including the desirability of negotiations.

Labelling for environmental purposes	The Doha decision instructs the CTE to give special attention, among other things, to 'labelling requirements for environmental purposes' (paragraph 32(iii)).
	  Deadline: 1 January 2005.
	  Work on these issues should include the identification of any need to clarify relevant WTO rules. The Committee shall report to the Fifth Session of the Ministerial Conference, and make recommendations, where appropriate, for future action, including the desirability of negotiations.

Trade measures under multilateral environmental agreements (MEAs)	The Doha decision contains an agreement to hold negotiations, 'without prejudging their outcome, on the relationship between existing WTO rules and specific trade obligations set out in multilateral environmental agreements (MEAs). The negotiations shall be limited in scope to the applicability of such existing WTO rules as among parties to the MEA in question. The negotiations shall not prejudice the WTO rights of any Member that is not a party to the MEA in question (WT/Min(01)/Dec/W/1 of 14th November 2001)'. Deadline: 1 January 2005.

SPS[16]

Longer time-frame for developing countries to comply with other countries' new SPS measures	Where a phased introduction is possible, the longer period allowed for developing countries to comply is now understood to mean, normally, at least six months. Where phased introduction is not envisaged, but a member government has problems complying, the two sides should consult, 'while continuing to achieve the importing Member's appropriate level of protection'. Implementation in the medium term.
Equivalence	Where possible, governments are supposed to accept that different measures used by other governments, which provide the same level of health protection for food, animals and plants, can be equivalent to their own. The SPS Agreement (Article 4) requires this, but does not say how it is to be achieved. In the lead-up to Doha, the SPS Committee settled this issue of implementation by deciding on an outline of steps designed to make it easier for all WTO members to make use of the SPS Agreement's equivalence provisions (decision of 24 October 2001). In the Doha decision, ministers instruct the SPS Committee to expeditiously develop the specific programme for the implementation of these equivalence provisions. Implementation: immediately.
Participation of developing countries in setting international SPS standards	The Doha decision notes the actions taken by the WTO director-general to help member developing countries participate more effectively. It also notes the efforts made to coordinate with the relevant organizations and to identify needs for technical assistance in the field. The ministers urge the director-general to continue with the efforts and to give priority to least developed countries. Implementation: immediately.
Review of the SPS Agreement	The Doha decision instructs the SPS Committee to review the operation of the agreements at least once every four years. Implementation: every four years or sooner.
Financial and technical assistance	The Doha decision calls for members to provide assistance to least developed countries so that they can respond adequately to new SPS measures that could obstruct their trade. It also calls for assistance to help them implement the agreement as a whole. Implementation: immediately.

and measures at the national and international levels. Enhanced understanding of the constraints developing countries face in meeting standards set by developed countries is of key importance for national trade policies, trade-related technical assistance and the SPS and Technical Barriers to Trade (TBT) Committees. The Doha Ministerial Declaration has also called upon the Committee on Trade and Environment (CTE) to give particular attention, among other things, to 'the effect of environmental measures on market access, especially in relation to developing countries, in particular the least-developed among them' (paragraph 32(i)).

EU Requirements

The European Union and its member states have enacted specific legislation concerning fishery products, which are also applied to imports. These include:[17]

- health conditions for the production and placing on the market of fishery products;
- freshness of fishery products;
- restrictions on veterinary medicines concerning aquaculture animals and products;
- the obligation to introduce a system based on the principles of Hazard Analysis Critical Control Point (HACCP) in fish processing companies.

Directive 91/493/EEC lays down the health conditions required for the production and placing on the market of fishery products in general. The key feature of this Directive is that all fishery products (whether fresh, chilled, frozen, canned, salted, smoked or dried) imported from third countries into the European Union must come from a preparation, processing, packaging or storage facility which is approved by a competent body in the country concerned. The list of approved companies will eventually be endorsed by the European Commission and published in the Official Journal of the European Union.

The Directive is based on the HACCP quality assurance approach. This system is based on the recognition that microbiological hazards exist at various points in the handling and processing of fishery products but, through a rational approach and by applying the necessary measures, it is possible to control them. Its main purpose is to avoid systematic detention, heavy sampling and laboratory checks at the point of entry in the EU. This means that a shift from traditional end-product inspection and certification to this preventive assurance approach is required. The actual control will thus take place in the third countries instead of at the point of entry into the European Union. This has various implications for developing countries. For example, regulations will have to be updated, inspection services need to be organized, and handling and processing will probably need to be improved.

Directive 91/492/EEC lays down the health conditions necessary for the production and placing on the market of live bivalve molluscs. It imposes strict recommendations on the building and construction of purification tanks, the equipment and the storage of products. Purification centres must also have the services of a laboratory that can carry out necessary microbiological tests. A record of each incoming batch of the product has to be carefully kept, and there should be a health mark on each package listing the name of the species, origin, dispatch centre and packing date.

As a consequence of the implementation of these two Directives, companies must allow certain investigations to be carried out during production and must record the data for a supervisory authority.[18] Countries exporting fishery products must also submit complete legislation to the European Commission concerning the export of live bivalve molluscs and other fishery products, as well as a complete report on the functioning of its controlling authority, including the infrastructure within which it operates. This documentation will be carefully studied by the European Commission and, if it is found to be satisfactory, a delegation will be sent to the exporting country, which will visit companies at random and depending on their findings in the third country, the European Commission may issue either a permanent approval or a provisional one for a limited time.

The Commission recognizes an official controlling body in a third country if its control procedures are up to a certain standard. This official body is held responsible for checking and monitoring that operators within the country correctly implement the procedures of internal control. This body must also select and submit to the European Commission a list of all the establishments that comply, or are implementing compliance, with the EU Directives. Only then will these establishments be issued with an official number that authorizes them to export to the European Union.

Specific legislation
Specific legislation has been enacted (both at the level of the European Union and at that of individual member states) concerning, for example:

- pesticide residues (maximum pesticide residue levels, MRLs)
- heavy metals
- polychlorinated biphenyls (PCBs)
- food additives
- radiological contamination of foods (irradiation of food)
- packaging

Countries authorized to export fishery products to the EU
In April 1997 the European Commission decided that as of 1 July 1998 fish
and fishery products could be imported only from a list of countries (Decision
97/296/EC, dated 22 April 1997). This list, which has been revised several
times, contains two groups of countries, as follows:[19]

Article I consists of countries that are approved to export fish and fishery
products to the European Union ('EC-harmonized countries'). This list
currently contains around 57 countries and territories, including, for example,
the United Republic of Tanzania and Uganda.[20]

Article II consists of countries that are not yet covered by a specific decision but qualify under Article 2(2) of Decision 95/408/EC as a 'provisionally-
approved' country. Imports may be allowed over an 'interim period' (this
period currently expires in December 2003). While imports from Article II
countries are authorized, each EU member state can still impose its own
specific import conditions and can have its own list of approved establishments.[21] Commission Decision 95/328/EEC establishes that health certification is required for fishery products from third countries in Article II of the list.
Currently there are around 45 countries and territories in Article II; for example, Kenya and Mozambique.

Until a common European regulation and code of practice is established,
traders have to follow the standards and regulations of individual countries in
the EU. Food laws regulate the production, processing and sale of food (which
includes spices) in each country. Though these laws vary from country to
country, they have two common objectives, namely the protection of public
health and the promotion of fair dealing in food commodities. Two types of
food law are generally recognized:

* horizontal regulations that regulate food standards, the use of additives,
  prevention of food contaminations, and labelling of food in the market
  in general;
* vertical regulations, which are product-wise application of regulations.

Apart from the food regulations, which have the force of law, the trade
has to respect ministerial orders and notifications, which are regarded as
high-level expert opinions. Some codes of practice and standards have
developed for fulfilling the requirements under good manufacturing practice
(GMP).

The maximum pesticide residue limits in Germany, Netherlands and United
Kingdom are very different. The microbiological standards fixed are so high
that compliance, in most cases, may not be feasible even in Europe. These
measures entail higher costs of analysis, investment in processing units and
upgrading competence of technicians.

With environmental trade regulations, developing countries must understand that they are gaining legal recognition at the WTO level. Prior to the Shrimp–Turtle dispute, WTO case law took the view that those environmental measures targeting non-product related production methods incorrectly distinguished between products that were 'alike'. Consequently, such measures were considered quantitative restrictions unjustifiable under GATT Article XX (exceptions). The Shrimp–Turtle case fundamentally changed this view. PPM-related trade measures are still considered a quantitative restriction. Yet such measures can be justified under the environmental exceptions of GATT Article XX, paragraphs (b) and (g).[22]

A country wanting to use the environmental exceptions in Article XX has three hurdles to overcome. It must first ascertain whether the policy purportedly embodied in the national measure serves to achieve one of the objectives established in paragraphs (b) and (g). These paragraphs comprise measures that are recognized as exceptions to substantive obligations established in the GATT, because the domestic policies embodied in such measures have been recognized as important and legitimate in character. After succeeding in this, the country has to prove that the national measure is necessary to achieve the policy objective. Finally, the issuing state must establish that the measure complies with the chapeau of Article XX.[23]

Once the above tests are met, the technical regulation must then pass the test of the chapeau of Article XX, which defines *how* the law is applied. The three tests in the chapeau to be met are whether, in its application, the measure is arbitrarily discriminatory, is unjustifiably discriminatory or constitutes a disguised restriction on trade. Although the Appellate Body did not try to define these terms, it arguably defined a number of criteria for *not* meeting the tests including:[24]

- Unilateral actions. International efforts and standards should be preferred.[25]
- One state cannot require another to adopt specific environmental technologies or measures – different technologies or measures that have the same final effect should be allowed.
- When applying a measure to other countries, regulating countries must take into account differences in the conditions prevailing in those countries.
- Before enacting trade measures countries should attempt to enter into negotiations with the exporting state(s).
- Foreign countries affected by trade measures should be allowed time to make adjustments.
- Due process, transparency, appropriate appeal procedures and other procedural safeguards must be available to foreign states or producers to review the application of the measure.

It is interesting to note that the Appellate Body basically states the requirements of recognition of international standards, equivalence and transparency for process-related standards.

SPS Measures

With the introduction of SPS measures and the liberalization of the agricultural sector through multilateral negotiations and regional agreements, certain trade barriers that were always present but remained unnoticed are now increasingly discussed. The core elements of the defensive international trade policy are changing very rapidly. In the past, the issue of SPS measures potentially forming barriers to trade was less important than it is today. There are several reasons for this: (a) the food sector was not fully integrated in the GATT disciplines and tariffs, and quantitative restrictions were abundant; (b) foreign trade in food products was relatively small in relation to domestic GDP; and (c) the main importers were also producers or strongly related to the chain of processing, therefore standards were closely watched by TNCs.

The increase in imports and exports, as well as in tourism, makes it easier to transfer pests from one region to the other. The recent cases of 'foot-and-mouth' and 'mad cow' diseases illustrate the ease with which infections spread from one place to another. Problems may also arise between neighbouring developing countries. Nations are more aware of such risks. Developed countries, in particular, have introduced more stringent testing requirements and the activities of laboratories expanded rapidly during the 1990s.

The SPS Agreement states that transparency in the establishment of animal and plant health measures is a cornerstone of international trade evolution (Article 7). Full knowledge of dispositions should help activate trade in a series of products. However, each country establishes its own health requirements within the framework of what it considers an 'adequate protection level', but this level is very hard to define. Thus, when one country objects to another's health requirement, the latter must simply justify why it feels that this particular measure is necessary. Thus countries have a wide scope to define health protection measures they deem necessary, and under bad faith or retaliating conditions they can become non-tariff barriers to trade.

On the issue of health requirements, the Agreement allows governments to impose more stringent import requirements than the international standards, and in pertinent cases they have to demonstrate scientifically exactly which international standards are deemed insufficient.

The important issue is that compliance with animal and plant health requirements implies a rise in the final costs, which may affect export competitiveness and could restrict access to certain markets. Therefore, technical and financial support from developed countries could help lessen the financial load that compliance with these requirements imposes.[26] However, within the current frame of the Agreement, the probability of this kind of aid is very restricted.

NOTES

1. Articles I and III deal with the most favoured nation theory and with national treatment, which advocates non-discrimination between contracting parties in trade. Article XX is the clause on general exceptions where contracting parties may, on the basis of some provision, restrict the free movement of goods and services.
2. It has sometimes been said that this provision is intended to ensure proportionality between regulations and the risks nonfulfilment of legitimate objectives would create, although this is not mentioned in the text.
3. Tsunehiro Otsukti, John S. Wilson and Mirvat Sewadeh, *Saving Two in a Billion: A case study to quantify the trade effect of European food safety standards on African exports*: Development Research Group (DECRG), The World Bank.
4. Bryan, Florence, *Diseases transmitted by foods*, Atlanta: Centre for Disease Control, 1982. Cited by Food and Agriculture Organization (FAO) in *The State of World Fisheries and Aquaculture*, Art I. 2000, available at www.fao.org.
5. Mead, Paul, et al., *Food-Related Illness and Death in the United States*, Centre for Disease Control and Prevention, Atlanta, Georgia, USA, www.cdc.gov/ncidod/eid/vol5no5, p. 1.
6. FAO Committee on Fisheries, Sub-Committee on Fish Trade, Sixth Session, Bremen, 3–6 June 1998, Report on important recent events concerning trade in fishery products, para. 24.
7. Centre for the Promotion of Imports from Developing Countries, *Eco Trade Manual*, February 1996, p. 19.
8. In a landmark decision on the turtle–shrimp dispute in 1998, the Appellate Body of the WTO, referring to Article XX(g) of the GATT on the exceptions based on conservation of non-renewable natural resources (the turtles), raised a series of arguments that make us think that environmental issues are somehow included in the WTO agreements: (i) the inclusion of live beings in the concept of natural resources, (ii) the fact that turtles were protected under another multilateral agreement (CITES), (iii) the fact that the same regulations applied to US ships. Therefore, the Appellate Body introduced the term 'environmental legitimate objectives', which makes it an interesting turn of events for the WTO (E. Gitli and C. Murillo, 'Factores que desalientan la introducción del tema ambiental en las negociaciones comerciales', in M. Araya (ed), *Comercio y Ambiente: Temas para avanzar el diálogo*, OEA, Washington, 2000).
9. See Charnovitz, Steve, 'A taxonomy of environmental trade measures', *Georgetown International Environmental Law Review*, **6**, 1993, p. 2.
10. Charnovitz, Steve, 'The environment vs. trade rules: defogging the debate', *Environmental Law*, **23**, (475), 1993, p. 490.
11. Process standards set regulations concerning how a product is harvested or produced. These standards are unrelated to the final characteristics of the product itself. It goes without saying that border verification is more difficult and reliance on some type of certification is required. Some may regard it as an import restriction. Nevertheless, technically, an import prohibition, to qualify as such, should have no internal counterpart. If it did, the obstacle would not be an external one, but an internal regulation or standard. Since the USA enacted the same prohibition for its nationals, we are in the presence of a process standard. Noncompliance causes import refusal.
12. Likeness is expressed by reference to physical similarity.
13. *United States – Restrictions on Imports of Tuna*, Report of the Panel, GATT Document DS21/R (3 September 1991), at 5.11–5.15; *United States – Restrictions on Imports of Tuna*, GATT Document DS29/R (16 June 1994), (not adopted), at 5.8–5.9; see also *United States – Standards for Reformulated and Conventional Gasoline* AB-1996-1, 29 April 1996, adopted 20 May 1996, WTO Document WT/DS2/AB/R at 5.19; *United States – Taxes on Automobiles*, GATT No. DS31/R (11 October 1994), (not adopted), at 5.52–5.54.

14. *United States – Import Prohibition of Certain Shrimp and Shrimp Products – Recourse to Article 21.5 by Malaysia*, WT/DS58/RW 15 June 2001, paras. 5.138–5.144.
15. For example, this chapter examines bans on imports of fishery products from Kenya, Mozambique, the United Republic of Tanzania and Uganda. Madagascar has also been affected by bans on fishery and meat products. In February 2000 the Commission of the EU decided that 'Given the seriousness of the deficiencies observed during an inspection visit to Cape Verde, imports of fishery products from this country should not be authorized' (Commission Decision 2000/170/EC of 14 February 2000 (Official Journal L 055 of 29 February 2000).
16. See WTO: http://www.wto.org/english/tratop_e/dda_e/implem_explained_e.htm#sps
17. Source: CBI *News Bulletin*, No. 256, June 1998.
18. See Chapter 4 for a description of similar requirements in the United States.
19. In 1996 countries in Article I represented around 73 per cent of extra-EU imports in value terms, while countries in Article II accounted for an additional 17 per cent. The remaining 10 per cent of extra-EU imports originated in countries which are not on the list. These imports will no longer be allowed after 1 July 1998. However, a number of countries, including Mozambique, submitted applications. Source: CBI *News Bulletin*, No. 256, June 1998.
20. A list of approved establishments in each of these (and other third) countries can be found on http://forum.europa.eu.int/irc/sanco/vets/info/data/listes/ffp.html
21. For example, France and Italy apply national regulations, which deviate from those stipulated by the European Commission. The consequence for exporters from third countries is that fishery products destined for those countries may be rejected by the national authorities, despite complying with the EU conditions (CBI, op. cit.).
22. See *United States – Import Prohibition of Certain Shrimp and Shrimp Products* – Recourse to Article 21.5 by Malaysia, WT/DS58/RW 15 June 2001, paras. 5.138–5.144. GATT Article XX states: 'Subject to the requirement that such measures are not applied in a manner which would constitute a means of arbitrary or unjustifiable discrimination between countries where the same conditions prevail, or a disguised restriction on international trade, nothing in this Agreement shall be construed to prevent the adoption or enforcement by any contracting party of measures: . . . (b) necessary to protect human, animal or plant life or health; (g) relating to the conservation of exhaustible natural resources if such measures are made effective in conjunction with restrictions on domestic production or consumption'.
23. See GATT Secretariat, GATT/WTO Dispute Settlement Practice Relating to Article XX, Paragraphs (b), (d) and (g) of GATT, WT/CTE/W/53, 30 July 1997, p. 5, and *United States – Standards for Reformulated and Conventional Gasoline* AB-1996-1, 29 April 1996, adopted 20 May 1996, WTO Document WT/DS2/AB/R, at 22.
24. See The United Nations Environment Programme, Division of Technology, Economics and Trade Unit and the International Institute for Sustainable Development, *Environment and Trade: A Handbook*, 2000, p. 30. If countries fail to take into account points 3–6, then standards would be discriminatory to trade.
25. At informal meetings and symposia, US authorities have issued the argument that their TED requirements have a legal ground in the Convention on International Trade of Endangered Species (CITES), since most sea turtles are included in its Appendices. We should remember that CITES works by subjecting international trade in specimens of selected species to certain controls. There is a licensing system to import, export, and re-export listed species. This argument is untenable for a very simple reason: CITES regulates trade in endangered species. In the Shrimp–Turtle case, turtles are not traded but incidentally killed. The TED regulation is aimed at incidental killing of sea turtles. Since turtles are not traded, CITES cannot apply. Besides, there is a multilateral control mechanism within the Convention. According to Article XIV, stricter domestic measures regarding the conditions for trade, taking possession or transport of specimens of species are allowed for contracting parties, but only at a domestic level.
26. For example, in Costa Rica a routine inspection on a national level to ensure the country is Newcastle-free costs approximately $3000.

3. South Asia

Veena Jha

INTRODUCTION

The South Asian component of this project has been designed to survey the impact of environmental standards and SPS measures on trade and explore policies that strengthen the capacity of developing countries to respond to such requirements. This chapter on South Asia has been prepared on the basis of the following:

- Empirical evidence in selected sectors, gathered by South Asian researchers. The methodology is set out in Annex III.
- Papers submitted to a regional seminar, organized jointly with the World Bank[1] (New Delhi, 11 to 13 January 2001), as well as interventions and ensuing discussions at the seminar. Participants from Bangladesh, India, Nepal, Pakistan and Sri Lanka took part in this seminar.
- Interviews with policy makers.
- Complementary research under other technical cooperation projects and UNCTAD secretariat studies.

Part of the information was collected through interviews conducted with representatives from approximately twenty fruit and twenty rice-exporting firms in the New Delhi area. The project also organized a brainstorming session jointly with the Federation of Indian Chambers of Commerce and Industry (FICCI), in which about forty members of the food processing industry from the Delhi area participated.

Five papers on the experiences of the countries were submitted at this seminar. These included the following:

- Bangladesh: Mr Sahadad Hussain, Member Director, Bangladesh Agricultural Research Council, 'SPS Measures and Environmental Management in Bangladesh'.
- India: Charles Kittu, Deputy Director, Spice Board, India, 'Issues on SPS and Environmental Standards for India – the case of spices', and Mr Basu, Principal Scientist, National Research Centre for Groundnut,

India, 'Issues on SPS and Environmental Standards for India – the case of aflatoxin in peanuts'.

The following papers presented at the seminar have also been used as a source of information and analysis for this chapter:

- Mr Sarfraz Khan Qureshi, Pakistan Institute for Development Economics, Islamabad, 'Agriculture and the New Trade Agenda in the Next WTO Round: Evaluation of Issues, Interests, Options and Strategies for Pakistan'.
- A.K.M. Abu Bakar Siddique, 'An Overview of Agriculture, Agricultural Trade in Bangladesh in the Context of Technical Barriers, SPS and Environmental Standards'.

Based on the above, the empirical analysis carried out under the project has focused on the following products:

- marine products (Bangladesh, India)
- peanuts (India)
- mango pulp (India)
- rice (India, Pakistan)
- spices (India, Sri Lanka)
- tea (India).

This chapter is organized as follows: Section 1 examines the impact of environmental requirements and SPS measures on exports of specific products from South Asia; Section 2 outlines the domestic policies of South Asian countries on these issues.

PRODUCTS

South Asian countries exporting the same products have had both similar and different problems in coping with SPS standards. This section aims to test the general propositions iterated in the last chapter and come up with a list of problems which are common to all South Asian countries. This will help in developing regional and national strategies for compliance with SPS and other environmental standards.[2]

Marine Products[3]

Stringent hygiene and sanitary requirements in developed countries, especially the provisions concerning the use of HACCP (Hazard Analysis Critical

Control Point), have affected marine exports from several South Asian countries. Failure to comply with such requirements has resulted in import bans in the European Union and 'automatic detention' in the United States.[4] The European Union imposed a ban on import of fishery products originating in Bangladesh (1997) and India (1997). The ban has subsequently been lifted. This section examines the experiences of India and Bangladesh regarding:

- their responses to the standards and the compliance costs;
- the opportunity costs of lost trade and the time taken to regain market shares;
- the perception of the protectionist nature of these standards;
- the policies put in place to meet the requirements of international markets;
- the recommendations made to strengthen the capacities of developing countries to respond to such standards at the national, bilateral and multilateral levels.

India
In August 1997 the European Commission banned fishery products from India. The EU stated that:

- The EU inspection in India had shown that there were serious deficiencies in infrastructure and hygiene in fishery establishments and not enough guarantee of the efficiency of controls by the competent authorities.
- There was a potentially high risk to public health in the manner of production and processing of fishery products in India. The results of the EU border inspection on fishery products imported from India indicated that these products may have been contaminated by micro-organisms, which may have constituted a hazard to human health.

Responses to standards The Seafood Exporters Association of India expressed the view that many of the standards adopted in the Order dated 21 August 1995 were either irrelevant for product quality or too stringent, given the Indian fishing conditions. They claimed that the legitimate objectives of the EU standards could be met through less cumbersome and less costly procedures. Some examples of the standards applied through this Order which are clearly beyond HACCP standards and, perhaps, not strictly relevant for product quality are given below:

- non-slip floor: structures and fixtures must have timber holds that are large enough not to be obstructed;

- walls and ceilings must be easy to clean;
- the floor of the food handling and cold room areas shall be waterproof;
- walls shall be free from projections . . . Junctions shall be rounded off;
- all windowsills shall be sloping inwards;
- an anteroom should be provided to the cold rooms/storage;
- potable water shall be used for all purposes, including cleaning the ceiling.

The producers felt that, while the concept behind HACCP is laudable, the adoption of stringent EU standards in developing countries such as India is not only difficult, but often indefensible. Producers feel that in some cases EU norms are too strict and, in several respects, irrelevant for product safety. For example, the EU standards require that even floors and ceilings be washed with potable water. Such standards are especially difficult to defend in places where potable water is in short supply, such as in the Cochin area where shrimps are farmed. The fish processing units often have their own treatment plants for water, but nevertheless ground water is depleted. Another example of over-strict regulations quoted by the producers is the requirement to undertake 62 tests to check water standards. The equipment required for some of these tests is not available in India.

Costs of compliance   The need to comply with the EU norms significantly increases the cost of production and entry into the EU markets, but does not result in price premiums. Before the EU norms were applied, exports from South Asia were mainly in bulk form; the equipment required was plate freezers, refrigeration equipment for freezing, processing, and cold storage. But the EU requirement involves heavy investment in infrastructure and equipment, apart from higher running costs. For example, it is now necessary for each factory to have a potable water system, continuous power (standby generators), effluent treatment plants, flake ice machines, chill rooms and a laboratory. It is estimated that such upgrading involves an expenditure of about US$250 000 to US$500 000 per unit as fixed cost.

The Seafood Exporters Association of India claims to have spent US$25 million on upgrading of their facilities to meet the regulations. Appropriate training of the personnel involved in various stages of production and processing are not included in this cost estimate.

Banks have been unwilling to provide loans, as most plants have recorded a poor performance for the three years between 1997 and 2000. The high cost of credit, at 18 per cent interest plus other running costs, is prohibitive for most small firms.

Opportunity cost: trade forgone   The total effect of the EU standards is very difficult to gauge at this point in time. What appears likely is that the small firms will become suppliers to large firms, which will then export their products. Thus the market premium that the small producers were able to obtain before the EU ban will fall drastically. Large firms may break even in five to seven years but small firms may go out of business. The standards appear to favour larger establishments rather than smaller ones, not only because of economies of scale but also because of the requirements of infrastructure and the space that it demands.

The EC-approved plants are normally bigger and have the capacity to process more than 10 tonnes of fishery products per day. According to Indian sources, the EC-approved plants in India are as good as, and in some cases even better than, any plant in Europe or the USA. There are 404 processing units in India, of which 84 are approved by the EC. The EC-approved plants have in-house peeling facilities and records are kept meticulously. A microbiological laboratory is also part of the facilities. Incoming material, as well as finished products, are regularly checked. Microbiological tests are also carried out in external laboratories to double-check the findings.

The second type of units are the ones that have applied for EC approval. These are units that were exporting to the EU before the ban came into effect, but are now exporting to the United States, Japan and other countries outside the EU. These units have reasonable facilities, though their standard is not the same as that of the units approved by the EU. Some of them also have laboratories. They normally have all the provisions required by the HACCP manual.

The third kind, typically, are small companies with an annual turnover of around US$0.5 million. These small structures do not have in-house peeling facilities. They may have laboratories, but few are functional. They have plenty of water and cleaning facilities. These companies are inferior to the EC-approved units, but can produce goods suitable for exports to other countries. A facility of this size generally cannot afford to install the expensive infrastructure required by the EU.

Thus, though fish exports from India to the EU have decreased since the introduction of stricter EU standards, there has been a structural change in the industry. Though the large companies continue to export to the EU, the middle-sized category, making up approximately 20 per cent of the units, has switched its exports to countries other than the EU. The smaller companies, which constitute approximately 75 per cent of the units and 80 per cent of total production, have now switched to domestic markets, where they are forced to accept, on average, 25–40 per cent lower prices. This may have led to higher poverty levels, but since the impact of these standards is recent, it is difficult to judge their overall effect.

Bangladesh

In the 1990s shrimps constituted over six per cent of all exports and more than 70 per cent of the value of export of primary products from Bangladesh. In

2000 38.7 per cent of Bangladesh's shrimp exports went to the EU, 38.3 per cent went to the United States and 11.2 per cent to Japan.

In July 1997 the European Commission imposed a ban on the import of shrimp products from Bangladesh on the grounds that the exported commodity did not meet the stringent provisions of the EC's HACCP regulations. The ban originated from (a) concerns about standards related to health safeguards, quality control, infrastructure and hygiene in the processing units, and (b) lack of trust in the efficiency of the controlling measures carried out by designated authorities in Bangladesh, in this particular case the Department of Fisheries (DoF).

Background   The problems with quality compliance in the shrimp industry in Bangladesh arise at different stages, including the pre-processing phase, the handling of raw shrimp (harvesting, sorting by size and colour, removal of heads and peeling) and the processing stage.

The handling of raw shrimp is often carried out in conditions and facilities that are hygienically unsuitable. The processing stage is affected by lack of high quality water and ice, irregular electricity supply, poor infrastructure and insufficient transportation facilities. These factors seriously constrain the ability of Bangladeshi firms to pursue modern sanitary practices. As in other LDCs, Bangladeshi plants also lack sufficient funds to invest in expensive mechanical equipment, fishing boats, quality control measures and adequately trained staff.

The EU concern about quality and safety compliance by Bangladeshi plants was justified and, in principle, conformed to the SPS provisions of the WTO. The plight of the Bangaldeshi shrimp industry shows that standards should be developed in cooperation with countries which lack the capacity to comply with stringent measures, so that solutions that meet the requirements of both the importer and the exporter may be found.

Compliance cost
It was estimated that the total cost of upgrading facilities and equipment and training staff and workers so that acceptable sanitary and technical standards could be achieved was about US$18.0 million. The annual cost of maintaining the HACCP programme was estimated to be US$2.4 million.[5]

Trade impacts   The ban remained in effect for five months, between August and December 1997. A World Bank study estimated that the cost of the EU ban for Bangladesh was about US$65.1 million. Some of the plants succeeded in diverting a large part of their intended EU shipment to the United States and Japan. Despite such efforts, the estimated net loss was equivalent to about US$14.7 million. These were evidently short-term losses. The medium- to long-term losses stemming from the slow-down of the sector's growth momentum, market diversions and erosion in the price offered to exporters were, in all probability, much higher.[6]

Shrimp exports from Bangladesh to the EU decreased from US$128.9 million in 1997 to US$48.2 million in 1998, while exports to the EU went up to US$89.3 million in 1999 and to US$124.9 million in 2000. Thus, the trade displacement effects in the dynamic sense may be larger than the immediate trade losses.

Policy responses   The government of India, in an attempt to meet standards following the EU ban, issued an Order dated 21 August 1995, specifying elaborate process standards, arguing that 'it is necessary to maintain the highest quality standards as per the health requirements of the importing countries that would encompass the standards like unified directive No. 91/493/EEC dated 22nd July 1991 of the European Community'.

As a result of the EU ban on Indian fishery products, and as a condition for the partial lifting of that ban, certain seafood processing plants and freezer vessels were re-inspected and approved for exporting to the EU countries. Standards for those still exporting to the EU, roughly 25 per cent of the original number of firms, have improved. It is difficult to judge the standards of firms that have shifted to domestic or the less stringent markets.

Summary

The trade displacements caused by the EU standards on fishery products have been significant. It has been difficult to restore exports to the levels before the ban. Little technical assistance has been made available by the EU to the firms to upgrade their standards. Most of the efforts, in the case of India, were domestic. There may have been some additional long-term effects, such as changes in the structure of the industry in favour of larger firms, which could meet these standards more easily. In most cases there was no government assistance, unlike in developed countries, where the fishery industry relies heavily on government subsidies.

Peanuts

Some EU countries have imposed alfatoxin standards that are more stringent than the international standards of the Codex Alimentarius Commission (that is, specific standards set for aflatoxin B I and the sampling procedures). This could have an adverse trade impact on developing countries. This section examines the potential effects of these EU aflatoxin standards on India's exports.

The EU Commission has specified tolerance limits for aflatoxin contamination in peanuts and also the testing methods to be used. The levels are 10 ppb (5ppb B1) for raw material and 4 ppb (2ppb B2) for consumer-ready products. The sampling plan is similar to the Dutch Code (see Box 3.2), that is, much more rigorous than the one currently in force.

The Codex Alimentarius Commission had proposed a maximum limit of 15 ppb. A report by the Joint European Commission Food Association (JECFA) mentions that aflatoxin contamination of foodstuff is very low among the EU nations and only a few members of the population suffer from hepatitis B, a precondition for liver damage by aflatoxins. The report estimates that the risk at 20 ppb is 0.0041 cancer cases per 100 000 persons annually. For 10ppb it is 0.0039 cases. This shows that the change in standard from 20 ppb to 10 ppb reduces the estimated risk of cancer by approximately two cancer cases per billion people annually.[7]

The JECFA had previously recommended that the maximum permissible aflatoxin levels should be fixed as low as possible. But now, on the basis of further data available, it has modified its recommendation to reducing the intake as far 'as is reasonably possible'.

In addition, it should be noted that the JECFA's risk estimates are based on data that made no allowance for the substantial reduction in aflatoxin contamination achieved by mechanical removal of the nut skins and by the use of optical and electronic methods for sorting the nuts. The risk computations of the EU are thus based on aflatoxin levels that are no longer applicable. In future, the new data should be taken into account when the EU tolerance limits are specified.

The implementation of the EU Commission's proposals would endanger the export of peanuts to the EU member countries, as:

• Europe represents 47 per cent of world's import of peanuts and peanut products – a value of $1.4 billion.
• Assuming all of Europe moves to a multi-test plan, the increase in cost of testing alone will be $4 million – this does not include re-testing costs in Europe.
• The government of the UK reported that compliance with the proposed EU directive would average eight per cent of turnover. Exporters will lose the ability to ship goods to an alternate European market when common European standards come into force. As a consequence, the overall cost of the lot will include the cost of rejected goods, which will have to be diverted to crushing mills or sold at a significant discount for animal feed. This makes Indian peanut growers less competitive. Exporters may be forced to absorb the costs of additional cleaning, re-sorting and blanching of rejected lots of peanuts. The implications of

increased costs of doing business in the European market could be more than $200 million, according to the Joint European Commission Food Association (JECFA).

• Indian peanut farmers experience other problems as well. For example, while there is no import duty in the EU on 50-kg bags, there is a duty on 5-kg bags. This is because the EU wants to discourage retail foreign consignments. Then there is the problem of genetically modified (GM) peanuts. Some years ago one foreign market encouraged the use of GMOs, but now another market wants an assurance that the peanuts supplied are not genetically modified.

Responses to standards

To tackle the problems caused by the introduction of new EU standards on aflatoxin, a number of pre- and post-harvest operations known to prevent afla-toxin contamination have been undertaken on a very large scale in five villages in the Ananatpur district of Andhra Pradesh, India, under a UNDP project on 'Food Quality in Peanuts'. The project successfully demonstrated aflatoxin-free peanut production for the first time in a high-risk area of the country. At the end of three years, 80 per cent of the samples (after three months of stor-age) had 0–5 ppb aflatoxin as against permissible limits of 15–20 ppb in some developed countries (Australia, Canada, USA) and 20–30 ppb in some devel-oping nations (India and China).[8] However, the exact cost of meeting the new standards, as well as the nationwide responses to this problem, are not avail-able at present.

While addressing the aflatoxin problem, the project also assisted peanut farmers in adopting low cost technologies to capture better yields in their rain-fed system of production. Besides, the farmers were taught to reduce depen-dency on plant protection chemicals by growing trap crops and using other integrated pest management approaches to make the produce free from residues. The steps that were undertaken for reducing aflatoxin contamination consisted of the following:

• selection of varieties which are suitable for the environment
• crop rotation between legumes, cereals and vegetables
• soil moisture management/conservation
• harvest at optimum physiological maturity
• quick natural drying of pods in small heaps
• mechanical separation of well-filled pods (by removing damaged and poorly filled or unfilled pods)
• bringing down pod moisture steadily
• storage of pods at 7–8 per cent moisture in dehumidified conditions.

This has been tried at district level and will require both investment and better management, but it may be necessary to develop a programme at the national level. Research conducted under the UNDP project has highlighted the need for:

- identification of a production system which will not lead to the development of the pathogens which cause aflatoxin;
- promotion of a new generation of confectionary grade peanut which has better seed coat resistance to bacteria which produce aflatoxin;
- an understanding of global requirements country-wise and development of a suitable production plan;
- a higher premium price, as paid to Argentina and the United States;
- introduction of better and more efficient processing and packaging equipment and improvement in cargo handling.

The Agricultural and Processed Food Products Export Development Authority (APEDA), the Ministry of Commerce, and the Government of India requested UNDP to organize special training for peanut farmers of Gujarat to improve their skill in management of aflatoxin. Several farmers were trained under this programme. The Australian Centre for International Agricultural Research (ACIAR) was interested in this project and wrote about it in the ACIAR Newsletter.[9]

The UNDP also helped the Sub-Programme Coordinator to visit the USA and the UK to interact with peanut scientists and learn about recent advances in aflatoxin research. This, in turn, helped to strengthen the national programme.

Some of the problems identified by the UNDP aflatoxin management programme were the following:

- The biggest obstacle for India is lack of financial and technical resources to implement stringent requirements.
- Stringent aflatoxin EU standards, which are like moving goalposts, have resulted in trade displacements.
- The permissible limits are different in different countries. The standards set may not be backed by scientific evidence. Several countries (such as India, Argentina, Malaysia, Cuba) have raised this issue at the Committee of the SPS.
- There is lack of mutual recognition of inspections and standards and non-involvement of developing countries in the standard-setting process.
- There is no rationality of the sampling size and testing procedures/ methods adopted. The smaller the sample size, the greater the risk of rejection of good lots (see Box 3.1).

BOX 3.1   SAMPLING PROCEDURE

The proposed sampling plan is similar to the Dutch Code (3 × 10 kg).

In the case of bulk raw nuts, the implementation of a regular monitoring policy presents difficulties because aflatoxin will seldom be evenly distributed throughout a given batch and only a few nuts may be contaminated. For example, the contamination rate is estimated at 1:10 000 for peanuts (peanuts).

The question is how large should the sample be in order to ensure that the test yields reliable data on the degree of aflatoxin contamination. Opinions differ on this point.

The FAO has recommended testing a single 20 kg sample for aflatoxin content from a batch of between 15 and 24 tonnes. The FAO is of the opinion that this sampling procedure will yield results that are reliable enough to eliminate the risk for the consumer and that stricter requirements would bring no significant safety measure.

The EU's sampling procedure requires that three samples of 10 kg each be tested from a batch of between 15 and 24 tonnes. According to the new regulation, the whole shipment will be rejected if only one of the three samples exceeds the tolerance level. It would be far more logical to calculate an average value from all three samples as an end result. On the basis of the risk estimate computed by JECFA, several experts are of the opinion that the new procedure would mean an unnecessary waste of good product without actually being necessarily safer.

It is also certain that this practice will lead to adverse effects on prices. The EU regulation is also criticized because it fails to specify how the sampling and testing of final products would be performed. Uniform criteria, which are binding for all EU member states, are also necessary for these products, but have not yet been adopted.

Source: Kaushik and Saqib, op. cit.

Cost of compliance

Some of the problems relate to different testing procedures and conformity assessment standards in different markets. Each test costs US$150. (For details of testing cost under the previous and the new system, see Box 3.2.)

BOX 3.2   TESTING PLAN COMPARISON – COST IMPLICATIONS FOR PEANUTS

Current single testing
procedure
Average MT cost: $800
Cost of testing: $50/lot
(Lot = 20 tonnes)

New EU multi-testing
procedure
Average MT cost: $800
Cost of testing: $200/lot
(Lot = 20 tonnes)

Further, tests are required by the EU markets only for exports from Egypt and India and not for exports from the USA and Argentina. This is because Argentinian exports are mostly through TNCs based in the USA.

Laboratory tests with small animals such as guinea pigs and rats, which were fed highly contaminated peanuts (B1) on a daily basis, showed that aflatoxin can cause cancer of the liver. But there is no clear evidence as yet to prove that aflatoxins are carcinogenic in humans. Besides, the fact is that, should a sample from a shipment of peanuts be found to contain aflatoxin, this does not mean that the whole lot is contaminated, since aflatoxin is concentrated in very few nuts. Statistically, one would expect to find one contaminated nut in a sample of 5000 to 10 000 nuts. Experts have concluded that 75 per cent of the lots rejected under the proposed procedure would be below the established tolerance level, that is, they would be uncontaminated because the infected nut can be easily identified and removed during the mechanical sorting.

In none of the countries all over the world where peanut consumption is very high, such as Argentina, China, India, South Africa, USA and Vietnam, have there been findings or reports which suggest an increased incidence of liver cancer.

Opportunity cost: lost trade
Indian peanut exporters often have to make distress sales, when foreign buyers do not accept supplies because of some unspecified standards in their domestic markets. The exporters feel, therefore, that they may have to depend upon their domestic market, or at most the regional market, for sustenance. According to their importers, higher aflatoxin standards than presently applicable were likely to come into effect in their export markets after 31 December 2000. Surveys have not been carried out after this date.

The suggestions to improve aflatoxin management included the following:

- joint monitoring of production sites by experts from importing, as well as producing, countries;
- issuing aflatoxin free tags certifying the quality and conformity with SPS measures;
- testing for aflatoxin status of the produce before shipment by the labs identified by the importing country;
- no retesting with subsequent rejection at the off-loading port;
- resorting to inexpensive but dependable and rapid tests like ELISA for detection of aflatoxin B1 and more financial support for establishing labs and processing facilities in producing countries.

Scientific data show that reducing aflatoxin levels for raw material (for example, from 15 ppb total to 10 ppb total) has little or no effect on the levels of aflatoxin found in the processed product.

The introduction of rigorous, expensive import requirements puts a burden on the suppliers. The resulting increase in cost will be reflected in the price. Depending on the price elasticity of demand, the total demand may drop, distorting trade from the level at which it was before the change in standards. The change may be especially large for some countries, where aflatoxin is more difficult to control than in other countries. Indeed, the export of peanuts may decrease from some countries and increase from others owing to such a change in standards.

Rigorous testing programmes are extremely difficult to monitor and enforce. If they are not applied uniformly, both the suppliers and the importers are at a disadvantage. When supplies are short owing to crop failures, there may be efforts to manipulate results or encourage alternative import schemes through markets where surveillance may be less stringent.

Assuming the need to increase the price to absorb anticipated rejections, European importers will be forced to consider the following options (which will result in an increase in price of the final product):

- blanch peanuts prior to importation (which adds to costs of raw materials and raises issues about splits and shelf-life)
- move production to a non-EU site, where stringent testing of raw materials is not mandatory, leading to job losses in both the manufacturing sector and ancillary businesses.

Lastly, none of the European countries produces peanuts and to enforce such stringent import restrictions on a commodity for which they are completely dependent on other countries, without considering the problems of the suppliers and recommendations of experts and the JECFA/WTO, will be unhealthy and perhaps even troublesome. The perception of the Indian producers is that these standards are meant to decrease producer prices, because peanuts are an important ingredient in the food industry. In fact, some retailers actually preferred to buy aflatoxin-containing peanuts, rather than aflatoxin-free peanuts, as the price of the former was lower. These peanuts were then mechanically sorted and sold through retail chains.

Therefore, the new legislation will not only be counter-productive both to the buyer and to the seller, but will also create numerous unnecessary problems and bottlenecks. In other words, the risk that non-fulfilment will entail is not commensurate with the costs incurred.

Indian producers perceived the stringency of the EU standards as well as the prescribed testing methods (known as the Dutch Code) as unjustifiable. The government and producers, nevertheless, adopted a proactive approach towards new market requirements. The government enacted domestic standards and promoted research and development as well as training through a UNDP project on aflatoxin management. India has managed to substantially reduce aflatoxin levels and has also developed reliable and affordable testing methods. The denial of an export market to farmers of a developing country like India could cause starvation deaths in many multiples of the estimated number of people in Europe who may be affected by aflatoxin.

Mango Pulp

Mango weevil in Indian mango pulp affects its export to the USA and the EU markets. This section analyses standards which deal with this problem. Although India is the largest mango producer in the world, and has the greatest variety of this fruit, its export of mangoes or mango pulp is insignificant.[10] This is despite the fact that India is also very competitive in the cost of production of mangoes. The major handicap is SPS measures relating to the presence of pesticides, which are used to rid the fruit of mango weevils.[11]

Quality–price problems
In India exporters of mango pulp have for years had fixed buyers, who have helped to sort out quality and other potential problems in the USA and the EU import markets. At the same time, the perception of the exporters is that these buyers have used quality requirements, such as shape, colour and the presence of fruit flies, to lower prices. Exporters claim that the issue of quality becomes a major hurdle only when the buyers have excess stock or prices have fallen below the agreed or contracted price in the international market. In such cases, the exporters have to accept price discounts, especially because of the perishable nature of the goods.

Cost of compliance

The lack of vapour heat treatment plants is a major constraint in exporting fresh mangoes to the EU and the USA. Several facilities do not have the infrastructure for this treatment and thus exports to the USA have not increased. Indian exporters claim that vapour heat treatment of mangoes is very expensive. The cost of labelling the product could be as high as 10 per cent of the total value, and the testing costs could be as high as 10–15 per cent of the total value. The relative cost of inputs varies according to the harvest – it is low when there is a good harvest and high when the harvest is bad. These cost differentials, which could be as high as 50 per cent, cannot be passed on to the consumer, largely because there is little correlation between producer prices and retail prices in commodities like mangoes. There may be long processing formalities after the shipment arrives at the ports, leading to demurrage and losses.

The technology costs may be too high: the cost of an imported gas chromatograph for evaluating pesticide residues may cost as much as 50 per cent of a consignment and the running costs may be an additional 2 per cent per consignment.

Transparency

Some exporters claim that there is a lack of clarity in the specification of SPS measures for mangoes. For example, exports to Jordan require a certificate stating that the product (a) is not radioactive, (b) does not contain dioxins and (c) does not contain certain pesticide residues. However, buyers are often unable to provide detailed specifications of the pesticide residues for which the fruit must be tested. This information is important since each pesticide may require a different testing method and it may be expensive to conduct. Even documentation may cost as much as 1.5 per cent of the total value of the cargo.

Summary

While it is difficult to get information on the mango industry, as producers are small and far apart and do not divulge costs, the survey carried out under this project showed that hygiene and health standards are of particular concern in this industry. Small growers find it difficult to export fresh mangoes, as the fixed cost of installing the equipment for testing and treatment is too high in proportion to the value of the consignment. Government help or subsidies are difficult to obtain.

Rice

This section is based on a survey of about 30 exporters of basmati and non-basmati rice. While the firms did not give exact figures, the survey does give a general picture of the problems facing Indian exporters of rice, especially to the USA. It examines standards affecting exports to the European Union, the United States and Japan. Pesticide residues are a major problem facing exporters to the EU and Japan. In the case of the USA, basmati rice faced larger compliance problems than other categories of rice, especially relating to the paper work on standards, raising the suspicion that standards are being used to protect domestic producers of this high-cost rice. The need to comply with the USA's pesticide standards significantly increases production costs.

Protectionist abuse
In the first six months of 2000, out of 80 consignments of basmati and non-basmati rice to the USA, nearly 20 consignments were rejected on the grounds that they were filthy and contained 'foreign' matter. Some problems relating to aflatoxins in the rice were also reported.

The problems were greater (they are difficult to quantify as the firms surveyed gave impressions rather than exact data) in the case of basmati or premium grade rice than for non-basmati rice.[12] The exporters were of the opinion that USFDA standards and the relative stringency of the standards for basmati rice were primarily because of the protection provided to domestic producers in the USA.

Cost of compliance
To comply with the US regulations, rice has to be manually sorted and fumigated, and dead weevils have to be blown out of it. This is not required for exports to the EU. The cost of all these processes is roughly 3 per cent of the fob (free on board) value per metric tonne of rice exported. The USFDA sampling and inspection costs are as high as 5–10 per cent of the total consignment. Some firms reported that just removing foreign matter as well as pesticide residues would increase costs by 8–10 per cent. Most of this has to be done manually. There is an average of three to six months delay in clearing rice consignments from a number of low-cost countries such as Thailand and Vietnam. This would thus incur interest costs. The price reduction after this wait may be about 5 per cent of the total consignment. Thus the incentive to export rice to the United States is very low.

Rice millers in India lack storage, transportation and testing facilities. The cost of modern milling facilities may be prohibitive. For example, the traditional two tonne rice mill costs Rs.10 lakhs or US$20 000, whereas the modern rice mill that would address all quality problems would cost about US$350 000. Of course, the capacity of such mills would be much higher, but they are often beyond the scope of small millers who dominate the rice milling industry in India. Upgrading of ports and roads is required. Problems of general infrastructure, such as the lack of laboratories for the testing for pesticides, radioactivity and dioxins, inhibit growth in exports from India.

Transparency
Import requirements for rice are not necessarily transparent. The problems in exporting to the Middle Eastern countries are very different from those that arise when exporting to Europe, Japan and the USA.

The difficulties of exporting to the Middle East arise primarily from a lack of clarity in the specification of standards and the extensive documentation required from their embassies. The problems in Europe and Japan relate to pesticide residues, frequent changes in standards and lack of clarity in the scientific justification of the standards. The problems of exporting to the United States are related to delays in clearing consignments, repeated tests, and bidding down of prices.

Pakistan's exporters of basmati rice have reported similar problems. The other countries of South Asia do not export rice, and may even be net importers.

Policy responses
At present, the Indian government has not formulated any technical assistance programme to promote rice exports. Since trademarks for basmati rice in the US markets have now been successfully challenged, basmati rice exports from India are expected to increase. However, SPS issues, specially relating to filth contamination, need to be comprehensively addressed by the producers. For this purpose good manufacturing practices or other comprehensive practices relating to HACCP need to be installed.

Summary
The complicated procedures necessary for compliance with the imposed standards are the main problems in exporting rice from India to the USA. Moreover, Europe has installed several mills for polishing rice and thus prefers to import paddy rather than polished rice. The value addition for paddy is very low. Rice imports also tend to be subject to different tariff rate quotas, which along with standards, complicate the procedures of export to the USA and the EU. The producers believe that the high cost of domestic rice in the USA, and the fact that Europe has moved to milling and polishing most of its own rice, has led to increased and more stringent standards including those relating to aflatoxin and pesticide contamination in these two markets.

Spices

The difficulties in complying with SPS measures greatly affect the export of spices to developed countries. The EU regulations, especially, are of great concern to developing countries. The main problems relate to the arbitrariness of the risk-assessment methodologies, as well as to the high costs of compliance.

The spice industry in Europe thrives mainly on trade in ground spices, which are used as food ingredients. Hence, the horizontal (general, non-product-wise) regulations concerning food processing and sale are directly relevant to spices. Though vertical (product-wise) regulations are not currently in place for spices, codes of practice and standards do exist.

The permitted levels of aflatoxin are a major problem faced by the chilli (red paprika) export to Europe. Different European countries follow different standards, which are very high. For example, aflatoxin contamination should be less than 4 ppb in Germany whereas Sweden and Finland allow 5ppb and Spain allows 10 ppb.

These measures entail higher costs of analysis, investment in processing units and upgrading of the competence of technicians. This is often beyond the capacity of most spice growers, who are small farmers.

Sri Lanka

Spices are important commodities both in the domestic and the overseas markets of Sri Lanka. They contribute US$70.2 million to the foreign exchange and provide employment for about 470 000 persons (which is about 10 per cent of the agricultural labour force). Cultivation and processing are labour intensive, and female labour is very important. Sri Lanka and other countries have shown that labour cost is over 50 per cent of the total cost of production (62 per cent for Indian pepper, 65 per cent for Indian clove, 51 per cent for Indian cardamom).[13]

There are no reported cases in Sri Lanka of a complete ban on the export of any categories of spices due to non-compliance with SPS requirements. However, the estimated rate of rejection due to substandard quality and non-compliance with SPS requirements is about 30 per cent of the total exportable volume (Sri Lanka Standards Institution). This figure has not been disaggregated by different kinds of standards. In addition, products affected with mould do not comply with SPS requirements, as this results in aflatoxin in the product. The SPS standards for aflatoxin are 4 ppb according to Codex Alimentarius.

The average fob price of Sri Lankan spices is much lower than the world market prices; for example, 20 per cent for pepper, 69 per cent for nutmeg and 30 per cent for cardamom.[14] This difference, according to exporters, is mainly due to non-compliance with stringent quality standards imposed by the importers.

Sri Lankan economists believe that quality and SPS standards may be more important than tariffs as a factor in determining market access conditions.[15]

For example, the major market for Sri Lankan cardamoms was Singapore, which has mandatory quality standards equivalent to the EU as it is a net re-exporter of cardamoms.

The main market for Sri Lankan pepper exports is India, which absorbed 80 per cent of the total black pepper exports from Sri Lanka in 2000. The remaining 20 per cent is exported to the UK and the USA, which use pepper mainly for oleoresin production, for which the SPS standards are not very restrictive. The high exports to India are due to the high quality standards prevailing in Europe and other major countries such as Singapore and the USA. The exporters fear that as there are several EU restrictions, the UK may also consider imposing high restrictions in time to come.

The higher standards in the EU imply that Sri Lanka is unable to export to the EU, but at the same time it diverts potential trade from EU to India. Access to Indian markets has been facilitated both by the lower standards in India as well as the Indo-Sri Lanka free trade agreement. The two main importers of clove are Saudi Arabia and India. India will provide preferential market access by reducing its import tariff by 50 per cent under an Indo-Lanka Free Trade Agreement. Even though developing countries are the main markets for clove, low quality has severely affected the export volume, as other developing countries supply higher quality products. Thus, even if markets are based only in developing countries, the quality of the product is important.

Currently, the USA and Mexico are the main importers of Sri Lankan cinnamon. According to the exporters, cinnamon undergoes heavy re-processing to improve its quality before export, particularly to the US market.

Problems of compliance   Sri Lankan spices are faced with SPS problems such as the presence of mould, high moisture content, aflatoxin and rodent droppings. These are primarily due to (a) poor weather conditions experienced by many producers with low-cost processing technology, (b) poor storage facilities, (c) the small-scale nature of production units and (d) early harvesting habits to meet family cash needs of resource-poor farmers. Farm-gate quality standards assessments based on Sri Lanka Standards Institution parameters are not equal to international standards. Therefore, a substantial proportion of the products that come to the exporters are of substandard quality. This leads to a direct loss of potential export volume due to non-compliance with SPS requirements. The estimated average volume loss was about 5500 metric tonnes during 1990–2000, 34 per cent of the total exports of spices and beverages. The corresponding total value of the products, estimated at its opportunity cost, was US$2.2 million per year, amounting to about 6 per cent of the foreign exchange earnings from spices and beverages. In total, the estimated value of foreign exchange loss due to non-compliance is US$2.9 million every year. Moreover, the lower price which actually accrued to the producers on account of non-compliance with SPS standards cost them an additional 0.7 million. This is about 7 per cent of the total foreign exchange earnings from spices and beverage crops in 2000.

Costs of compliance   Apart from poor storage facilities, leading to problems caused by moisture and a high percentage of mammalian and other excreta, the small scale of production leads to heterogeneity in quality standards. In order to eradicate these problems, high investment is necessary, which is unaffordable for many small-scale growers. The investments would be needed for:

- Machinery and equipment: drying floors, processing sheds, threshers and hand pulpers are popular facilities, in that order of priority. The cost of most of this can be equal to or more than the annual income of the growers. A government scheme, which offered 50 per cent of the price of machinery as a grant, began in 1999. However, only large producers have managed to purchase the facilities.
- Inadequate scale of production for mechanization: many producers operate on a scale which is smaller than the capacity of available machinery. To overcome this problem the government is organizing group processing, but the effectiveness of such activities has only been marginal.
- Availability of machinery: the mechanization of the system of processing of spices and beverage crops is relatively new. Most of the technology for the process was obtained from India and from a few other countries. Improving the availability of these machines for all growers will take time.
- Information gap: nearly 60 per cent of the exporters involved in the study[16] reported that the products are of an inferior quality and that they would not meet SPS requirements. A much lower percentage of village collectors, retail buyers and wholesale buyers reported the quality of the same products as being inferior. The total cost of training the farmers according to this study is approximately US$2 million for two training programmes covering all the traders. The annual budget allocation for training of stakeholders in this sector is US$24 400, 2.4 per cent of the requirement. This appears exorbitant if we take account of all the other costs involved, such as technology costs. Given that the total value loss due to lack of quality is US$2.9 million per year, the fixed costs in attaining these standards appears inordinately high.

Policy responses   A financial assistance scheme was launched by Sri Lanka. Under this scheme 230 producers have constructed drying floors, 483 have built processing sheds, 26 have obtained various types of machinery, 9 have purchased dryers and 26 have established oil distillation units, with total assistance of US$1.0 million in 1999 and 2000. While this shows the magnitude of processing investment, compared with the total number of producers and processors this contribution was marginal.

India

Standards Complaints have been received from Indian spice exporters about the lack of uniformity in regulations in the EU. The efforts of the European Spice Association (ESA) to lay down uniform standards and codes of practice in collaboration with the spice trade associations of individual European countries are yet to find wider acceptance at EC levels.

Italy and Germany have detained Indian spice consignments on the grounds of pesticide residue.[17] However, both countries failed to justify the changes they made to their existing regulations on microbial contamination and contamination due to pesticide residue.[18] No action has been taken in the WTO, as the developing countries are wary of getting into disputes. Variability in standards, as in the case of acceptable levels of aflatoxin and pesticide residues among countries within Europe, has been a cause of great difficulty for exports from India.

Response strategies In the case of spices, the Spices Board conducts various quality awareness meetings and seminars. Open house meetings, task force meetings and training programmes are some of the means through which information on standards is passed on to the exporters, processors, manufacturers, traders and farmers. Regular post-harvest training programmes are conducted, benefiting farmers, traders, processors, and workers in manufacturing units, exporters, NGOs and extension officials. On average 40–45 000 persons are trained under this programme annually. This would cover roughly 50 per cent of the spice growers in some districts.

Cost of compliance The cost of compliance with standards for aflatoxin and pesticide contamination is very high. The investment in improvement of infrastructure is prohibitive since, for example, high performance liquid chromatography machines needed for detecting pesticides cost Rs.12–20 lakhs or US$30–50 000, whereas the income of a small farmer is approximately US$750 to US$2000 per year. Similarly, operational costs of, for example, chemicals, procedures for compliance with standards and skilled technicians, are very high. A rough estimate of the cost of setting up a moderate lab for testing and analysing samples is US$100 000, which is not only beyond the scope of small farmers but also beyond the scope of government budgets. There is a wide gap between technology used in domestic units and that used in units in developed countries. The difficulty in accessing technology from abroad and its prohibitive cost are other reasons for poor adoption of new technologies by the Indian food industry. A sterilization unit of moderate capacity for spices would cost about US$1 million. Similarly, the technologies needed for the supercritical CO_2 extraction, cryogenic powdering, freeze drying and other processes necessary to produce quality spices are costly.

There is an insufficient supply of certain products, such as chemicals that cause less damage to the environment. Ethylene oxide (ETO) is widely used in the USA as a sterilizing agent, though not in Europe and Japan. Pressure groups are working to bring about a ban on this product, since it is environmentally more damaging than others that are available, though they are less cost effective. Steam sterilization and irradiation are options, but they are expensive. Besides, irradiated products are not universally accepted. There is also an attempt to replace hazardous chemicals like hexane, used as a solvent in spice extraction units, with environmentally less damaging materials like carbon dioxide. However, they are not popular because of their prohibitive cost.

Imported inputs required for processing and analytical work are exorbitant in developing countries. The imported inputs used in chromatography are many times costlier than equivalent local products; however, the local product may not be acceptable to the importing countries.

The investment to effect quality improvement has a longer payback period for small-sized enterprises. This is because their average earning is lower than that of large enterprises, whereas the cost of some of the equipment and procedures is the same for both. There is also a shortage of funds and technical personnel to manage a unit with modern gadgets. Only a few small-scale enterprises can adapt to quality requirements.

This industry is dominated by small producers who find it difficult to apply good manufacturing practices, as well as test their products, before export. The equipment and recurring costs of testing tend to be high. As the domestic consumption of spices is very high, in most cases small producers, who are by and large quite clean, revert to domestic markets. Of course, the price realization in the domestic markets is lower, but the uncertainties of the export markets make it a difficult proposition for small producers. The main grievance of the Indian producers is that since spice is used in very small quantities, there is little scientific justification for applying to it the same standards on aflatoxin or pesticide residues as are applied to rice and peanuts. They, therefore, propose that different standards be developed for spices from those for other products.

Tropical Beverages: Indian Tea

This section explains how large sellers may be able to develop better coping strategies than small exporters.

In recent years, there have been growing reports of pesticide residues in Indian tea, affecting its market access. For example, Germany complained about high residue levels of ethion in Darjeeling teas. Complaints were also received about high levels of bicofol in Assam, Terai and Booras teas. In response to these complaints, the Indian government banned the application of DDT, BHC, aldrin, aldrex, endrine, heptachlor, chlordane and tetradifon in the mid 1990s. Moreover, there are government guidelines which state that if chemicals such as thjiomton, dimethoate, monocroptos, fenicyphermethrin, fenvalerate, phorat, phosphomodon, formothian, acephate and carboxin are applied during the plucking season, the lot plucked immediately after such spraying should be discarded.

Varying standards
In the past, doubts have been raised about the justification of some of the objections about pesticide residue in the European market. In 1995, the German limit of 0.01 mg of tetradifon and 2 mg of ethion per kg of tea were somewhat arbitrarily imposed because of lack of data from India on its pesticide safety limits for tea. Later that year, the Teekanne Darjeeling Gold brand of tea was rejected because it contained 0.24 mg of tetrafidon per kg, 24 times the limit set by Germany. The rejection was soon followed by a report by the German Institute of Environment Analytics, Messzelle, branding it as unsafe. On the other hand, there were no rejections from the UK, another European market, which continued to import it. This led some to believe that the German ban was protectionist, as they were using the standard as an instrument to control prices, or that there was no ban in the UK because most of the Indian tea firms follow British principles of production, devised during the colonial era.

The tea estates are largely well managed and employ sufficiently educated people to follow government guidelines. The production process is sophisticated enough to ensure compliance with these standards. However, testing and conformity assessment for these standards are difficult. There is only one institute, the Pesticide Residue Laboratory, which can test commercial samples of tea in India, and testing itself is very expensive. The test required for clearing a consignment for Germany costs roughly US$234 per analysis (see Saqib, 1999).[19] This is unaffordable for the bulk tea exporters, who get a much lower price than specialized tea producers.

The Tea Research Association now monitors pesticide residues. Exporters apply the ISO 3720 standard. The Indian standards are even more stringent than the ISO and the standards of all other countries, except Japan. The best tea is supplied to the UK and Japan, while the lower quality goes to countries such as Russia, Poland and Iran. The stricter EC standards apply to exports to the UK, while for Japan an EIC inspection suffices.

Summary

The cost of tests required for tea to meet the necessary standards for export to European countries is exorbitant. Producers question the appropriateness of the standard. The tea markets are dominated by multinationals, which have evolved their own brands and load the market premiums at the retail end. Tea is bought at auctions where costs of products can vary and the high cost of complying with standards can easily lead to lower price realization. It has proved difficult for TNCs to emerge from India even though India is the largest exporter of tea. However, this industry is relatively well organized and has devised strategies for compliance, including the setting of its own standards rather than meekly accepting international ones.

Conclusions

Meeting SPS standards demands acquisition of technology, heavy investment, training of personnel, and better management from the level of procurement of raw materials to packaging and selling. Only a few processing/manufacturing units follow good manufacturing practices (GMP) and a small number are accredited to ISO 9000 and 14000 series. Thus, the overall preparedness of South Asian countries is low.

The infrastructure for testing and certification available in South Asia is insufficient to meet the needs of the region. Apart from the laboratories of the Directorate of Marketing and Inspection, the Export Inspection Agencies and the Commodity Boards/Export Promotion Councils, there are only a few laboratories in the private sector which can undertake analytical work. Some manufacturing/processing units have developed in-house laboratories for quality evaluation. Certification cost, especially for inspection and testing, is beyond the reach of small and medium enterprises. Most exporters also complain that standards may be frequently protectionist or used to bid down prices. A lower price realization has been reported by almost all producers, primarily due to poor standards. Risk assessment strategies have not been very useful, since they are usually not applicable to conditions of production in South Asian countries. Capacity problems, especially the lack of technology and finance, have been found to be important bottlenecks.

Lack of clarity and transparency in the implementation of standards has been another major problem. What is most distressing to producers is that compliance with SPS standards does not ensure better price realization. In fact, as the markets are commodity markets, they are driven by supply and demand factors rather than by quality. Thus, meeting SPS and environmental requirements is a minimum condition for market access but not a sufficient condition for higher prices.

DOMESTIC STANDARD-SETTING

One of the views emerging strongly in the 'Standards and Trade' debate is that SPS and other standards must be implemented at the domestic level for domestically produced and sold goods, rather than just for exports to developing countries. This is because realizing economies of scale, as well as maintaining higher standards, requires a holistic rather than a narrowly focused, export-oriented approach. This section thus examines the domestic standard setting processes and institutions in South Asian countries that could assist in upgrading domestic standards.

Bangladesh

In Bangladesh the Ministry of Agriculture, the Ministry of Livestock and Fisheries and the Ministry of Health and Family Planning look after the sanitary and phytosanitary measures of the country at present. The Director of the Plant Protection wing of the Ministry of Agriculture is responsible for execution and implementation of the existing national or international Plant Quarantine Legislation and Agreement. Aquatic animal health and health of livestock are looked after by the Directorate of Livestock, which arranges for inspection of imported animals, poultry birds and fisheries and looks for signs and symptoms of diseases and pests, and puts animals under quarantine.

The import and export of agricultural commodities in Bangladesh are regulated by the 'Destructive Insects and Pests Rules, 1966 (Plant Quarantine), amended in July 1989.[20] This is based on the FAO guidelines on sound plant quarantine principles and procedures for trade. The Plant Protection wing of the Department of Agricultural Extension (DAE) under the Ministry of Agriculture is responsible for implementing this guideline. At the national level, a Director General heads the DAE. He is assisted by a 'Director' from each of the wings, namely Plant Protection, Field Service, Food Crops, Cash Crops and Training. Personnel and Administration (P&A) and Planning and Evaluation (P&E) are the two other wings directly linked with the director general, DAE.

There are five sections in the Plant Protection wing, namely Plant Quarantine Section, Pesticide Administration and Quality Control, Operation (Aerial and Ground), Surveillance and Forecasting, and Integrated Pest Management.

At present 16 plant quarantine stations are functioning at different entry points to Bangladesh. Some of these are equipped with moderate plant quarantine facilities. Bangladesh and India signed a bilateral memorandum of understanding in 1978. According to this, about 15 land border check-posts were surveyed to study the feasibility of opening new plant quarantine stations. Bangladesh established nine land border check-posts, three airports, two seaports and one river port for plant quarantine. New quarantine stations are to be established by both India and Bangladesh at the borders.[21]

Environment Policy, 1992, encompasses different sectors such as (a) agriculture, (b) industry, (c) health and sanitation, (d) energy and fuel, (e) water development, flood control and irrigation, (f) land, (g) forest, wildlife and biodiversity, (h) fisheries and livestock, (i) food, (j) coastal and marine environment, (k) transport and communication, (l) housing and urbanization, (m) population, (n) education and public awareness and (o) science, technology and research.

The government has also undertaken a wide range of initiatives such as enacting the environment bill in 1995, and the Ministry of Science and Technology has prepared the Bio-Safety Guidelines for Bangladesh in 1999. The objectives of the bio-safety guidelines are to ensure safe transfer, handling and use of living, modified organisms, with special focus on safeguarding human and animal health, the environment, biological diversity and the socio-economic welfare of societies, including trans-boundary movement of any of these organisms.

The present plant inspection and quarantine rules of Bangladesh are out of date and should be completely renewed in order to fulfil the needs of the country and to comply with the FAO convention and the Application of Sanitary and Phytosanitary Measures (WTO SPS Agreement). A list of important plant diseases occurring in Bangladesh will be of considerable value not only to the country itself but also to importers from Bangladesh. At present, there is no coordination between plant health inspection and quarantine services in Bangladesh and the corresponding ones in the neighbouring countries. Thus, there is great demand at all levels for more information about the work and importance of plant health inspections and quarantines.

India

There is no comprehensive body that sets SPS standards in India. The domestic standards, which correspond to SPS standards, operate under the Prevention of Food Adulteration (PFA) Act 1954; the AGMARK standard, which is a voluntary grading system operated by the Directorate of Marketing Inspection under the Ministry of Agriculture; the Bureau of Indian Standards; and the Export Inspection and Quality Control Act, among others.

The Government of India has set up a National Codex Committee under the Department of Health, Ministry of Health and Family Welfare, which has identified six major areas, namely:

- fish and marine products;
- meat and meat products;
- fruits and vegetables;
- spices and condiments;
- milk products and cereal;
- nuts and oil seeds.

Base papers on these subjects were prepared by the Spices Board, the Agricultural and Processed Food Products Export Development Authority (APEDA), the Directorate of Vanaspathy, Vegetable Oils and Fats, the Central Food Trade Research Institute and other such bodies. The observations emanating from these papers have led to the establishment of institutionalized training programmes in areas of HACCP and GMP (fisheries, fruits and vegetables); a revision of PFA standards based on grade specifications for export (spices and condiments) including parameters for microbial limits; the establishment of maximum tolerance limits/MRLs for pesticide residue and aflatoxin; an emphasis on physical characteristics and cleanliness; the allocation of food identifier codes (spices); strengthening of analytical laboratories in all food sectors; improving existing laboratories to reach BIS levels; harmonization of maximum tolerance limits for different pesticides for different food groups/foods under PFA and Codex and a multicentric study on use of edible colours in food products (CFTRI and NIN). A Shadow Committee on general principles and a Steering Committee for setting up standards for organic foods and so on have also started work.

These standards are comparable with international standards for all major agricultural crops, especially where chemical and microbiological standards are concerned. The standards followed by sectors like spices and marine products are compatible with international standards. The Government of India is attempting to develop national standards that encompass all areas of operation, but the pace of formulation and implementation is slow, because coordination between various ministries is often difficult.

Though there are a number of laws on food standards, enforcement is a critical problem. The departments responsible for their enforcement often do not have adequate resources, testing facilities or trained personnel, and the penalty provisions are not strong enough to have the desired deterrent effect.

Nepal

Nepal has implemented the Agriculture Perspective Plan (APP) for the overall development of the country. The history of food control in Nepal began with the Food Act of 1966, which was implemented through Food Regulations in 1979 by the Department of Food Technology and Quality Control (DFTQC) under the Ministry of Agriculture. Five regional laboratories are assigned the responsibility of conducting inspections and laboratory investigations.

The Food Standardization Board has so far formulated 84 mandatory food standards under the Food Act for milk and milk products, edible oils and fats, fruits and vegetables, spices and condiments, grains and legumes, cereal products, bakery and confectionary, sweetening agents and some other products.

Inadequacies of inspection, laboratories and enforcement units limit the application of national standards. The strengthening of the National Food Control Agency is seen as an important step in enhancing Nepal's capability in food trade as well as in implementing WTO's SPS and TBT requirements in the country.

Pakistan

Pakistan has a number of regulations and standards to prevent food adulteration and to ensure hygiene and quality. These are used at both the domestic production level and the import level. The WTO Secretariat's Report on the Trade Policy Review of Pakistan, conducted in 1995, observed that the country has made some efforts to base its standards on international norms. It further remarked that national standards on only a small number of items are inferior to international norms, owing to domestic non-availability of the required technology, and Pakistani standards do not seem to constitute a major impediment to trade. In some cases, controls on imports have been made more lenient. For example, in its trade policy for the year 1995–96 the prescribed shelf life of imported edible oil products was reduced from 75 per cent to 50 per cent at the time of import. It has been observed that the exporting countries have often taken an undue advantage of the poor local and physical infrastructure of Pakistan to enforce SPS standards.[22]

Sri Lanka

The Sri Lanka Standards Institution (SLSI) is the national body responsible for setting and monitoring food standards and it is also a national enquiry point for the implementation of the SPS Agreement. In this capacity SLSI is responsible for the dissemination of information to exporters regarding changes to trade partners' product standards in various industries.

In the case of food items, SLSI adheres to international health and safety standards and guidelines, such as Codex standards, as strictly as possible. Sri Lanka is a member of the Codex Alimentarius Commission, which has set 237 food commodity standards, 41 hygienic practice codes, and over 3200 maximum residue limits for pesticides. The control of pesticides is by the Department of Agriculture under the Authority of Registrar of Pesticides. The

Ministry of Health, through the Food Act No. 26, 1980, exercises general control on the health aspects of the food industry. Testing and inspection procedures are also harmonized with international procedures.

SLSI has three categories of certification: voluntary adoption schemes, voluntary SLS certification and mandatory certification. Certain food items such as canned fish, fruit cordials, drinks and condensed milk come under the compulsory certification schemes. Other products have also been brought under this scheme in 2001. SLSI has also certified around 10 auditors for HACCP. Food manufacturing organizations intending to get ISO 9000 need to comply with the food hygiene requirements. There is a proposal to bring imported products under the SLS certification schemes.

In addition, SLSI has recently proposed the initiation of an independent national accreditation body, which will facilitate the smooth flow of exports. It will, specifically, be an umbrella organization governing a national standards body, a national measurement laboratory, other testing laboratories and conformity assessment bodies.

The Plant Protection Act has recently been revised and is due to be gazetted shortly, in line with some of the SPS requirements. The biggest constraint facing the government in amending the plant quarantine regulations is the inability to provide the necessary and complementary testing facilities, due to resource constraints.

There is no government-managed system in Sri Lanka to provide compulsory quality certification for spice and beverage crops (tea is a special case where the Tea Board provides compulsory quality certification). The pre-shipment quality testing process is optional for the exporter. However, the exporters make arrangements with their international importers on a private basis to provide information on the quality of the products being traded. The required facilities for quality testing are available at the Sri Lanka Standards Institution (SLSI) and a few other laboratories belonging to private organizations. The government does not subsidize the cost of the quality certification process.[23]

A national enquiry point (NEP) to obtain quality parameters for spices and beverages has not been formally established for Sri Lanka. SLSI functions as a focal point for the information, but the online linkages of SLSI and international standard setting organizations are very poor. The Director of the Department of Animal Health and Production has been appointed as an NEP for animal products. The most appropriate government institution for this purpose, in the case of spices and beverages, is the Department of Export Agriculture (DEA), which has linkages with growers, traders and exporters. Infrastructure facilities, human capacity development, and increased and systematic interactions with all stakeholders of the industry are required at a sustainable cost for the purpose.

Conclusion

In most South Asian countries the legal framework for developing and monitoring SPS and environmental standards has already been set up. However, implementation and monitoring remains a challenge, largely on account of the lack of technical, financial and monitoring capacities. The shortage of equipment and laboratories also remains a critical problem.

NOTES

1. 'A New WTO Round – Agriculture, SPS and the Environment – Capturing the Benefits for South Asia', New Delhi, January 11–13, 2001. The agenda and the list of participants are attached as annexes to this report.
2. For additional information on South Asian exports subject to SPS and other quality requirements, see S. Subasinghe, 'Promotion of export processing of value-added fishery products from Bangladesh: a success story of an integrated project', and V.C. Mathur, 'Export potential of onion: a case study of India', prepared for Regional Workshop on Commodity Export Diversification and Poverty Reduction in South and South-East Asia (Bangkok, Thailand, 3–5 April 2001), organized by UNCTAD in cooperation with ESCAP under project 'Capacity building for diversification and commodity based development'. See also http://www.unctad.org/infocomm/Diversification/bangkok/bangkok.htm#
3. The study on marine products draws upon an exhaustive survey done by Atul Kaushik and Mohammed Saqib for UNCTAD under project IND/97/955.
4. India's marine exports attract automatic detention in the United States. Automatic detention means the product must be sampled and tested before it gains entry into the country, which means delays, storage costs and a substantial refusal rate. According to some estimates at present the value of detained fishery products in the US is valued at US$14 million (or 15 per cent) out of total exports of US$108.2 million to the country in 1996–97 (Chemonics-ACE Project 1998).
5. 'EU Ban on Shrimp Imports from Bangladesh: A Case Study on Market Access Problems Faced by the LDCs', by Professor Mustafijur Rahman, presented at the CUTS Seminar on SPS Standards and Trade, April 2001.
6. Ibid.
7. Kausik and Saqib, 2000, Rajiv Gandhi Institute for Development Studies, mimeograph
8. Basu, M.S and Radhakrishanan, 'Capacity Building in Peanut Farms: A Success Story', paper presented at the UNCTAD/World Bank workshop on 11–13 January 2001.
9. Basu, M.S., 1999, 'UNDP project successfully reduces aflatoxin in Indian peanuts', in the Australian Centre for International Agricultural Research Food Legume Programme Newsletter, February 1999.
10. Data from APEDA.
11. Primary research with questionnaires was carried out for 30 mango pulp exporting firms for this project. The author is grateful for the research assistance provided by Ms Shilpi Kapoor for this survey.
12. Primary information was collected from approximately 20–25 rice-exporting firms. The author gratefully acknowledges the research assistance provided by Mr Chandrasekhar for this survey.
13. *A Study of Compliance of Sanitary and Phytosanitary Requirements in Beverages and Spices in Sri Lanka* by Anura Herath, 2000, Economics Research Unit, Department of Export Agriculture, Sri Lanka.
14. Ibid.
15. Ibid.

16. Study conducted by Anura Herath, quoted above.
17. Exporters considered this to be a denial of their rights under Article 7 of the Agreement on the Application of SPS Measures, dealing with transparency. In accordance with the provisions given in Annexure – B, the members shall notify changes in their SPS measures and shall provide information. These provisions insist on publication of regulations and establishment of *enquiry points*. Apart from ensuring prompt publication of all SPS regulations for the benefit of the members of WTO, the member country has to offer sufficient time to others to implement the changes suggested, especially in adopting the changes to their products and methods of production.
18. Kittu, C., Deputy Director, Spices Board, 'Issues on SPS and Environmental Standards for India', paper presented at the UNCTAD/World Bank Conference on 11–13 January 2001.
19. M. Saqib, 1999, 'Impact of standards on Indian trade', study prepared for UNCTAD under project IND/97/955.
20. Hussein and Shahadad, paper presented in the workshop, 'A New WTO Round – Agriculture, SPS and Environment: Capturing the Benefits for South Asia', sponsored by UNCTAD and the World Bank in partnership with the SAARC Secretariat, 11–13 January 2001, New Delhi, India. The authors are Member-Director and Principal Scientific Officer of Agricultural Economics & Rural Sociology Division, Bangladesh Agricultural Research Council, New Airport Road, Farmgate, Dhaka-1215, Bangladesh.
21. Md. Muslehuddin Faruque, Sanitary and Phystosanitary Specialist, BGD/98/008 FAO of UN, who prepared the 'Report of the Agreement on Sanitary and Phytosanitary Measures'.
22. Sarfaraj Khan Qureshi, paper presented at the UNCTAD/World Bank Conference, 11–13 January 2001.
23. Ginige, S.L., 2001, 'Implementation of Food Sanitary Standards in Sri Lanka', paper presented at the UNCTAD/World Bank workshop, 11–13 January 2001.

4. Costa Rica

Eduardo Gitli, Max Valverde and María Pérez-Esteve

INTRODUCTION

This chapter examines the implications of sanitary, phytosanitary and environmental requirements on exports from Central America, in particular Costa Rica. It also examines trading conditions for organic agricultural products. The objective is to make recommendations for future trade negotiations and strategies at national and international levels, to strengthen the capacity of Central American countries to respond to health and environment related requirements and opportunities, and to improve their participation in the world trading system. The project conducted studies on the following sectors:[1,2]

- poultry, a case of the application of SPS regulations against specific avian diseases and HACCP, in the context of trade within Central America and with the United States;[3]
- fisheries, with an emphasis on shrimps, which are subject to environmental measures as well as Hazard Analysis Critical Control Point (HACCP) and stringent testing requirements.[4]

The two cases examined are different in scope. In the poultry industry there are different degrees of tariff protection practically everywhere. However, it is the presence of animal diseases and sanitary requirements that make free trade difficult. The trade in fishery products, in this case shrimps, is a case of environmental barriers, which are important, especially for some countries; but testing and HACCP requirements also have important implications for exports.

The two cases under review, though sometimes mixing tariff and non-tariff barriers, strengthen the point that a better participation in the world trade system implies much more than so-called 'modern' or new generation agreements. In the absence of a number of conditions, comparative advantages alone do not guarantee trade possibilities (see, for example, the poultry industry in Costa Rica). These conditions may include strong mechanisms of international cooperation, negotiators' awareness, domestic association between private and public sectors, and specific public investments to be able to comply with the standards and guidelines set by importing countries.

POULTRY[5]

International trade in poultry products is subject to a series of tariff and non-tariff barriers and often appears to elude the rules of the MTS, resulting in very specific and fragmented markets.

The poultry industry must comply with SPS measures and other requirements in order to gain access to international markets. These include the recognition of Newcastle disease-free regions or countries (Newcastle disease is an exotic disease affecting birds) and certified implementation of Hazard Analysis Critical Control Point (HACCP) approaches.

Exports of poultry products by Central American countries are very small and mostly confined to trade within the region. Costa Rica, the principal poultry exporter, sells to several countries in and outside the region. It has been targeting the US market. El Salvador, the second largest exporter, does not export poultry products to markets outside Central America. Nicaragua and Panama export very low levels of poultry to other countries in the region. This could explain why only Costa Rica has made efforts to be declared Newcastle disease-free, a pre-requisite to enter the United States market. In the case of other countries, the entrepreneurial sector seems to be primarily concerned with maintaining its 'hegemony' in the domestic market. Producers seem to feel that the internal market is large enough to develop their businesses and do not wish to enter international competition.

The domestic poultry industry in Central America is controlled by two or three firms in each country which satisfy the local market needs and even export if there is an open market. It is estimated that poultry production holds between 1 and 2.5 per cent of the gross domestic product (GDP) of Central American countries. It represents between 9 and 15 per cent of agricultural GDP in these countries. Foreign trade, at an average of only 1 per cent, represents a very small share of Central American apparent consumption.

Domestic prices of whole chicken meat in the USA are not substantially different from those in Central America, but the dark meat (thighs and legs) is considerably cheaper, whereas breasts are more expensive because of greater demand for them. In Central America, the situation is the opposite. One would thus expect Central American countries to specialize in exporting breasts and the US producers to export thighs and legs. However, since the US market is closed for Central American poultry meat (for sanitary reasons), such trade flows are unlikely. If the Central American countries open their markets, they risk inundation with US exports. In other words, free trade will result in substantially reduced prices in the domestic market, driving a large number of local producers out of the market, without providing outlets for poultry breasts in the US market. Thus, there is pressure to keep the markets closed. Producers in Central America argue that the absence of free trade in international markets results in artificial price differentials in poultry meat (dark part against white part). Therefore, they justify high tariffs for the 'poultry part'. In Costa Rica, legs and thighs have a tariff of 154 per cent, compared to 40 per cent for whole chicken. With some exceptions, this is the general trend in Central American countries (and most of the world). In the United States tariffs are around 12 to 15 per cent, but SPS measures exclude certain countries from the market. If a true real price-arbitrating international market could be achieved, prices of different parts of chicken would tend to converge.

Poultry products have been excluded from most regional free-trade agreements (FTAs), such as the Costa Rica–Mexico FTA and, more recently, the Chile–Costa Rica FTA. This shows how sensitive regional poultry farmers are to liberalization. Negotiations between Central America and the Dominican Republic, leading to an FTA, also exclude poultry products from the bilateral treaty. Nonetheless, Costa Rica and the Dominican Republic negotiated a quota, established solely by the latter, to be applied to chicken breast imports from Costa Rica, with a preferential tariff of 12.5 per cent. This represents half the general tariff applied in all other countries. Chicken meat has been included in the Mexico–Nicaragua FTA, although Nicaragua's poultry sector argues that the country was left at a disadvantage because of the cost of raw materials and the presence of large US companies in Mexico which were rapidly overtaking the business. Regarding the Central America–Dominican Republic FTA, Nicaragua's position is noteworthy. This country decided not to ratify the agreement after negotiations concluded in 1999, because it felt that opening the Dominican market to certain agricultural products was against its interests. However, should the treaty be ratified, Nicaragua would be assured of preferential quotas for its chicken meat in this market. Guatemala did not include poultry products in its FTA negotiations with the Dominican Republic.

Health Norms

The presence of diseases in certain products has given rise to the important concept of regionalization or *free areas*. This designation, contained in the SPS Agreement, is crucial for international trade, because it suggests that countries must have the opportunity to export from areas declared free from a particular plague or disease, or from areas with low incidence of the disease, even if the disease should exist somewhere else within the country. This concept represents a leap forward in the policies of certain countries, where zero risk tolerance used to be a common practice. In order to be declared plague- or disease-free, countries are required to undergo a lengthy process of data collection for pertinent analysis and evaluation.

Export and Health Problems

Newcastle disease-free
One of the fundamental requirements for a country wishing to export poultry products to the United States is to be declared Newcastle disease-free. To gain this status, a country must undergo a lengthy procedure.[6] For example, it took Costa Rica five to eight years and at least \$1 million in expenditures to be declared Newcastle disease-free.[7] The process involved joint and individual efforts among representatives from the entrepreneurial sectors and the governmental institutions concerned: the Ministry of Agriculture and Livestock (MAG) in Costa Rica and the United States Department of Agriculture (USDA) through its Animal and Plant Health Inspection Service (APHIS). See Box 4.1.

BOX 4.1 COSTA RICA AS A NEWCASTLE DISEASE-FREE COUNTRY

The United States requires countries wishing to export chicken meat to its market to be included in a list of countries recognized by the USDA. Exports are allowed only from countries or regions declared free of Newcastle disease.

Efforts by Costa Rica to be declared free of Newcastle disease sprang from a governmental and private initiative. The whole process took eight years. A Newcastle Commission was established in 1991 (Executive Decree 2055-MAG, 2 July 1991). It was composed of four government representatives (Ministry of Agriculture and Livestock), two private sector representatives and one USDA-APHIS official. The process required participation from many sectors involved in the poultry industry, as well as a series of activities, including the following:

- preparation of a handbook for preventing, controlling and eradicating Newcastle disease, to be used in case of an outbreak;
- preparation of a handbook on procedures for regulating imports of poultry products and sub-products in Costa Rica;

- seminar – rehearsal of a Newcastle outbreak for official and poultry industry veterinarians, with USDA participants;
- answering and translating the USDA-APHIS questionnaire required to apply for the Newcastle disease-free declaratory (sent to Washington in June 1993, it obtained US approval in September 1993);
- several informative talks, including varied teaching aids for small, medium and large poultry producers;
- preparation and publication of informative brochures for producers, aimed at keeping them watchful for the disease;
- visit from the USDA-APHIS authorities, in February 1994, who in turn met with the Newcastle Commission in order to evaluate progress in the declaratory; in April 1994 the USDA sent its report on its previous visit to Costa Rica;
- national sampling of backyard birds (in high-risk areas such as those near the northern border, in areas containing large poultry farms and near the Juan Santa Maria International Airport) and industrial enterprises including laying hens;
- implementation of the Epidemiological Vigilance sampling in poultry breeding farms and backyard birds in hazard-prone areas;
- serological laboratory diagnosis;
- sampling of 426 farms, of which 17 were industrial enterprises, 405 were households with backyard birds and 4 were other sorts of birds; a total of 3,065 birds were sampled nationwide.

Costa Rica unilaterally declared itself Newcastle disease-free on 26 April. However, it had to wait one additional year for official recognition by the United States. This came on 6 June 1997, when the United States included Costa Rica in its list of eligible countries.

Sources: B. Olga Marta Vargas (1996) Muestreo Nacional Enfermedad Newcastle V-V. Informe Final, Dirección de Protección Agropecuaria, Gerencia de Salud Animal, Comisión Newcastle, Heredia, September 1995; USDA-APHIS (1997), 'Change in disease status of Costa Rica because of exotic Newcastle disease', *Federal Register*, **62** (99), May, pp. 27938–40, www.aphis.usda.gov:80/ppd/rad/OldRules/96-077.2.f, accessed 1/10/99.

Hazard Analysis Critical Control Point

The Hazard Analysis Critical Control Point (HACCP) was documented in the United States at the beginning of the 1970s[8] and food industries in the European Union and the United States started using it in the 1980s. The Codex Alimentarius Commission has recognized the HACCP as a requisite for food treatment. In a recent communication, the Commission states that:

> The Hazard Analysis Critical Control Point system (HACCP) was conceived as a way of ensuring food safety. Governments are responsible for encouraging the industry to apply the HACCP system to analyse potential hazards, identify the points where these can be controlled and describe process parameters and their critical limits, as well as follow-up procedures. Operators are trained to control the part of the process they are responsible for, to follow-up the efficacy of their controls and to adopt adequate corrective measures in the case of deviations. (FAO, 1999).[9]

The HACCP was introduced into the US poultry sector in 1996 to avoid contamination through identification and control of certain procedures of the production process prone to contamination hazards (USITC, 1998:16).[10] The system is now used in the entire US poultry industry.

The HACCP has not yet been widely implemented in Costa Rica. Therefore one of the requisites for exporting to the United States had not been fulfilled in 1997. In fact, according to a communication from the USDA, the USA did not expect any significant changes in imports of poultry products from Costa Rica despite the country having been declared Newcastle disease-free (USDA-APHIS, 1997).[11]

After being declared Newcastle disease-free, Costa Rica began formal procedures to prove compliance with the HACCP.[12] To achieve this goal, the country must comply with a series of forms or protocols prior to an inspection of the production plants by USDA officials. Sources from the MAG told the research team (in 2001) that the protocols had been submitted more than two years earlier, in 1998, while others said that they were sent in the first months of the year 2000. Sources from the United States informed the researchers that the documents had actually been sent at the end of 2000 and that inspections from the USDA were therefore delayed. Finally, the research team found out that official communication of the remittance was sent from Costa Rica on 18 December 2000. It specifies that the first protocol was submitted on 16 June 2000.[13] Thus, it seems that delays in accreditation of Costa Rica for the HACCP are due to the time it took the Costa Rican authorities to submit the protocols. But Costa Rican producers and national authorities insist that the problem was due to the fact that each time they complied with a requirement a new one came up, and new requests for information and new criteria for inspections caused the delays.

BOX 4.2 PROCEDURE REQUIRED TO EXPORT
MEAT AND CHICKEN TO THE UNITED
STATES

The United States requires that poultry products exported to its market must be produced under standards equivalent to its own regarding safety, wholesomeness and labelling. The authorities responsible for enforcing these measures are the United States Department of Agriculture (USDA) and the Food Safety Inspection Service (FSIS). The FSIS oversees livestock, products such as sheep, pigs, goats, horses and all poultry products. The last include all processed products which have more than two or three per cent poultry meat as a basic ingredient.

The competent authorities in the United States must approve countries' exports and plants. The process by which a country may be declared eligible to export to the USA involves the evaluation of information requested from the country, followed by on-site inspection. The evaluation covers the exporting country's laws and regulations, focusing on five key hazard areas: contamination, disease, processing, residues and economic fraud. If the result is satisfactory, in the next stage a US technical team visits the country in order to carry out an exhaustive evaluation of equipment, laboratories, training programmes and inspection systems, and an inspection of plants. Once this phase is concluded, if the FSIS deems the system 'equivalent' to that of the USA, the country becomes eligible for exporting poultry meat to the USA. Periodical inspections take place later on to ensure that this equivalence continues between both the countries.

Once a country holds a stamp of approval it may export poultry meat to the United States, subject to import inspection requirements. One of these concerns labelling. Import inspections require labels on the containers as well as labels detailing the product. The latter must comply with requirements for household products.

Certified export plants must have their labelling approved before they prepare the product for export. Labels must be in English and include name of the product, establishment number and country of origin, name and address of the manufacturer or distributor, net amount, list of ingredients and handling instructions. Large shipments do not require pre-approval, but they are inspected at the port of entry. For meat and chicken shipments, the FSIS requires (i) an original certificate from the country of origin, indicating that the product was inspected by the national inspection service and is eligible for export to the USA; (ii) an import inspection report and form (FSIS form 9540-1).

Afterwards, through the Automated Import Information System, the country's plant and product are examined to determine whether it may export to the USA. There are two alternative results. First, it can be concluded that preliminary inspection was sufficient and no further inspection is required (cases with a good history record). Second, a series of inspections may be required, including detailed checking of net weight of packages, examining container conditions, searching for defects in the products, and laboratory analysis of product composition, microbiological contamination, residues and species. During these inspections, a certain amount of product is randomly selected and examined by FSIS import inspectors. When product samples are sent to FSIS laboratories for analysis, the shipment is usually released before the test results are received. However, if the plant has a record of previous violations or a problem is suspected, the shipment is held until laboratory results are known. When a shipment passes inspection, each shipping container is stamped with the official mark of inspection and released into the USA's commercial stream. From this point, the shipment is treated as domestic product.

If a shipment does not meet US requirements, the containers are stamped 'U.S. Refused Entry,' and the entire shipment must be exported, destroyed, or – with the approval of FDA – converted to animal food within 45 days.

Source: USDA, Food Safety and Inspection Service, *Importing Meat and Poultry to the United States: A Guide for Importers and Brokers* (http://www.fsis.usda.gov:80/OA/ptograms/import.htm), 20 September 1999.

Import Requirements

In December 2000 the Costa Rican government modified import requirements for poultry products, which were required to be free of (a) Newcastle disease, (b) avian influenza, (c) *Salmonella pullorum*, (d) typhoid fever and (e) ornithosis. Foreign processing plants and slaughterhouses were obliged to undergo official inspection and obtain authorization to export poultry meat to

Costa Rica. They also needed official certification from competent authorities in their own country stating that the poultry products were suitable for human consumption.

The new requirements came into force on 1 January 2001, and since then poultry imports from the United States have been suspended. The USA has argued that this measure is unjustified, because previously USDA inspections sufficed. However, Costa Rican authorities point out that the new legislation is to be applied and that plants exporting to Costa Rica, therefore, are to be inspected by national (Costa Rican) authorities.

Summary

In its quest to sell poultry to the USA, Costa Rica's largest problem was to prove that it was free from Newcastle disease and that it fulfilled HACCP requirements. In 1997, the USA declared Costa Rica Newcastle disease-free. The compliance cost for this declaration was estimated at a minimum of $1 million, and the process was considered to have been time consuming. However, it was with the process of being accepted as complying with HACCP requirements that considerations of purposeful delays on the grounds of protectionism were suspected. Checks for HACPP compliance seemed to take inordinately long owing to new requirements being made when previous ones were met. Opportunity costs were estimated at loss of trade for the five to eight years that it took to be declared Newcastle disease-free.

The problems have now been overcome, and Costa Rica can export chicken parts to the USA. Meanwhile, requirements for imports of chicken parts from the USA into Costa Rica have been tightened.

FISHERIES[14]

Introduction

Costa Rica is a minor player in the world trade in fishery products. Approximately 80 per cent of the Costa Rican fishing fleet consists of small boats. In 2000, Costa Rica earned US$103.4 million from exports, which was a significant decrease from 1999. While the export of some products, such as fresh, frozen and preserved fish, increased, there was a decline in the export of shrimp.

The United States has applied several environment-related trade measures to Costa Rican exports of fishery products. For example, between 1992 and August 2000, Costa Rica could not export tuna to the United States because of the United States' well-known dolphin conservation measures taken against tuna producing countries. Despite the long period, Costa Rica was in no hurry to negotiate the standard, since most of its production went to the Central American or the European market[15] even before the trade measure came into force. However, shrimps were exported largely to the USA.

The United States enacted legislation in 1987, which became fully operational in 1990, to protect an associated species harmed during shrimp-catching operations: turtles. This legislation affected the international shrimp trade and took the form of an environmental trade measure. It led to a dispute under the WTO Dispute Settlement Understanding and has had important repercussions on the Costa Rican catching techniques.

Costa Rica also faces problems in complying with standards imposed by the HACCP requirements for exports to the USA and the EU.

Turtle Excluder Devices

Pursuant to the United States Endangered Species Act (ESA) of 1973, all sea turtles that occur in US waters were listed as endangered or threatened species. The drowning of sea turtles in shrimp trawls was identified as a serious problem in the 1970s. In 1980 the National Marine Fisheries Service (NMFS) devised a solution to the problem: the turtle excluder device (TED). Finally, in 1987, the United States issued regulations pursuant to the ESA that required all United States shrimp trawlers to use TEDs or tow-time restrictions in specified areas where there was a significant mortality of sea turtles associated with shrimp harvesting.[16]

After delays due to challenges in state and federal courts, the 1987 Regulations became fully effective in 1990 and were modified to require the use of TEDs at all times and in all areas where shrimp trawling interacts in a significant way with sea turtles. In the beginning, these regulations affected only US operations and boats. However, environmental groups filed judicial complaints demanding that turtles be protected outside the US borders owing to their highly migratory nature. Several environmental organizations acted as plaintiffs: the Earth Island Institute, the American Society for the Prevention of Cruelty to Animals, the US Humane Society and the Sierra Club. In addition to the environmental arguments, there were also commercial concerns. The US shrimp fishing industry complained that fishing operations in countries exporting to the USA were not subject to these requirements, placing them at a competitive disadvantage with trawlers based abroad. Therefore, the Georgia Fishermen's Association Inc. decided to join the cause and acted as plaintiff with the environmental groups.[17]

Developing countries were immediately anxious because of the effect this would have on trade and competition. One of the few NGO websites to mention a possible benefit to the US industry was that of the Friends of the Earth. According to them,

[s]ome might argue that this is a case of 'green protectionism' (that is, using an environmental measure to protect a domestic industry). However, given the fact that this measure left imports of shrimps from aquaculture, non-sea turtle areas and non-trawler areas unimpeded, the US shrimp fishing industry still faced ample competition. Thus, the claim that this was a case of 'green protectionism' is probably erroneous.'[18]

This statement is not completely accurate. It is true that aquaculture shrimp, non-sea turtle areas and non-trawler areas were unrestrained. It is also true that some big exporters like Ecuador (19 per cent of the US market in 1995) used aquaculture techniques and remained unaffected.[19] Nonetheless, at the time it was estimated that as much as 30 per cent of the US shrimp imports were going to be affected by the restriction.[20] The US fishing vessels supply only a third of the shrimp consumed in that country,[21] so a potential 30 per cent reduction in import competition is not negligible.

In a former study, a group of researchers from the Centre for Economic Policy on Sustainable Development (CINPE) based in Costa Rica established that the group of countries potentially affected by the new measures represented approximately 75 per cent of the *domestic consumption* in the USA.[22] This explains the ambiguous position of the US government in this matter. In the beginning, administration officials did not pay much attention to the new rules, but as pressure mounted they hardened their controls. They tried to find different ways to solve the problem for Latin American suppliers. However, no efforts were made to tackle this problem for Asian producers.

Section 609 of the United States Public Law No. 101-162 provides that shrimp harvested with technology that may adversely affect certain species of sea turtles protected under US law may not be imported into the USA, unless the President annually certifies to the Congress: (a) that the harvesting country concerned has a regulatory programme governing the incidental taking of such sea turtles in the course of such harvesting that is comparable to that of the USA, and that the average rate of that incidental taking by the vessels of the harvesting country is comparable to the average rate of incidental taking of sea turtles by US vessels in the course of such harvesting; or (b) that the fishing environment of the harvesting country does not pose a threat of incidental taking of sea turtles in the course of such harvesting.

The United States issued guidelines in 1991 and 1993 for the implementation of Section 609.[23] Pursuant to these guidelines, Section 609 was applied only to countries of the Caribbean/Western Atlantic. In September 1996, the United States concluded the Inter-American Convention for the Protection and Conservation of Sea Turtles with a number of countries of that region.[24] As mentioned, environmental groups complained that turtles should be protected outside the US borders and elevated the protest to the US Court of International Trade (CIT).[25]

It is worth noting that the US Department of State, wary of the diplomatic implications, had counter-argued that the Convention may have sought some degree of international protection for turtles, but it did not want to disrupt global markets or unhinge diplomatic relations, a position that was effectively overruled.[26] The tougher US line stems from a series of far-reaching decisions by the CIT. In December 1995 the CIT found the 1991 and 1993 Guidelines inconsistent with Section 609 in so far as they limited the geographical scope of Section 609 to shrimp harvested in the wider Caribbean/Western Atlantic area. Then it directed the US Department of State to prohibit, as of 1 May 1996, the importation of shrimp or shrimp products wherever harvested in the wild with commercial fishing technology, unless otherwise certified by a US agency.

In April 1996, the Department of State published revised guidelines to comply with the CIT order of December 1995. The new guidelines extended the scope of Section 609 to shrimp harvested in all countries.[27] On 25 November 1996 the CIT clarified that shrimp harvested by manual methods that did not harm sea turtles, by aquaculture and in cold water, could continue to be imported from non-certified countries.[28] The 1996 guidelines provided that certification could be granted by 1 May 1996, and annually thereafter, to harvesting countries other than those where turtles do not occur or that exclusively use means that do not pose a threat to sea turtles

> only if the government of [each of those countries] has provided documentary evidence of the adoption of a regulatory program governing the incidental taking of sea turtles in the course of commercial shrimp trawl harvesting that is comparable to that of the United States and if the average take rate of that incidental taking by vessels of the harvesting nation is comparable to the average rate of incidental taking of sea turtles by United States vessels in the course of such harvesting.

For the purpose of these certifications, a regulatory programme must have included a requirement that all commercial shrimp trawl vessels operating in waters in which there was a likelihood of intercepting sea turtles used TEDs at all times. TEDs had to be comparable in effectiveness to those used by the United States. Moreover, the average incidental take rate had to be deemed comparable to that of the United States if the harvesting country required the use of TEDs in a manner comparable to that of the US programme.

India, Malaysia, Pakistan and Thailand asked, in January 1997, for the establishment of a Dispute Settlement Panel against the USA under the WTO Dispute Settlement Procedures. A number of countries submitted third-party statements.[29] Costa Rica participated as a third party to the dispute but chose not to submit a statement. The Panel ruled against the United States since Section 609, as was being applied, was a measure conditioning access to the US market for a given product on the adoption by exporting members of conservation policies that the USA considered to be comparable to its own in terms of regulatory programmes and incidental taking.[30] Then it states,

> it appears to us that, in light of the context of the term 'unjustifiable' and the object and purpose of the WTO Agreement, *the US measure at issue constitutes unjustifiable discrimination* between countries where the same conditions prevail and thus is not within the scope of measures permitted under Article XX.[31]

On 13 July 1998, the United States appealed certain issues of law and legal interpretations in the Original Panel Report.[32] The Appellate Body issued its Report on 12 October 1998.[33] It found that Section 609 qualified for provisional justification under Article XX (g), but that it failed to meet the requirements of the chapeau of Article XX, as it was applied in a manner that constituted arbitrary and unjustifiable discrimination.

The Appellate Body opposed the text of Section 609 on the one hand and the implementing guidelines and the practice of the United States authorities on the other hand. The former only provided that conservation programmes should be comparable, whereas the latter required them to be essentially the same as the US programme. Furthermore, the Appellate Body opposed the application of a uniform standard throughout the US territory, which was acceptable, and the application of the same uniform standard to exporting countries, which was not.[34] Also, the USA had granted a longer 'phase-in' period for Latin American countries. Besides, some differences were found in the level of efforts made by the United States to transfer TED technology successfully to exporting countries.

In response to all this process, the United States instituted a range of procedural changes in the manner in which it makes certification decisions under Section 609. It issued the 1999 Revised Guidelines introducing modifications.[35] The process is more predictable and transparent, providing opportunities for rebuttal and appeal. For example, the Department of State now notifies governments of shrimp harvesting nations on a timely basis of all pending and final decisions and provides them with a meaningful opportunity to be heard and to present any additional information relevant to the certification decision. Even prior to that Appellate Body's ruling, on 28 August 1998, the Department of State reinstated the policy of permitting importation of shrimp harvested with TEDs in countries not certified under Section 609.[36] For instance, Australia has been granted permission to export shrimp from the Northern Prawn Fisheries and the Spencer Gulf even though Australia is not certified under Section 609.[37]

Nevertheless, on 19 July 2000 the CIT issued a decision that found that this policy violated that statute.[38] The US Executive Branch did not agree with the court's interpretation, and the issue is currently under review by the US Court of Appeals of the Federal Circuit. This appellate process will take considerable time to reach any conclusion. In the meantime, the United States plans to maintain its current policy.[39] In its ruling, however, the CIT refused to issue an injunction to reverse that policy, as it deemed that the evidence was insufficient to show that the policy was harming sea turtles.

Malaysia believed that this decision obliged the USA to continue applying the guidelines in a way contrary to the Dispute Panel findings and recommendations. Therefore, it requested the establishment of a dispute settlement body. This body issued its report on 15 June 2001.[40] It concluded that the USA is now applying Section 609 in a manner that no longer constitutes a means of unjustifiable or arbitrary discrimination.[41] It then went on to state that Section 609 violates GATT's Article XI, but it is justified under Article XX (g).

Costa Rica has prior legislation concerning turtles. For example, a 1948 law prohibits the killing of turtles and the sale of their eggs.[42] Costa Rica is also a signatory to international conventions dealing with this species; for instance, the 1973 Convention on International Trade in Endangered Species of Wild Fauna and Flora (CITES).[43] CITES recognizes all seven species of marine turtles as threatened with extinction and lists these species in Appendix I.

With the introduction of the TED requirements in the USA, Costa Rica decided neither to initiate litigation in the WTO nor to join the subsequent dispute.[44] Instead, the Instituto Costarricence de Pesca (INCOPESCA), which grants permits to fish and shrimp, issued a Board Resolution requiring the use of TEDs for shore trawl shrimp fishing from 1 May 1996. After an inspection by US authorities, Costa Rica was certified for the first time in May 1996.

The fishermen's reluctance to use TEDs made enforcement more difficult. They set forth arguments not against the use of TEDs, but against the technical specifications by which they were being built. The main reason was that the TEDs required by the USA were not suitable for the biological conditions of Costa Rican coasts. On the basis of their experience in the Gulf of Mexico, the USA set bar spacing at 4 inches. However, the Costa Rican marine environment presents different circumstances. The main difference is that, contrary to the Gulf of Mexico, the Costa Rican shoreline receives water from short but highly torrential rivers. Therefore, a significant amount of organic material is carried by the rivers to the shoreline where shrimp fishing takes place.

Imported from the USA at a cost of $300 each, TEDs were constantly blocked by organic waste. This meant that the escape gate for the turtles normally got blocked. The blockages also resulted in economic losses. First of all, jammed TEDs required more engine power in the trawling process, which translated into increased fuel costs. But most important, it was estimated that out of the total catch 70 per cent was waste and 30 per cent shrimp. This fact made shrimp fishers unwilling to use TEDs. In April 1999, a US inspection team composed of technicians and representatives of the Department of State and the US Embassy visited the port of Puntarenas and inspected six docked vessels and six vessels at sea. The team found serious problems on almost all of the six boats inspected at sea. When discussing the national enforcement programme with the local fisheries personnel, the team also found that the TEDs enforcement regime was not as comprehensive as it should be.

In order to prevent a trade measure under Section 609, Costa Rica then began a series of diplomatic efforts. In spite of these, Costa Rica was not certified to the US Congress. Therefore, the USA communicated to the country that, from 30 April 1999, it could no longer export shrimp to the American market.[45] Yet, in that same communiqué, after a diplomatic intercession by the Costa Rican Ambassador to the US Department of State, another inspection trip was scheduled for 10 May.[46] This assessment resulted in the Sub-Secretary of State certifying to the US Congress Costa Rican shrimp operations as compliant with Section 609 on 18 May.[47] As a consequence, the country could reinitiate shrimp exports.

After the crisis, Costa Rica initiated formal procedures to seek permission to change the TEDs' measurement. Two important studies were initiated in order to support this petition. These scientific studies led to a specific modification proposal by Costa Rica, the Tico-TED, more acceptable for the biological systems in the area.[48] The US Department of State finally agreed to a modification in the technical specifications of the TEDs, allowing, on 16 August 2000, an increase in the escape holes by 2 inches, for a maximum distance between deflection bars of 6 inches (15.2 cms).

HACCP Requirements for the USA and the EU

According to the US and the EU regulations, all imported fish products sold in these markets must come from plants with an HACCP plan. These regulations make entrepreneurs (processor, trader) fully responsible for the quality of their product.

In relation to fish and other food products, the HACCP is basically a plan with preventive actions that the processor can apply to control those identified food safety hazards that are reasonably likely to occur. An HACCP plan shall be specific to (1) each location where fish and fishery products are processed by that processor and (2) each kind of fish and fishery product processed by the processor.

In many cases, countries that have signed a memorandum of understanding (MOU) with the FDA are considered to have an equivalent inspection system to that of the USA. They do not need plant inspections. But in the absence of an MOU, the importer must provide documentation proving that the products imported by the USA were processed in accordance with the Federal Regulations. As a general rule, the on-site plant inspection is a necessary step.

Logically, the best way to ensure compliance with the HACCP regulations is to ensure conformity with the FDA's assessment guidelines. They are compiled in 'Fish and Fishery Products Hazard and Control Guide'[49] as well as the 'Regulator's HACCP Training Manual'. The problem is that sometimes inspectors give different interpretations, introducing uncertainties into the system.

Cost of compliance

TEDs
The TEDs cost $300 each.

HACCP
After an inspection conducted in 2001, the EU required that Costa Rican authorities should implement a sanitary control of fishing vessels supplying whole as well as de-headed shrimps and fishery products to the on-land establishments. The corrective action suggested by the EU is basically an extension of the HACCP plan to fishing vessels and collecting centres. Until then, the HACCP plan had been a responsibility of processing plants. Compliance with sanitary standards may create a problem for small fishing vessels in Costa Rica. For example, 80 per cent of the Costa Rican fishing fleet consists of just light barges, which have no space for refrigerating or sewage facilities on board.

Costa Rican processing plants have largely adapted well to HACCP necessities.[50] This is partly a result of heavy investment in infrastructure. During 1999 and 2000, the tuna processing companies invested US$15 million in refurbishing, expansion and, of course, sanitary controls.[51]

The mandatory tests required for exports are very expensive. For sales in the domestic market, national authorities in Costa Rica require processing companies to conduct at least 16 histamine tests per consignment in official laboratories. The costs for these may amount to US$500 a year (= 500/16 = $30 per test). However, in the case of exports, the much larger number of compulsory tests required by foreign authorities significantly increase costs. FDA rules require at least two tests per tonne of fish. A large Costa Rican processing plant can export an average of 15 000 kilos of mahi mahi a week. Adherence to FDA regulations would thus require 30 tests per week, costing US$1000 each week. This implies that, in order to export, the company would have to incur a cost of US$52 000 per year on histamine tests alone, 100 times the cost of tests required for the domestic market. And this does not include the cost of other microbiological and microchemical tests required.

Opportunity Costs: Lost Trade

TEDs

Thailand and India challenged the US regulations directly at the WTO level. Pakistan and Malaysia acted also as joint applicants. Australia, China, Ecuador, El Salvador, European Community, Guatemala, Hong Kong, Japan, Nigeria, Philippines, Singapore and Venezuela submitted third-party allegations either at the first or second instance. With a few exceptions, all the applicants, as well as the third parties had, and continue to have, a significant share of the US market. In 1995, they supplied 74.2 per cent of the market, while in 1999 it was 70 per cent. For instance, Thailand's contribution shrank from 33.1 per cent in 1995 to 23.1 per cent in 1997. In relative price dynamics, these countries show stable behaviour. The impact of the TED norms is relatively low, or none at all, on the third parties. For example, Ecuador's market participation fell by 1.6 per cent. And even this cannot be attributed directly to the TED constraint, since there were other factors such as the shrimp 'white spot disease' and 'El Niño'.

Nations in the 'other countries' category have benefited from the reduction in market share of some of the exporting countries. For instance, Indonesia, with a significant aquaculture industry, gained a part of the market lost by the applicants and third parties. By contrast, the Central American countries kept up a constant market involvement. In fact, there was a relative increase in their competitiveness in 1996. In that year, their market share improved by 1.6 per cent, since it increased from 10.2 per cent in 1995 to 11.8 per cent in 1996. Nevertheless, since 1996 Central America has stagnated, probably owing to natural production limits and an incipient aquaculture development.

What conclusions can be derived from the preceding data? Perhaps it is more important to state the conclusions that cannot be derived. It cannot be proved that the TED regulation had a significant impact on the structure of the US import market. But there were countries whose competitiveness was affected by this rule, and other exporting countries rapidly filled the spaces that opened up. As a consequence, there have been changes in the players in the market (changes that can or cannot have the TED regulations as one of the causes) that did not result in an overall increase in the US shrimpers' competitiveness. After all, US shrimp imports and suppliers have remained constant over the past five years. Naturally, American shrimpers have not benefited from the environmental measure, since they continue to provide a third of the national consumption. In other words, even if it is claimed that TED regulations were aimed at protecting the US based shrimp industry or at least at levelling the playing field between the national and the foreign producer, the environmental trade measure did not produce such a result.

Costa Rican market participation expanded from 0.5 to 0.6 per cent, and relative prices from 1.1 to 1.3, between 1995 and 1999. There is no way of knowing how this would have developed without the introduction of TEDs.

HACCP

The opportunity costs of the application of HACCP have not been calculated, although 80 per cent of the fleet does not have the required sanitary (cooling and sewage) facilities. Some of the costs of forgone income are due to inconsistencies in inspection results, which may make exporters wary of staying in the exporting business.

Responses to Standards

TEDs

Costa Ricans involved in the production of shrimps seemed to be angrier at being forced to use an inappropriate device for local circumstances than about the fact that devices needed to be used at all. More recently, more appropriate devices have been approved.

HACCP

All of the exporting plants have designed an HACCP plan that, according to the best of their abilities, minimizes the occurrence of the hazards associated with fish. The 'HACCP Team' has aided this process.[52] This team is composed of the civil servants from INCOPESCA and ZED (zone for export development). They have created a training module for the design and proper follow-up of HACCP plans. INCOPESCA, together with the National Chamber of Fish Exporters, works primarily for the incorporation of HACCP plans on ships and in collecting centres. The ZED deals with processing plants. In the year 2000, this team trained over 350 people in HACCP operations.

As the main interested party, the private sector has also taken responsibility for its HACCP compliance. Each plant has to have an HACCP manager. Plants also pay for annual training of their personnel by national HACCP experts. When the requirement was introduced in 1997, some plants brought in HACCP experts from the USA to assess and help them draft their HACCP plans in the FDA format.[53]

There has been no clear strategy regarding the expansion of HACCP to boats. The biggest processing plants own collecting centres and sometimes even boats. At landing, fishermen must present a record of the temperatures on board at which the fish are stored. This record has to be signed by them. But most of the companies buy from independent collecting centres and they have no way of ensuring the accuracy of the temperature record, if any, while at sea or during transportation.

INCOPESCA and CANNEP are in the process of drafting a project to address this problem.[54] They will identify ships that feed processing plants which export to the EU. Thereafter they will look for national and international funds (probably Canadian) to implement an HACCP plan on those vessels. At present, exports to the EU are small, hence tracking the boats is not difficult. The initial investment may be done only on a few vessels. However, it is expected that the USA will soon follow this procedure. In that event, the whole fleet will have to be refurbished, but there is no real economic possibility of this happening.

Meanwhile, private companies have found that the best way to deal with the EU and the US inspections is through a joint effort between the companies and the public agencies (ZED and INCOPESCA). It is felt that mediation of public bodies eases problems and improves communication with foreign authorities.

Are Standards Protectionist?

TEDs
It is curious to note that the shrimp fishing industry does not see these environmental requirements as barriers to trade. 'They set forth arguments not against the use of TEDs, but against the technical specifications by which they were being built.' The feeling is that if the USA requests it, they should comply and there is nothing wrong or abnormal about it. It is a part of the game, not an obstacle to playing the game. They see no gain in opposing the measure. Perhaps because it is rooted in this conviction, the Costa Rican strategy in all these cases has been non-confrontational.[55] Costa Rica did not even submit any claim as an interested third party in the WTO litigation process. Instead, the country embarked on a series of negotiation processes defined by:

1. engagement in international negotiations with the issuing country, leading either to international agreements or to certification programmes;
2. enactment of national legislation;
3. seeking approval by showing commitment to internationally accepted norms (for instance, the recent adoption of the FAO Code);
4. seeking recognition of differing national circumstances that render US regulations inapplicable by issuing scientific reports on the issues concerned (substantial equivalence).

HACCP
The issue of protectionism of HACCP has not been mentioned.

Summary

Until 1995 there were no problems with shrimp exports from Costa Rica to the USA. The 1991 US Guidelines limited the geographical scope of the ban on imports imposed by Section 609, concerned with TEDs, to countries in the wider Caribbean/Western Atlantic region,[56] and granted these countries a three-year phase-in period that, in practice, was extended beyond the specified time limit. In 1994, the Caribbean countries initiated cooperative efforts with the USA by negotiating the Inter-American Convention for the Protection and Conservation of Sea Turtles. These TED requirements constituted a problem for Costa Rica, but have been sorted out over time. However, some issues still persist.

The compliance cost of using TEDs in the shrimp industry is US$300 per device.

The tests that products must undergo before export to comply with HACCP standards cost a hundred times more than tests for the domestic market. The tuna processing companies invested US$15 million in refurbishing, expansion of facilities and, of course, establishing sanitary controls to comply with HACCP requirements.

Despite the TED and HACCP restrictions, the quantity and price of shrimp exports from Costa Rica to the USA between 1995 and 1999 have increased. However, the supply of shrimps for export is distributed among different vessels, as 80 per cent of the Costa Rican fishing fleet is unable to comply with HACCP requirements.

The responses to the TED standards were against the appropriateness of the specifications for the device rather than against the device itself. The responses to HACCP are not recorded as being protectionist.

RECOMMENDATIONS TO STRENGTHEN DEVELOPING COUNTRIES' CAPACITIES

Almost every new regulation implies some change in the production process and costs. In some cases, this is accepted as a normal and unavoidable part of the conditions for export. In other cases, a new regulation may be seen as an unjustified barrier to trade aimed at protecting competing industries. It is very difficult to draw a precise line between protection and protectionism. Strategies to deal with the trade measures of trading partners vary from case to case. For example, the case study on fisheries indicates that the Government of Costa Rica considered the TED requirements of the United States a 'part of the game'. However, in 1996 the Costa Rican government had strongly opposed the United States textile quotas and Costa Rica had been the first WTO member to request the establishment of a panel, which ruled that the United States' quotas breached the Agreement on Textiles.[57]

It may be suggested, at the risk of oversimplification, that when there is strong competition from domestic producers in the destination market, it is likely that environmental and sanitary regulations are perceived as disguised trade barriers.

Environmental Requirements

In the case of shrimp, the Costa Rican authorities and exporters opted to focus on compliance with a new market requirement rather than contesting the measure. Compliance increased competitiveness vis-à-vis suppliers who were not in compliance. Some issues should, nevertheless, be raised. For example, in order to grant the country certification, US regulations required all Costa Rican fishery boats to comply with TED requirements. It did not make any difference if the fishing boats were operating in turtle-free areas. Even when environmental norms and regulations can be defended from the point of view of the importing country, the importing country should not impose its criteria on *all* production units, independent of the market of destination of the products.

SPS Measures

When there is a politically strong domestic industry competing with imports, there is a temptation to use SPS measures as a protectionist device. Even an authentic and legitimate SPS measure may cause an exporting country to suspect that it reflects nothing more than the interest of the importing country's firms.

From the technical viewpoint, animal health measures established for poultry products on a regional level are justified because they prevent the spread of disease. This brings us face to face with a situation where measures look after human, plant and animal health and therefore are justified within the WTO frame. The measures cannot be dismissed as non-tariff trade barriers, because, if a country can prove it is disease-free and at the same time it complies with HACCP, it should be able to export products to its chosen destination. In this sense, there would be no discrimination between countries. On the contrary, the same measures would be imposed on all countries as a requisite for the export of their products, which would concur with the SPS Agreement.

Structural Problems

There are several elements which, although they are not costs in themselves, turn into restrictions. For example, the process of convincing both the entrepreneurial and the public sectors of the need to advance towards compliance is costly enough. The typical instability of high-ranking government posts bears a cost, since changes in government generally imply a change of direction. Thus there are neither long-term policies nor a clearly defined, credible policy.

In short, we observe that the SPS Agreement offers some disadvantages to developing countries. For one thing, because they generally lack the technical staff needed to deal with the decision-making process within the Committee on Sanitary and Phytosanitary Measures, most of the proposals come from developed countries. Secondly, the institutional capacity of developing countries is limited by the scarcity of resources available to comply with export requirements for certain products, such as poultry. Thirdly, technical and financial support from developed countries may be conditioned by the need these countries have for new suppliers, not necessarily by the desire of developing countries to export the product.

Therefore, although health norms for trade in poultry products within Central America and to the USA do present a scientific justification, it is also true that nothing guarantees that the measures will not become non-tariff barriers to trade.

In the case of the TED requirements, there were considerable arguments in the international arena concerning the legality of this process standard, since it was not related to the physical characteristics of the product. There is no ground for such a claim in relation to HACCP, since the Codex Alimentarius Commission recognized it as an internationally accepted standard.[58] The basic problem is compliance. The case studies on the poultry and fisheries sectors indicate that problems in the use of HACCP in Costa Rica and other Central American countries have to be overcome to gain access to the US and EU markets. The problems with HACCP requirements must be seen against the way production is structured in Central American countries. When transnational corporations (TNCs) or large domestic companies handle the production and/or export process, HACCP is generally considered as a part of the export business. However, when small and medium-sized enterprises (SMEs) deal with the process of production and exports, the situation is often different.

There may be a kind of perverse shift in the structure of public expenditure to the extent that such expenditure is necessary to comply with very specific requirements emerging from external markets without it having a clear impact on the overall competitiveness and export promotion. This kind of expenditure competes with the efforts to improve social safety nets for structural adjustment or industrial policy. For example, according to the fisheries case study, INCOPESCA admitted that the major enforcement problems were due to the lack of resources and the low pay of inspection personnel. Addressing these issues should be a priority.

Yet public expenditure to strengthen compliance with specific requirements in external markets may serve as an export promotion device when not every country complies. Thus, for complying countries this acts as a sort of externality covered by the state. But it takes away resources that otherwise could be geared toward improving technology for the domestic exporting firms. If the (private) fisheries are forced by the market to increase their costs because of environmental rules, this may translate somehow into higher prices and exporting firms may not lose profits. But it is not clear how public expenditure may be recovered if this does not generate higher fiscal yields. If it is a new measure that does not generate new exports, it may be seen as a new burden on the public budget. Therefore, an environmental measure geared towards a new requirement only to keep (already existing) exports going on will have a negative impact on developing countries, unless the environmental measure impacts highly on the domestic priorities of the exporting country.

A General Strategy

Certification is an increasingly important issue for marketing purposes. There will be social certification, as in 'no sweatshop' or 'fair trade' and environmental certification as in 'dolphin safe' or in 'organic produce'. But even more complicated will be the pyramid of accredited and fully recognized national certifications superseded by national seals suggesting that other nations' certifications are accepted but not 'good enough'. Therefore, each country will need to build its own strategy, which should be national and coordinated with the different segments of the private sector.

For a country like Costa Rica, which is known for being 'environmentally healthy', a national seal could be an interesting opportunity to promote its products, but for other developing countries it will not be easy, because the national image does not sell well in the relevant markets.

When a developing country finds itself restricted by environmental or sanitary measures, where the political and organizational cost of changing domestic behaviour is easy to bear, the best strategy is:

* to engage in international negotiations with the issuing country, leading either to international agreements or to certification programmes;
* to enact national legislation and regulation that, while taking into account the need to compensate net losers in the process, allows for a smooth administration of the systems;
* to participate in multilateral negotiations and to commit to the accepted norms, which is the case of the different FAO agreements;
* to engage the support of the local scientific community in the country to study the new rules proposed, their logic and possible alternatives, to reach the same objectives under different systems to achieve substantial equivalence;[59]

- to rally the private sector in support of the necessary strategies to overcome the problem, although this may backfire when the domestic private sector considers that the current status is safer for them.

Actions at the national level

Proactive approaches
Central American countries should adopt proactive approaches to environmental quality and good sanitary conditions, which are increasingly important factors determining competitiveness in the process of globalization. The private sector should fully understand that the process of globalization will continue and that the quality of the national insertion into the world is changing. A defensive stance is not the best way of dealing with the new realities. For example, efforts to continue excluding the poultry sector from the process of global and regional trade liberalization, such as the FTAA (Free Trade Agreement between the Americas), may not pay off in the long run. The sector should be prepared to compete in international markets as well as at home, when this sector is liberalized. Therefore, efforts to improve sanitary conditions and avoid Newcastle disease should be strengthened. This example should be generalized to include other sectors.

Developing countries should seek to focus on preventive rather than corrective actions. Therefore, they must anticipate and seek to influence new standards. Thus, developing countries should insist on a strict application of the WTO notification mechanisms. They should also ensure that the private sector adjusts to new conditions. In accordance with their obligations under the SPS and TBT Agreements, developing countries should create and support national enquiry points and promote dissemination of information on new standards and regulations in export markets to the private sector. Finally, while WTO notification mechanisms are important, developing countries should take advantage of private initiatives, such as the Central Bureau for the Promotion of Imports from Developing Countries (CBI), to gather information and analyses on emerging standards and market trends.

Standard setting
Setting domestic standards and creating conditions allowing developing country producers to compete successfully in international markets requires strong cooperation and sustained efforts by the government and the private sector. The poultry case study shows that in order to be declared 'Newcastle disease-free', Costa Rica had to sustain a process over a total of eight years, which included a five-year formal process of cooperation with the US authorities. Similarly, continued efforts are necessary to introduce HACCP in the poultry and fisheries sectors.

Establishing national standards and regulations addressing SPS issues is very important. The preparation and enactment of standards in major markets are an indication of future requirements and new trends. One important question that the public and private sectors in developing countries have to address is the extent to which stringent standards emerging in international markets should also be implemented at home, that is, for sales in their domestic market. Some standards must, by necessity, be strictly applied throughout the country. For example, the fight against Newcastle disease must necessarily be national (or 'regional'). But in the case of the TED the certification should be on a firm or association basis. This argument should be strongly defended, as some countries are learning 'the hard way' that forcing a whole country to abide by rules that could be in the interest of a few exporters could be costly.[60]

Capacity building
Capacity building of public and private sectors is one of the most important features of the new universe of exports. In our modern, globalized world the exporter should have the assurance that the public sector is supporting the building of knowledge and infrastructure where the private sector, for reasons of scale or externalities (being public goods), cannot produce results alone. For example, building laboratories necessary to certify products and processes, staffing them, and making information available for everyone are impossible tasks for individual firms. The government should work mainly through producers' associations and complete the institutional arrangements through its own network.

Industry cooperation
SMEs should associate to pool their exports as a means of cost sharing. This will facilitate the process of being accepted in the destination markets. In these cases, it will be easier and cost-effective to hire someone to be in charge of reviewing the entire HACCP process.

Government
The government should stand behind the domestic producers in supporting their efforts to certify enterprises. It has been shown that in many cases the inspector has a wide margin of interpretation for standards. In these cases, a strong government posture may be a helpful complement for the producer's efforts. In other words, trade negotiators should be aware of what is going on in the area of technical standards and SPS measures that creates specific problems, in order to solve them at a higher level in the trade community.

This matter was obvious on 30 April 1999, when the USA communicated to Costa Rica that it could no longer export shrimps to the American market. But, after a diplomatic intercession by the Costa Rican ambassador, another inspection visit was programmed for 10 May (only ten days later). On 18 May Costa Rica was able to reinitiate shrimp exports.

National seal
A national seal may be an important promotion mechanism for some countries, for example, Costa Rica. This country has an international image of being ecologically friendly. It is the tourism destiny of hundreds of thousands of people annually, attracted by this precise feature. They may distinguish this stamp seal and it may be an important source of product recognition. There is a growing trend towards the multiplication of certifying agencies that are recognized in each country, but such proliferation makes it increasingly difficult to point out the real differences between them. Even if you have a national certifying private firm with a good standard, with government approval, and even with international recognition, the certifying firms are unknown to the consumers in developed countries. A national 'country seal' may remove this obstacle, if it does not add to the firm's costs. On the other hand, such a move could unify the promotion costs and make it easier for the state to invest in it, because it would not come up in support of specific firms.

Germany is working on such a scheme, which may even have a protectionist undertone. If the country's authorities were forced to accept all the European certification firms that are nationally accredited, a new way to distinguish local German products would be to put a national seal on them vowing to comply with stricter standards.

Some states in the USA (Florida, Maine and Texas) have enacted country-of-origin labelling laws for fresh produce (conventional or organic). Florida requires all imported fresh produce to be identified by the country of origin by, for example, marking each produce item or placing a sign or label adjacent to the bin. Maine requires country-of-origin labelling for fresh produce at the retail level when it has been imported from countries identified as having special pesticide violations (that is, even after they have been authorized by APHIS). Texas requires country-of-origin labelling for fresh grapefruit. In addition, labelling laws for fresh produce have been proposed in five other states: California, Connecticut, Oregon, Rhode Island and Virginia.[61]

Actions at the international level

Cooperation
A review of the literature and the experience of the case studies indicate that many cases fall in grey areas, where measures to address environmental concerns or threats to human or animal health are bound up with red tape and changing requirements that are perceived as unjustified. Such measures are hard to contest through the dispute settlement mechanism of the WTO. Grey

area cases, in particular, are difficult to address without cooperation between importing and exporting countries. This points to the need for strengthened cooperation.

Technical assistance

The SPS Agreement, in Article 9, paragraph 2, encourages developed countries to provide technical assistance:

> When substantial investments are required for a developing member country to comply with animal or plant health requirements posed by a developed member, the latter shall consider the possibility of giving technical assistance necessary to enable the developed country to maintain and increase its access opportunities for the product at hand.

The Agreement establishes the *possibility* of developed countries offering technical assistance to developing countries. Whether or not this will be done in practice is likely to depend on political will and the need to import certain products. It has been noted that 'much of the technical assistance is reactive – it is provided once compliance problems with the SPS Agreement have been identified – instead of being part of a strategy leading to the improvement of the country's existing capacity.'[62] Thus, developed countries' interest in assisting developing countries in complying with animal or plant health requirements may be limited to situations where other suppliers would be unable to satisfy the demand. Under other conditions, what incentives could a developed country have to provide technical assistance to developing countries, if it does not really need them to supply the product?

In this regard, the technical capacity installed in the developing country becomes crucial, because the possibility of carrying out all the tests necessary in the long process of acquiring a disease-free status depends on it. In this case, cooperation between the private sector and the government within the country is indispensable, as the Costa Rican case proves. Here all expenses to finance a technical supervisor of procedures leading to the Newcastle disease-free declaratory were undertaken by the private sector. It would be interesting to think about the possibility of developed countries helping developing ones to increase their technical capability and face the process of disease-free declarations or to comply with requirements in general. Again, however, this would only be possible if developed countries needed more suppliers of the product at hand; otherwise, only the traditional structure of suppliers will continue to exist.

Besides changing the language of the SPS agreement with respect to technical assistance, it may be interesting to explore the possibility of establishing a multilateral fund to support implementation of Article 9. This would overcome the problem of asking a country to support imports in a protected sector.

UNCTAD, UNIDO and/or the World Bank could administer such a special fund. It may be one way of using official development assistance to fully include developing countries in the benefits of free trade. This new deal could be negotiated under the next round of multilateral negotiations, as part of improved SPS and TBT agreements. The administration of this facility would be completely separated from the WTO and would be comprehensive; that is, it would cover physical infrastructure as well as technical assistance. It would also emphasize regional components.

Central American governments could elaborate a proposal to create such a facility at regional level, which could take the form of a fund managed by the Central American Bank of Economic Integration.

Equivalence

According to Article 4 of the SPS Agreement, WTO Members shall accept the SPS measures of other Members as equivalent, even if these measures differ from their own, if the exporting Member objectively demonstrates to the importing Member that its measures achieve the importing Member's appropriate level of phytosanitary protection. One problem is that equivalence is often interpreted as 'sameness'.[63] Such interpretation deprives Article 4.1 of its function, which is to recognize that different measures may achieve the same level of SPS protection and, therefore, countries can enjoy a certain level of flexibility regarding the kind of measures they adopt. This could be spelled out more clearly in the Article.[64]

HACCP 'is in no way a binding set of requirements. Processors may choose to use other control measures, as long as they provide an equivalent level of assurance of safety for the product.'[65] Yet, in practice, HACCP requirements in import markets may force specific changes in national legislation, imposing conditions that are *equal* rather than *equivalent* to those in importing countries.

To demonstrate an equivalent level of control is not easy. Costa Rica worked to promote a different TED that would provide the same end results. Nevertheless, the process took over a year. Such a process will normally require the presentation of scientific information or studies, which may be a burdensome task.

While helpful, equivalence is not a panacea. Under the SPS Agreement, any Member is free to establish the 'appropriate level of protection.' For example, the United States has argued, 'In the end, the choice of the appropriate level of protection is a societal value judgment. The [SPS] Agreement imposes no requirement to establish a scientific basis for the chosen level of protection because the choice is not a scientific judgment'.[66] So, even if a developing country achieves equivalent SPS regulations and enforcement capacity, an importing country could choose zero risk and this could adversely affect a specific product. Besides, even when standards are equivalent, the certification and accreditation process can still pose obstacles.

Participation in international standard-setting processes

Participation in international standard-setting processes is important because the resulting standards determine the requirements that developing countries' exports will have to comply with. The Codex Alimentarius Commission is the most important standardization body for food and agricultural products.

The Codex Alimentarius Commission was established in 1962 to recommend minimum food safety standards in order to protect public health and ensure fair practices in food trade. The establishment of the WTO has raised public awareness of Codex standards, because the Agreement on Sanitary and Phytosanitary Measures recognizes that trade measures based on them are considered prima facie WTO-consistent.

Codex standards are supposed to be based on authoritative scientific evidence. However, as a consequence of its heightened role in the international trade context, Codex decision making has become more politicized.[67] In addition, developing country participation at Codex meetings – and therefore their input into its standard-setting activities – remains insufficient. While Codex membership is open to all representatives from member nations and associate members of FAO and WHO (presently 165 member countries representing 98 per cent of the world's population), in practice most delegates come from developed countries.[68] It can be argued that developing countries do not have the financial capacity to have a permanent representation in all the committees. In other cases, countries are simply not aware of the importance of these meetings and the potential health and trade effects of the standards adopted.

A report made by the Ambio Foundation of Costa Rica[69] illustrates this point. On the basis of the attendance list of the 29th session of the Food Labeling Committee (Ottawa, 1 to 4 May), country participants were classified according to the country and stakeholder representation (that is, government, trading and consumer associations, producers, manufacturers and others). Less than 50 countries, out of 144 participating in the WTO, were present. Out of a total of 211 delegates, 71 per cent were civil servants whereas 21 per cent represented the private sector. Among the public sector delegates, 42 per cent were developing countries and only 20 per cent were from the private sector. Costa Rica was the only Central American country with representatives from the private sector, and one producer and one representative of a consumer organization.

If Central America were to move away from being 'standard-taker' and towards becoming 'standard-setter', the creation of a regional Central American institution for standards would be important. This institution could then represent Central American countries, although this would not exclude the possibility of a specific country participating directly. This would allow Central American countries to be fully informed about new developments and take part in relevant decisions in a cost-effective manner.

NOTES

1. Eduardo Gitli and Randall Arce, 'Considerations on the International Marketing of International Products in Central America: Some Ideas on Costa Rica', March 2001.
2. The study by Roxana Salazar (2001), 'Barriers to Organic Agriculture: The Case of Costa Rica', has been included in Chapter 6 of this publication.
3. Eduardo Gitli, Randall Arce and Eliana Villalobos, 'Central America and the International Trade of Poultry Products', August 2001.
4. Max Valverde, 'Sanitary and Environmental Barriers to Trade in Fisheries: The Case of Costa Rica', July 2001.
5. From work by Eduardo Gitli.
6. In 2000, the countries declared Newcastle disease-free by the USDA were Australia, Canada, Chile, Costa Rica, Denmark, Fiji, Finland, France, Great Britain (England, the Isle of Man, Scotland and Wales), Greece, Iceland, Luxembourg, New Zealand, Ireland, Spain, Sweden and Switzerland (Code of Federal Regulations 9CFR94.6).
7. Estimation made by the Costa Rican Executive Manager of the Chamber of Poultry Producers.
8. NASA first used the HACCP in 1958 to ensure sanitary conditions for food taken into space.
9. FAO (1999), Conferencia sobre Comercio Internacional de Alimentos a Partir del Año 2000: Decisiones basadas en criterios científicos, armonización, equivalencia y reconocimiento mutuo, ALICOM 99/10.
10. USITC (1998), Industry and Trade Summary: Poultry, USITC Publication 3148, December.
11. USDA-APHIS (1997), op. cit.
12. It is important to point out that some of the people we consulted said that the fact that the entrepreneurial sector did not seek earlier implementation of the HACCP implies that expectations of exporting to the USA were not a priority for the sector.
13. Specifically, on 18 December, the following formularies were submitted: *Regulations for Meat and Poultry Products Inspection, Slaughter/Processing, Compulsoriness Questionnaire, Health Questionnaire, Animal Disease Questionnaire*. In turn, the questionnaire *Criteria for Assessing the Adequacy of the Residue Control Program* was submitted on 16 June 2000.
14. This part was written by Max Valverde, who prepared the paper for UNCTAD as part of the Central American Component of the Project on Standards and Trade.
15. See www.procomer.com
16. Hereafter the '1987 Regulations' (52 Federal Register 24244, 29 June 1987).
17. See *Earth Island Inst.* v *Christopher*, 913 F. Supp. 559 (CIT, 1995).
18. See http://www.foei.org/activist_guide/tradeweb/turtle.htm, Friends of the Earth.
19. Aquaculture provides 90 per cent of Ecuadorian shrimp exports. See Skou, Lene, 'Rules to protect sea turtles could block shrimp imports', 30 April 1996, *Journal of Commerce*, p. 4.
20. Ibid.
21. See Samocha, Tzachi, 'More seafood, please', *Journal of the American Society of Agricultural Engineers Review*, **6** (4), April 1999, pp. 11–12.
22. See Conejo, C., Díaz, R. Furst E., Gitli, E. and Vargas, L, *Comercio y Ambiente: el caso de Costa Rica*, CINPE, Heredia, 1996. Study prepared for UNCTAD.
23. See 56 Federal Register 1051, 10 January 1991, and 58 Federal Register 9015, 18 February 1993.
24. The Convention entered into force on 1 May 2001. As of 15 May 2001, the Convention has nine parties: Brazil, Costa Rica, Ecuador, Honduras, Mexico, The Netherlands, Peru, Venezuela, and the United States. Costa Rica ratified the Convention on 14 May 2000. To

implement this international and other national commitments for the conservation of sea turtles, Costa Rica also adopted on 8 May 1998, together with Nicaragua and Panama, the Cooperative Agreement for the Conservation of Sea Turtles of the Caribbean Coast of Costa Rica, Nicaragua and Panama. An important part of it is the execution of a Regional Management Plan for the Caribbean coast of these countries.

25. The CIT has jurisdiction over unfair trade practices and other import issues.
26. See Skou, Lene. op. cit., p. 4.
27. See 61 Federal Register 17342, 19 April 1996, Section 609(b)(2).
28. See *Earth Island Institute* v *Warren Christopher*, 948 Fed. Supp. 1062 (CIT 1996).
29. Australia, China, Ecuador, European Community, Hong Kong and Nigeria acted as third parties in both the first and second instances. El Salvador, Guatemala, Japan, Philippines, Singapore and Venezuela acted as interested third parties only during the first instance, while Mexico only participated during the second instance.
30. See *United States – Import Prohibition of Certain Shrimp and Shrimp Products*, Report of the Panel, at 7.48.
31. Ibid. at 7.49.
32. See WT/DS58/11, 13 July 1998.
33. See Appellate Body Report, *United States – Import Prohibition of Certain Shrimp and Shrimp Products*, adopted on 6 November 1998, WT/DS58/AB/R (hereafter the 'Appellate Body Report').
34. See Appellate Body Report, para. 5. 9.
35. See US Department of State, *Guidelines for the Implementation of Section 609 of Public Law 101–162 Relating to the Protection of Sea Turtles in Shrimp Trawl Fishing Operations*. Federal Register, Vol. 64, No. 130, 8 July 1999, Public Notice 3086, pp. 36949–52.
36. See US Department of State, *Notice of Proposed Revisions of the Guidelines for the Implementation of Section 609 of Public Law 101–162, Relating to the Protection of Sea Turtles in Shrimp Trawl Fishing Operations*. Federal Register Vol. 64, No. 57, 25 March 1999, Public Notice 3013, pp. 14481–5.
37. See *United States – Import Prohibition of Certain Shrimp and Shrimp Products*, Recourse to Article 21.5 by Malaysia, WT/DS58/RW, 15 June 2001, para. 5.124.
38. See *Turtle Island Restoration Network* v *Robert Mallett*, 110 Fed. Supp. 2d 1005 (CIT 2000).
39. See *United States – Import Prohibition of Certain Shrimp and Shrimp Products*, Recourse to Article 21.5 by Malaysia, WT/DS58/RW, 15 June 2001, para. 3.150.
40. Ibid.
41. Ibid., para. 5.137.
42. See Article 28 of the Fish and Marine Hunting Law No. 190, 1948.
43. Adopted on 3 March 1973 and entered into force on 1 July 1975, with 152 parties as of 15 May 2001. Appendix I includes all species threatened with extinction which are or may be affected by trade. Trade in these species is subject to strict regulation through both import and export permits. See www.cites.org.
44. Costa Rica reserved its third-party rights in accordance with Article 10 of the WTO Dispute Settlement Understanding, but it did not submit any allegations; see Report of the Panel, at 6.
45. 4 May 1999 communiqué from US Embassy Minister Richard Baltimore to Esteban Brenes, Costa Rican Agriculture Minister.
46. Ibid.
47. 20 May 1999 communiqué from US Embassy Minister Richard Baltimore to Esteban Brenes, Costa Rican Agriculture Minister.
48. 'Tico' is the gentile for a Costa Rican citizen. The Tico-TED reports a shrimp loss of only 10 per cent, compared to a 40 per cent loss reported when using the US design. See Marine Turtle Restoration Program, Costa Rica, informative leaflet, (pretoma@racsa.co.cr).
49. US Food and Drug Administration, *Fish and Fisheries Product Hazards and Control Guide*, second edition, January 1998, hereinafter 'FDA's Guidelines'.
50. As of 16 June 2001, there were 33 processing facilities with permission to export to the EU and the USA.

51. See *La Nación*, national newspaper, 2 July 2001, p. 21/A.
52. 12 June 2001 interview with Roland Ramírez, Director of INCOPESCA's Statistics Department.
53. 7 July 2001 interview with Miguel Jiménez, Veterinary and HACCP Manager of PMT, one of the biggest exporting companies.
54. 11 June 2001 interview with Patricia Arce, CANEPP Executive Directress.
55. This is not a general rule in Costa Rican trade policy. For instance, in 1996 Costa Rica was the first WTO member to request the establishment of a Panel to demand the removal of a US safeguard measure conditioning access of cotton underwear manufactured in the country. The Panel ruled that the US quotas breached the Agreement on Textiles. See Costa Rica, *Examen de las Políticas Comerciales, Informe del Gobierno*, World Trade Organization, 9 April 2000.
56. Specifically, Mexico, Belize, Guatemala, Honduras, Nicaragua, Costa Rica, Panama, Colombia, Venezuela, Trinidad and Tobago, Guyana, Suriname, French Guyana and Brazil.
57. See Costa Rica, *Examen de las Políticas Comerciales: Informe del Gobierno*, WTO, 9 April 2000.
58. Recognizing the importance of HACCP to food control, the twentieth session of the Codex Alimentarius Commission, held in Geneva, Switzerland from 28 June to 7 July 1993, adopted *Guidelines for the application of the Hazard Analysis Critical Control Point (HACCP) system* (ALINORM 93/13A, Appendix II). The revised version of the *Recommended International Code of Practice – General Principles of Food Hygiene* [CAC/RCP 1-1969, Rev. 3 (1997)], adopted during the twenty-second session of the Codex Alimentarius Commission, held in Geneva from 23 to 28 June 1997, incorporates the *Hazard Analysis Critical Control Point (HACCP) system and guidelines for its application* as Annex.
59. For example, technical studies made by two independent groups of national experts concluded that the American technical specifications for the TED (4 inches width) were not suitable for the Costa Rican shoreline, which receives water from highly torrential rivers, and that it was possible to augment the width. An arrangement was achieved for a 6-inch Costa Rican TED to avoid killing turtles when catching shrimps.
60. This may be the case for foot-and-mouth disease in Uruguay, where a non-vaccination policy was necessary to ensure the status of 'country free of f-a-m disease'. This standard benefited only those who exported to the US and Europe, as neighboring countries and other customers accepted beef coming from vaccinated animals. When f-a-m disease arrived through Argentina, it attacked all the herds, negatively affecting everybody.
61. See GAO, *Fresh Produce: Potential Consequences of Country-of-Origin Labeling*, United States General Accounting Office, Washington, April 1999.
62. See Henson, S. and Loader, R., 'Barriers to agricultural exports from developing countries: the role of sanitary and phytosanitary requirements', *World Development*, **29** (1), 85–102.
63. See Zarrilli, Simonetta, Veena Jha and René Vossenaar (eds), 1999, *Ecolabelling and International Trade*, New York: UNCTAD. See TED and HACCP examples above.
64. Ibid.
65. See FDA Guidelines, p. 2. This Guide does not provide specific guidance to importers of fish for the development of required importer verification procedures, but it is mentioned that this need will be addressed in a future edition. Yet the information contained in the text may prove useful for this purpose.
66. See Administrative Action Statement accompanying The Uruguay Round Agreements Act (P.L. 103-465; 8 December 1994) at A.3.b. This statement describes significant administrative actions proposed to implement the Uruguay Round Agreements. It represents an authoritative expression by the US Administration concerning its views regarding the interpretation and application of the Uruguay Round Agreements, both for purposes of US international obligations and domestic law. We should bear in mind that according to the SPS Agreement, 'members should, when determining the appropriate level of sanitary or phytosanitary protection, take into account the objective of minimizing negative trade effects.'

67.   'Bridges between Trade and Sustainable Development', *ICTSD*, first issue, 2000.
68.   'Ensuring Food Safety: it's a question of standards', Food Policy Briefing Paper, *Consumers International*, November 2000, No. 1, p. 1.
69.   Ambio, 'Consumer Participation in the Codex Alimentarius Commission: the case of the 29th session of the Food Labeling Committee', Costa Rica, 2000.

5. Eastern and Southern Africa: the Experience of Kenya, Mozambique, the United Republic of Tanzania and Uganda

Cerina Banu Issufo Mussa, René Vossenaar and Nimrod Nakisisa Waniala

INTRODUCTION

Issues

The possible effects of environmental standards and regulations (see Box 5.1) as well as SPS measures have been an issue of key concern to African developing countries. The African component of this project seeks to address the following issues:

- How can governments and the private sector in African developing countries, including the least developed countries (LDCs), address existing constraints in responding to environmental and health requirements in external markets and implementing national policies on food safety and environmental quality?
- How can developed countries take account of the special conditions and needs of African developing countries in framing policies concerning environment and food safety?
- How can bilateral and multilateral aid agencies assist African developing countries to strengthen their capacities to respond to environmental and health requirements in international markets and to take full advantage of trade liberalization under the WTO negotiations and initiatives in favour of Africa and/or LDCs?
- What are the key trade issues in the area of trade rules, in particular in the WTO post-Doha work programme (Doha Development Agenda)?

This chapter draws on papers prepared by national experts from Kenya, Mozambique, the United Republic of Tanzania and Uganda.[1] These papers focus on SPS measures, especially in the European Union, the largest export market for African countries.[2]

BOX 5.1   ENVIRONMENTAL MEASURES WITH POTENTIAL TRADE EFFECTS ON COUNTRIES IN EASTERN AND SOUTHERN AFRICA

Pesticide residues: Standards for maximum residue levels for pesticide may be based on both consumer health and environmental grounds.

Packaging requirements: African exporters have been concerned about the effects of packaging requirements on their exports.

Eco-labelling: Eco-labelling may have effects on exports of some product categories. For example, eco-labelling may become more important in the cut flowers and fisheries sectors.

Timber: Timber exports may be affected by consumer boycotts and/or timber certification. On the other hand, several African countries (for example, Mozambique) see timber certification as a means to promote exports as well as the sustainable use of forests.

CITES: Certain trade measures under the Convention on International Trade in Endangered Species are of key relevance to African countries. A well-known example is the ivory trade.

Montreal Protocol: It was agreed to have a freeze in consumption and phasing out of methyl bromide, used in agriculture and crops, such as cut flowers.[3]

In several cases, exporters perceive that SPS and similar measures applied in developed country markets are unjustified. For example, it has been noted that environment-related trade measures are applied only to selected sectors, while ignoring others, like gold, whose market access has not been subject to environmental requirements despite negative effects of mining on the environment.[4]

Case studies carried out under this project also mention a number of such cases. For example, when the European Union implemented a ban on imports of fishery products following the outbreak of cholera, the World Health Organization (WHO) and the UN Food and Agriculture Organization (FAO) issued statements arguing that there was no documented evidence of risk of human illness in non-cholera regions resulting from exposure to food products imported from areas where cholera is endemic or the epidemic level is low.

Notwithstanding these doubts about the validity of the claims made about certain SPS measures, non-compliance with SPS or TBT standards is not a reasonable option; instead, capacity building is required to assist in complying with these standards.

The Papers

All four countries covered in this chapter have faced problems in exporting fishery products, particularly to the European Union, their traditional export market. New standards for maximum permissible levels of pesticide residues have generated concern among exporters of horticultural products, especially in Kenya and Uganda. The studies focus on these cases.

Policies and measures aimed at strengthening the capacities of developing countries in dealing with SPS requirements were also examined. Options were considered based on appropriate action at the national level (such as development of infrastructure, training and awareness raising), in international cooperation (bilateral, regional or multilateral) and in the area of trade rules.

The export performance of Sub-Saharan Africa, including Eastern and Southern Africa, has been below that of other developing regions, despite significant trade liberalization and economic policy reform. Market access remains an issue of key concern.

KENYA[5]

Agriculture (Horticulture)

Kenya produces approximately 3 million tonnes of vegetables, fruits and cut flowers annually, approximately 100 000 tonnes of which are exported, with the European Union receiving 90 per cent of the exports.

Since agriculture is the mainstay of the Kenyan economy, standards and regulations concerning the quality of agricultural inputs (seeds, fertilizers and agrochemicals) and produce are essential. Such standards and regulations are also essential for compliance with consumer health and environmental requirements in international markets. The Kenyan government and private sector have taken several steps to strengthen capacities to respond to such requirements, but Kenyan producers and exporters still face a range of constraints.

The responsibility for administering the various regulating Acts of Parliament governing the agricultural sector was fragmented in the past. In order to consolidate regulatory Acts and strengthen their enforcement mechanisms, the Kenya Plant Health Inspectorate Service (KEPHIS), a state corporation, was established in 1996. Its activities were subsequently consolidated for the improvement of the quality of agricultural inputs, plant health and plant breeding materials for use in agriculture. KEPHIS is the government enforcement agency that handles matters related to quality control of agricultural inputs, produce, and plant health. In addition, it aims to eliminate the regulatory bottlenecks in a liberalized market economy.

As far as the horticultural industry is concerned, adherence to the maximum residue level (MRL) requirements is the main concern. Pesticides play an important role in many food production systems. They also pose a potential risk to both human beings and the environment. To effectively control crop pests without necessarily endangering the ecosystem, good agricultural practice (GAP) is important when using these chemicals. MRL is an internationally agreed concept of pesticide residue level that should not be exceeded on any consumable portion of the plant. It is also necessary to monitor the environment for presence of these harmful chemical residues, which may ultimately find their way into the food chain.

Kenyan fresh produce exporters are concerned about the new European Union regulations on pesticide application that should have come into force in July 2000 but were postponed by one year. These regulations may, under certain conditions, fix MRLs at 'analytical' zero value, requiring that there be no trace of pesticide residue in fruits, vegetables and cut flowers intended for the European markets. Exporters must also provide information on the types of pesticide used.

In Kenya's tropical climate, frequent applications of pesticides have, over the years, proved to be effective. Halima Noor argues that the EU regulation forces Kenyan producers to discontinue such applications. Kenyan producers fear that, because of lack of experience and other factors, this will result in wrong pesticide application by farmers and low quality crops. Changing from one type of pesticide, already in use, to another type that may prove less effective or require more frequent application may be expensive. New pesticides may also turn out to be equally toxic to the consumer, the operator or the environment. However, unless Kenyan horticultural producers and exporters adapt rapidly to the new measures, they will lose their market share built up over the years.

The study argues that the impact of stringent consumer health requirements on large corporations will be quite different from that on small-scale farmers. Large corporations are in a much better position than small-scale farmers to quickly adapt to new measures, such as the zero pesticide residue regulations in the European Union. In fact, European markets have favoured larger producers and exporters, who are able to have some control over their production practices, particularly with regard to the interval between pesticide sprays and picking. Larger producers are also benefiting from the more value-added pre-packs, where French beans, in particular, are packaged ready for supermarket shelves and immediate cooking.

Problems of small-scale farmers
The study on Kenya highlights the lack of rural infrastructure, high transportation cost and insufficient support services that constitute major problems for small landholders in the agricultural sector. Small landholders also suffer from limited access to credit and technical information, which is often tied to contracts with particular exporters or embodied in costly, often expatriate, consultants. The contributions of research and extension systems to the levelling of the information playing-field between large- and small-scale producers has been less than exemplary. Small farmers, who form the majority of producers, have to resort to a process of trial and error to obtain technical information from their neighbours, because limited public resources cannot be contributed to this area. Credit through exporter- or farmer-organized groups has failed largely owing to difficulties in enforcing contracts.

Awareness about SPS measures
The knowledge of SPS issues, both within the relevant government departments and in the horticultural supply chain is, with a few exceptions, limited. Education and training will have to be undertaken to familiarize relevant ministries and producers. There are 60 000 such producers who are small-scale farmers in areas where compliance with SPS requirements of importing countries can be very problematic.

While Kenya supports the overall objective of SPS measures and recognizes the long-term benefits, there is concern about compliance costs. The expense of implementing the new measures will lead to increased costs for the exporters in the form of:

- training/sensitization of exporters and officials on SPS requirements;
- capital costs associated with changing from one type of pesticide to the recommended types;
- pest risk assessment and management;
- delays in shipping because of rigorous inspections and increased handling costs;
- bureaucratic complications in the importing countries;
- community fees paid by farmers for plant health checks.

Agricultural policies and institutions
The Kenyan government wants to introduce a Bill in Parliament to regulate this sector. One of the key aims is to give legal muscle to the semi-governmental

Horticultural Crops Development Authority (HCDA) that will enable it to discipline the sector. The Bill also proposes a levy of one per cent of the turnover to finance the new bureaucracy. The industry feels this is punitive, and has strongly opposed such a plan. It believes that attempts by the government to have a bigger say in this area would strangle private enterprise. It feels that horticulture is the last bastion of growth in an economy that shrank by 0.3 per cent in 2000. The lobby maintains that they have adhered to the MRL rules of the EU and continuous training of growers and enforcement of the Code of Practice. It further believes that the government has achieved growth through the hands-off policy and the government's belated attempts at involvement can only breed market inefficiency and lethargy, as has been witnessed in the coffee and tea sectors.

Fisheries

For the fisheries sector, the Ministry of Health is the competent authority. However, it has delegated the responsibility of inspection to the Department of Fisheries and the auditing role to the Kenya Bureau of Standards.

Of an annual production of 180 000 tonnes of marine and freshwater fish and fish products, 120 000 tonnes go to fish processing establishments, which in turn export 18 000 tonnes of fish and fish products, earning the country nearly US$55 million. Ninety-two per cent of Kenya's total fish production comes from Lake Victoria, and approximately 50 per cent of it is Nile perch.

Traditionally Kenya relies on the European Union market for her fish exports. Until 1996, when Spain and Italy imposed import restrictions on Kenyan fishery products, the European Union absorbed 70 per cent of Kenyan exports, with Spain importing the bulk of the commodity.

MOZAMBIQUE[6]

Standards and Competitiveness

Mozambique's traditional exports (maize, cashew, cotton, wood, prawns and fish) are vulnerable to international pressures (in terms of price, politics and quality) and high cost of imported inputs and transportation to global markets. Mozambique still faces numerous socio-economic problems. Among them are an unstable growth rate, the unstable condition of two-digit inflation, decline and stagnation of agricultural and industrial output and a poor commercial network, a poor to moderate export performance and high foreign debt.

Under these circumstances Mozambique, like many other developing countries, faces serious problems in complying with stringent SPS measures and environmental requirements in international markets. Thus, there is concern that such requirements may cause significant adverse economic consequences in terms of financial costs, unemployment and human suffering.

Yet Mozambique, as a country interested in international trade, should follow international market trends. Mozambique has had greater exposure to international competition in recent years. The conclusion of the Uruguay Round of Multilateral Trade Negotiations in 1994 and the subsequent creation of the WTO, as well as the gradual reintegration of South Africa into the world economy after the 1994 elections, have contributed to this development. The return of South Africa as the dominant southern African exporter increases the importance of cost and quality factors for all the other potential African exporters, including Mozambique. South Africa's relatively well-developed transport, communication and agro-processing infrastructure provides its exporters with a competitive edge over the other regional exporters. Building capacities to improve grades and standards will be a critical element of Mozambique's export strategy.

The African Growth Opportunity Act (AGOA) should open new opportunities for 39 targeted African countries to export textile and agricultural products to the United States market. In order to take advantage of new trading opportunities, existing production and export constraints (see below) have to be overcome. Many of these constraints are already clear. Other constraints are likely to emerge or to become visible when Mozambique begins to take advantage of the trade concessions being offered by the United States (AGOA) and the European Union (see Table 5.1).

The government of Mozambique has put in place a number of macroeconomic policies designed to improve its export position. Mozambique continues to depend strongly on its agricultural exports to SADC and other international trading partners. The increased stringency of SPS/food safety requirements by developed countries, in particular, compels Mozambique to increase its capacity to deal with such matters.

Grades and standards in Mozambique

This is an enormous task. The study on Mozambique elaborates a series of structural weaknesses in the areas of grades and standards. First, the current system of grades and standards in the domestic market in Mozambique is weak. A low cost/low quality culture permeates all the sectors owing to very low income levels and the poor economic climate overall. The weak system of grades and standards in Mozambique encourages imports of poor quality products and of products beyond their expiry dates. It creates export discouragement and increases transaction costs. The problem of quality is circular in that exports and processing capacity are low because quality is low, and quality

Table 5.1   Mozambique: factors adversely affecting the ability to comply
with SPS measures and environmental requirements in external
markets

Ranking	Factor	At present	Likely to be important in future
1	Insufficient access to technology	**	*
2	High cost of imported imports	**	*
3	Lack of awareness of or access to information on the part of the exporter	**	*
4	Insufficient domestic infrastructure (lack of testing facilities)	**	**
5	High compliance cost	**	**
6	Legal factor (lack of enforcement)	*	***
7	Stringency of the measure (which may be perceived as unreasonable)	n/a	**
8	Firm size	n/a	*
9	Insufficient supply of environment-friendly inputs, prescribed chemicals	n/a	**
10	Lack of transparency in the design and implementation of the measure in the importing country	n/a	*

cannot be improved because the income earned from exports and processing is low.

Secondly, there are practically no government standards for agricultural inputs currently in place, which causes several problems. It is difficult to obtain good-quality seed for many commodities. The lack of seed certification programmes leaves farmers with no guarantee that what they are buying is actually what they think it is and that the seeds will actually germinate. In addition, there is no pesticide registry in Mozambique, which means there is no control over what is allowed into the country or regulations on pesticide labelling and usage. Pesticides such as DDT are banned in most countries but can be found in Mozambique. The lack of government regulation on pesticides has led non-governmental organizations to press for conformity with international standards.

While the regional markets are less demanding with respect to standards than global markets, standards are still an important element in trading relationships.

The same categories of standards exist for the regional market as for the global market. Standards across countries are in the process of harmonization in accordance with regional trade agreements, which will facilitate trade.

Export Constraints

Mozambique faces a variety of constraints in effectively and efficiently dealing with trade in agricultural and food products. These may be summarized as follows:

- *The low level of technical education of the staff involved as well as the technology used for inspection processes.* This contributes to the low level of implementation of international standards, guidelines or recommendations.
- *Lack of pertinent, trade-related information for importers and exporters.* This often results in traders attempting to move goods without the required documentation, at great economic cost.
- *Lack of consultation among national SPS/food safety authorities.* The flow of information from national enquiry contact points is poor; as a result authorities 'downstream' from the enquiry/contact points are not provided with the data they need to effectively fulfil their operational mandates.
- *Lack of technical resources.* Mozambique's capacity to apply international standards and regional requirements of conformity assessment, risk assessment, data provision and so on are limited at present owing to lack of technical and adequately qualified human resources.
- *Inadequate exchange of animal and plant disease information among SADC member states.* The poor flow of relevant information among SADC member countries severely impedes regional trade, and makes national efforts to contain plant and animal diseases difficult.
- *Lack of adequate conformity infrastructure.* This includes laboratory facilities for the analysis of pesticide residues.

Summary and Conclusions

The structural weaknesses mentioned above imply that Mozambique has to strengthen its capacities to compete in international and domestic markets in order to be able to reap the benefits of trade liberalization. In the short run, import liberalization may put heavy pressure on domestic industry. Therefore, the study on Mozambique recommends that:

- Companies and agricultural producers likely to be most negatively affected by trade liberalization should receive special attention and preferential financial and technical assistance from donors to assist them in becoming as competitive as possible before new trade regulations come into full effect. Insufficient attention has been paid to implementing measures to reduce the predicted negative consequences (economic and political) expected in some sectors owing to accelerated trade liberalization.

Trade rules should allow for periodic review and adjustments of the rate of liberalization and other key trade issues through specific legal mechanisms. This will enable poorer nations like Mozambique to become more willing to take risks in trying new initiatives.

UNITED REPUBLIC OF TANZANIA[7]

Since the mid-1980s the Tanzanian economy has undergone a gradual but fundamental transformation that has redefined the roles of the government and the private sector. These changes have paved the way for the withdrawal of government involvement in direct production, processing and marketing activities, which can be performed better by the private sector. The government liberalized the marketing of agricultural products and inputs; price controls and subsidies have been removed; monopolies of cooperatives and marketing boards have been eliminated; and private traders now participate in crop procurement and input supply. Some institutions have been streamlined to cater to the new emerging roles. The government has now retained the core functions of policy formulation and maintenance of law and order. These reforms have necessitated major changes in the Agriculture and Livestock Policies of 1983. The National Agricultural and Livestock Policy of 1997 has been drawn up taking into account the broader economic and social objectives of the country and the need to have policies which are clear in their objectives and feasible to implement.

The study on the United Republic of Tanzania SPS Agreement is crucial in providing market access, while allowing the government to protect its people, plant and animal health and general environment. The United Republic of Tanzania has initiated measures which aim at ensuring that agricultural production, processing and export is undertaken under strict SPS conditions. The 1997 Act is based on the standard developed under the International Plant Protection Convention (IPPC). The IPPC has now been modified to suit the WTO agreement. However, Tanzania still needs assistance to develop sanitary policy and legislation.

The agricultural sector faces the following challenges:

- *Low investments in the agricultural sector*. The agricultural sector has consistently received 3 per cent or less of the total public budget. These allocations have been declining in real terms over time. Similarly, the private sector investments have been low owing to high risks attached to the sector.

- *Poor rural infrastructure.* Poor rural infrastructure, including roads, limits farmers' access to markets for inputs and produce, increases the cost of transportation and often causes deterioration of produce resulting in poor quality products. Similarly, inadequate and poor storage facilities cause substantial post-harvest losses, estimated to be between 30 and 40 per cent of the produce. The absence of communication in rural areas is a serious constraint to the dissemination of knowledge and market information, both of which are vital to the survival of farmers in a free market economy.
- *Limited capital and access to financial services.* Smallholder farmers, most of whom produce food for subsistence, dominate Tanzanian agriculture, which is characterized by food insecurity and low cash income.
- *Inadequate supporting services.* Supporting services, which are vital to agricultural growth, are insufficient. They consist of agricultural research and extension services, agricultural information services, veterinary services and plant protection services.
- *Agricultural research.* Weak research–extension farmer linkages have limited the diffusion of research results and restricted researchers' ability to diagnose and respond to farmers' real problems.
- *Agricultural data and information services.* Agricultural data and information services are essential for making the liberalized market transparent to both traders and farmers and for effective management of a sector. The market information currently produced and disseminated by the Ministry of Agriculture and Food Security is not comprehensive in terms of its coverage of products, inputs and areas.
- *Weak and inappropriate legal framework and taxation policy.* The current legal framework, land tenure and taxation policy do not enable Tanzanians to fully exploit the production and marketing opportunities created by the emerging free market environment.

FISHERIES

Background

For developing African countries, the establishment of a system for sanitary and quality assurance of fish products that is compatible with and equivalent to the systems of the developed countries, such as that of the EU, can be very difficult.[8] Such a system gives the industry the responsibility to implement its own quality control and provide proof that their procedures and products are reliable and comply with the regulations, while the inspection services carry out check-up programmes.

Kenya, for example, has experienced a number of problems in gaining approval from the European Commission to export fish to the EU and did not obtain 'Part 2' status until January 1999. Since 1997, the Commission has undertaken a series of inspection visits to Kenya. Subsequently, it questioned the procedures by which plants were approved to export to the EU and export health certificates were issued for individual product consignments as well as for overall standards of hygiene in the supply chain. An area of particular concern was hygiene standards on boats and on landing sites, many of which lack jetties, potable running water, cooling facilities, fencing and so on.[9]

Mozambique faces numerous problems in complying with SPS and TBT requirements of developed countries. Specifically, it lacks:[10]

*   human and institutional capacity needed to address SPS issues;
*   specialized equipment needed for analysis;
*   technical information on SPS/TBT and mechanisms to disseminate this to stakeholders;
*   a mechanism for consultations among national SPS/food safety authorities and other stakeholders;
*   overall conformity infrastructure, such as laboratory facilities for the analysis of pesticide residues.

In the United Republic of Tanzania industrial fishery is mostly practised by trawlers engaged in shrimp fishery. Currently, there are approximately 16 commercial vessels operating in the country. Despite its potential of fish allowable biomass of 710 000 metric tonnes, the average fish catch is estimated at 350 000 tonnes annually. Lake Victoria's potential is estimated at 200 000 metric tonnes. Compared with other East African Community (EAC) member states, the United Republic of Tanzania has better chances of increasing the present fish production without exceeding the allowable biomass potential.

The Tanzanian fisheries sector is constrained in the following areas:

*   inadequate fishing gear and craft;
*   inadequate extension services to fishermen, leading to poor handling and management of fish products;
*   unreliable/inadequate data on fishing;
*   inadequate infrastructure facilities, including processing and storage facilities.

The case study on Uganda lists the following problems:[11]

- The structure of the competent authority (CA): there were unclear lines of command, which in turn led to conflicts. The two quality assurance bodies for fish belonged to different parent ministries, the Uganda National Bureau of Standards (UNBS) under the Ministry of Tourism, Trade and Industry (MTTI) and the Department of Fisheries and Resources (DFR), which reports to the Ministry of Agriculture, Animal Industry and Fisheries (MAAIF).
- The Fish and Crocodile Act has not been upgraded to meet the present challenges of the fast growing fisheries industry.
- With the policy of decentralization, District Fisheries Officers (DFO) were not answerable to the DFR and therefore did not follow instructions regarding hygiene and handling of fish.
- The inspectors of the DFR were not able to perform their duties owing to lack of guidelines and standard operating practices for landing sites.
- Most fish landing sites had not been upgraded and their facilities did not meet EU requirements.
- Non-availability of suitable laboratories for pesticide residue analysis: the performance and capacity of the Government Chemist were considered totally inadequate by the EU inspection team in spite of the fact that the government had invested close to US$160 000 in improving its facilities.

In November 1996, Spain and Italy imposed a ban on Kenyan fish, claiming that salmonellae were present in it. No other European Union member state was affected by the ban and they continued importing fish from Kenya. The ban caused a reduction in foreign exchange earnings by 13.1 per cent, with total exports to Spain decreasing by 86 per cent. Since 1997, Eastern African and Mozambican exports of fishery products have been affected by several specific problems, in particular (a) the presence of salmonellae in Nile perch from Lake Victoria, (b) an outbreak of cholera and (c) fish poisoning in Lake Victoria as a result of pesticide residues. In each of these cases, the European Union imposed import restrictions (testing and/or bans); see Table 5.2.

The papers highlight several concerns. First, the fact that exports of fishery products from Kenya, the United Republic of Tanzania and Uganda have been subject to successive rounds of restrictions illustrates the complexity of the problems and may have contributed to the perception that SPS measures act as 'signposts' to be shifted when reached (see above).

Secondly, there have been doubts about the scientific justification of the measures imposed. With regard to the cholera case, the papers on Kenya and

Table 5.2   Specific problems affecting East African and Mozambican exports of fishery products

Issue	Countries affected	Measure taken	Source
Presence of salmonellae in Nile perch from Lake Victoria	Kenya, United Republic of Tanzania, Uganda	Each consignment of Nile perch fillets tested for the presence of salmonellae	Commission Decisions 97/272/EC (Kenya), 97/273/EC (Uganda) and 97/274/EC (the United Republic of Tanzania) of 4 April 1997 (Official Journal L 108 of 25 April 1997)
Outbreak of cholera	Kenya, Mozambique, United Republic of Tanzania, Uganda	Each consignment of frozen or processed fishery products subject to checks capable of detecting, in particular, the presence of salmonellae and vibrios (*Vibrio cholerae* and *Vibrio parahaemolyticus*); prohibition of imports of fresh fishery products (because of time required to carry out microbiological analyses)	Commission Decision 98/84/EC of 16 January 1998 (Official Journal L 015 of 21 January 1998)
Fish poisoning caused by the presence of pesticides in the water of Lake Victoria and by fishery malpractice	Kenya, United Republic of Tanzania, Uganda	Suspension by Uganda of exports of fishery products caught in Lake Victoria to the European Union Suspension of imports by the European Union of fishery products caught in Lake Victoria from Kenya and the United Republic of Tanzania	Precautionary measures by Uganda itself Commission Decision 1999/253/EC of 12 April 1999 (Official Journal L 098 of 13 April 1999): restrictions on imports from Kenya and Tanzania

Mozambique argue that there was insufficient scientific evidence to justify the ban. The World Health Organization (WHO), for example, had issued a *note verbale* explaining that despite the fact that at least 50 countries had been affected by epidemic or endemic cholera since 1961, there had been no documented evidence of any case of cholera resulting from commercially imported food.[12] The *note verbale* clarified that *Vibrio cholerae 01*, the bacterium that causes cholera, can be transmitted to humans via food.[13] Cases of cholera had occasionally occurred as a result of eating food, usually seafood, transported across international borders by individual travellers, but WHO had not documented cases of cholera resulting from commercially imported food.

Similarly, the Food and Agriculture Organization (FAO) noted that the cholera bacterium does not survive proper cooking or drying, and cooked, dried or canned products are considered safe from cholera transmission. Furthermore, the FAO report held that 'Epidemiological data suggest that the risk of transmission of cholera from contaminated imported fish is negligible. Only rare and sporadic cases of cholera have occurred in developed countries as a result of eating fish transported across international borders by individuals'.

In Mozambique, the government and fisheries sector were convinced that there was insufficient scientific evidence to justify the ban. The authorities, however, tried to resolve the underlying problems and to obtain the removal of the ban through consultations with the European Union. Consultations both on a bilateral basis and at the level of ACP countries took place in early 1998.

Thirdly, the papers express the view that insufficient attention was paid to the ongoing efforts of African countries. Both the papers on Kenya and Mozambique argue that in the cholera case the ban was unfortunate, since curative and preventive measures had been put in place. With regard to the case of fish poisoning caused by the presence of pesticides in the water of Lake Victoria and by fishery malpractice, the government of Kenya had imposed a two-week ban on fishing in the lake to stamp out the illegal practice. When the ban expired, the government was satisfied that fish caught from Lake Victoria was safe for consumption. The European Commission, however, argued that 'Kenya and Tanzania have taken precautionary measures but not suspended the exports of fishery products to the Community. These precautionary measures are not enough to assure, in the current situation, the safety of the fishery products'.[14]

In August 1999, three inspectors from the European Union visited Kenya to assess the capacities and resources of the competent authority in relation to pesticide residues in fish and to assess the reliability of the system of certification for freedom from pesticide residues. The professionalism with which the analyses were carried out in the KEPHIS laboratories impressed the inspectors, but, despite the results of monthly sampling and analysis procedures that did not detect pesticide residues in fish caught in Lake Victoria, the ban continued for 20 months before it was lifted.

Responses to the Standards, and Costs of Import Restrictions

Kenya

The 1998 ban (cholera outbreak) resulted in a significant drop in the production and export of fish, which in turn negatively impacted on the fishing communities, in particular through loss of employment. Nile perch exports were particularly affected, dropping by 66 per cent. This resulted in a 24 per cent drop in total fish exports and 32 per cent drop in value. The third ban, on account of suspicions that fishermen were using chemicals to catch fish, saw further loss of incomes, jobs and foreign earnings. Factories operated below capacity, while many closed down, affecting approximately 40 000 artisan fishermen.

Kenya will need large sums of money to upgrade its fish export infrastructure if it is to be put on the EU's Part I list. It will have to invest in manpower development, capacity building of fishermen and fish handlers, upgrading of its landing sites and factories, and putting in place appropriate monitoring systems. In particular, Kenya will need a scientific and technical establishment with experience to defend or challenge any adverse decisions under the SPS measures; collection of scientific data; capacity building of small-scale fishermen; dissemination of information to artisan fishermen and fish handlers on any amendments to measures already in place; adequate inspection, communication and documentation facilities; trained operators, processing and cleaning personnel; effective monitoring and properly equipped laboratories to support regular routine and monitoring programmes.

One study[15] estimates that the cost of upgrading a single landing site on Lake Victoria to provide potable running water, cooling facilities and so on is around $1.2 million (Lake Victoria Management Project). Given that there are five main beaches that supply fish for export (Ministry of Health), the total cost is estimated to be $5.8 million. The cost of upgrading laboratory facilities for chemical and microbiological analysis is estimated to be $1.1 million (Lake Victoria Management Project). The Kenyan government has discussed with the European Commission the possibility of receiving technical assistance and funds, at least in part, for these improvements. A summary of the costs is shown in Box 5.2.

BOX 5.2   IMPACTS OF EU RESTRICTIONS ON FISH EXPORTS FROM KENYA[16]

Fish exports from Kenya

The European Union is a very important market for Kenyan exports of fish, accounting for 59 per cent of exports by volume during the period immediately prior to the introduction of the restrictions. It is not surprising, therefore, that the EU measures have had a significant impact on Kenyan fish exports, particularly during the two periods in which exports of particular types of fish were prohibited.

During 1998, when exports of fresh fish were prohibited for a period of six months, the total volume of exports was 29 per cent lower than in 1996, while exports to the EU were 69 per cent lower. Similarly, in 1999 total fish exports were 21 per cent lower than in 1996, while exports to the EU were 64 per cent lower. This indicates a significant trade diversion effect, whereby Kenyan exporters were able to partially offset the impact of the EU restrictions by pursuing alternative markets, in particular in Israel, Singapore, Japan and the United Arab Emirates. Despite this, however, the total value of fish exports (in nominal terms) was significantly lower in 1998 (37 per cent) and in 1999 (24 per cent) than in 1996.

The EU restrictions have had a particularly significant impact on exports of fresh fillets, for which the EU typically accounts for over 95 per cent of exports and for which few alternative markets exist. In 1998 and 1999 exports of fresh fillets were around 86 per cent lower than in 1996. Conversely, in the case of frozen fillets, for which the EU accounted for 60 per cent of exports in 1996, the decline in exports to the European Union has been progressively offset by increased exports to other markets. Thus, in 1998, exports were 30 per cent lower than in 1996. In 1999, exports were 13 per cent lower than in 1996.

Impact on the fish processing sector

The EU restrictions have had a significant impact on fish processors, in terms of both the economic performance of individual companies and the manner in which the sector as a whole is organized. First, the performance of fish processing companies has declined as a direct result of the loss of exports to the EU.

Given that there are few alternative markets for fresh fillets, processors have had little choice but to switch to the production of frozen fillets, although market prices are typically 60 per cent lower and have been further reduced by intensified competition among exporters. Many processors claim that during the periods that restrictions were applied, the returns from exports of Nile perch were barely sufficient to cover costs. Indeed most have been operating at lower levels of capacity and have shed labour in an effort to minimize operating costs. Furthermore, four processing plants have subsequently suspended operations and two companies have gone into receivership. These companies typically had the lowest hygiene standards and/or lacked the necessary processing facilities to switch from production of fresh to frozen fillets.

Many processors have had to invest significant sums (at interest rates of over 20 per cent) to upgrade their processing facilities and to improve their procedures so as to meet the EU hygiene requirements. According to the Kenyan government, only two plants that processed Nile perch were in compliance with the EU hygiene requirements in November 1998 (Ministry of Health). The improvements required to obtain approval for export to the European Union, as identified by European Commission inspection visits and the competent authority, include upgrading of buildings and/or equipment, improvements to laboratory facilities, implementing HACCP plans and training of staff. The necessary investment undoubtedly contributed to the poor financial performance of many processing companies.

Third, the fish processing sector has also been forced to improve the manner in which it manages the supply chain for fresh fish. Traditionally, processors have been supplied through traders and although some have provided finance and/or fishing equipment to fishing boats on the lake in an attempt to foster dependency among fisher-folk and to guarantee supplies, their role in the management of the supply chain has been limited. However, as a result of the EU's criticisms of hygiene conditions at landing sites, processors were forced to improve these, not only in their own plants but throughout the supply chain. A number of processors, for example, invested in cold storage facilities on the landing beaches and routinely provide ice for use by traders and for the transportation of fish to their factories. While this undoubtedly increased their power to dictate terms of supply to fisher-folk through the traders, it necessitated further investment at a time when competition was particularly intense.

Fourth, as a result of the EU's restrictions and demands for improvements in hygiene conditions throughout the fish supply chain in Kenya, the processing sector recognized the need to share information and to cooperate with the Kenyan government and the European Commission. Consequently, in 1998 the Kenya Association of Fish Exporters and Processors was formed, involving all of the main fish processing companies. Members of the association were prominent in negotiations with the European Commission, and accompanied Kenyan government officials to meetings in Brussels. It is conceded by many processors that the sector benefited as a result of this heightened level of cooperation, not only in dealing with the EU restrictions, but also in the long-term management of the sector. It is believed that this would have been unlikely if normal market conditions had prevailed.

Finally, the closure of or reduction in output of industrial fish processing plants has, in turn, led to a decline in the supply of skeletons and other waste products. This has had significant consequences for those individuals, mainly women, who have built up a livelihood around the processing of these products. In Obunga, one of the largest communities dependent on the processing of waste products from fish processing plants, a women's group responded to this threat to their livelihood by collectively absorbing the impact. The group, which organizes the processing activities of 800 women, rations the supply of skeletons available to each of its members. This meant that during 1999 each woman was typically allocated less than 50 per cent of the skeletons that she processed before the introduction of the restrictions.

Conclusions
In the case of fish exports from Kenya, a supply chain that is highly reliant on the EU market for fresh fillets, the economic impact of prolonged prohibitions on exports has been significant. At the macroeconomic level, fish exports declined, with consequent reductions in foreign exchange earnings. At the microeconomic level, industrial fish processing companies closed or reduced capacity and employment in the sector declined. Furthermore, the livelihoods of fisher-folk and others in local fishing communities, who have limited access to alternative economic activities, in part as a result of the progressive export-orientation of the sector, have suffered as market prices for fish have declined.

Mozambique
The ban on fresh fishery products reportedly resulted in a loss of about $60 000 a month in hard currency earnings. Mozambique's main fisheries exports, deep-frozen prawns, were not banned but subject to testing. The trade impact is not known. The study by Cerina Mussa mentions that for Mozambique the ban was unfortunate, since it had already put in place curative and preventive measures well before the imposition of the ban.

Uganda
Following successive bans on fish exports to the EU, volumes and earnings were severely curtailed, and negative multiplier effects to the fishing communities and overall economy ensued. In particular:

- An estimated loss of $36.9 million was posted over the period of the ban and loss to the fishermen's community in terms of reduced prices and lower activity of fishing was estimated at $1 million per month.
- Out of 11 factories which were operational at that time, 3 were closed and the remaining 8 operated at about 20 per cent capacity. As a consequence, 60–70 per cent of the directly employed people were laid off.
- People involved in various fishing activities became jobless and those that had some work to do earned less than a third of their normal earnings – this directly affected the families and dependants of the people involved in fishing and supplementary activities.
- Other related industries, such as packaging and transport, were affected, with subsequent effects on other sectors.
- The restrictions concerning trade in Nile perch, which had been considered a proper substitute for cod in low season in Europe before the ban, had a negative impact on its popularity. An expensive marketing campaign is required to restore its former acceptance levels.
- As a result of the ban government and fish exporters were compelled to spend huge sums of money to upgrade fish handling facilities from the lake – fishing gear and transporting boats containers – to landing sites and factory floors/facilities. Specifically, the UNBS microbiology laboratory had to be fully equipped. Eighteen thousand dollars were invested in a monitoring programme on Lake Victoria and ten inspectors were recruited to supervise fish production at factories. In order to create capacity to analyse pesticide residues, a privately run laboratory – Chemiphar (U) Ltd – was set up, at considerable cost, with support from UNIDO. Two pilot boats were constructed to conduct trials for assessment of socio-economic impact on boat building and design.

Building Capacities: The Current Situation

Kenya
The Kenyan government has undertaken a number of initiatives to have the restrictions suspended and ultimately to get full (Directive 91/493/EEC, Annex I, Part I) approval for the export of fish to the EU. This involved both legislative change and reform of procedures for the approval of plants which could export to the EU and the issuing of health certificates (see Box 5.3). For example, the Kenya Bureau of Standards (KEBS) published a code of hygiene practice for the handling, processing and storage of fish, which applies to all fish, both for export and for the domestic market. This standard essentially harmonizes Kenyan hygiene requirements for fish with those of the EU.

BOX 5.3   MEASURES TAKEN BY THE KENYAN GOVERNMENT TO COMPLY WITH EU REGULATIONS[17]

The Kenyan government has undertaken a number of initiatives to meet the demands of the European Commission. It introduced legislative changes and reformed procedures for the approval of plants for exports of fish to the EU and the issuing of health certificates. Regulations were introduced to ensure hygienic fish handling and processing, in order to assure the safety of Kenyan fishery products to consumers. After the publication of the Fisheries (Fish Quality Assurance) Act, the Ministry of Agriculture and Rural Development, whose mandate is to ensure food safety, quality and security, became the competent authority (CA) for fish and fishery products, effective 11 August 2000.

The Kenya Bureau of Standards (KEBS) published a code of hygiene practice for the handling, processing and storage of fish, which applies to all fish for both export and the domestic market. This standard essentially harmonizes Kenyan hygiene requirements for fish with those of the EU.

In addition, the Fisheries Department planned and implemented a number of activities, including:

Landing beaches. The improvement of landing beaches is being implemented through community/stakeholder participation. Ten strategic landing sites have been earmarked, with the first phase aimed at fencing, paving of the reception area, improvement of the drainage system, the provision of insulated fish boxes, and improvement of the sorting sheds. The second phase of beach improvement will include provision of electricity and water, construction of landing jetties, modernization of fish reception, and improvement of access roads.

Analytical laboratories. Building capacity for both chemical and microbiological analysis of fish and environment (water and sediments) is essential to help develop databases that would be used to assure consumers of the safety and quality of Kenya's fish. To this end, construction and renovation laboratories will be used for routine analysis of the necessary parameters, which will provide the database that will be the reference point for fish safety and quality assurance.

Training. The training and refresher courses for fish inspectors and industry quality managers is an ongoing programme aimed at upgrading fish quality in the country. The Department is also planning to conduct courses for trainers on fish quality control to build training capacity. This is expected to assist in upgrading fish quality through training of frontline fish inspectors, fish handlers and quality managers. The trained trainers of quality will therefore be instrumental in enhancement of fish product marketability.

Collaborative approach. The need to collaborate with local and international fisheries researchers is being emphasized and several memoranda of understanding have been prepared and signed to this effect. Demand driven research and survey are being promoted to improve the flow of information and build a database for better management of fishery resources. The same approach is being developed for all the stakeholders in the fishing industry, with fisheries taking a lead role.

Despite the hardship caused by the import bans there have been some positive developments in the industry:

- a code of practice has been established and private sector operators are involved in the maintenance of SPS services;
- quality assurance programmes for sustainable exports have been developed;
- health conditions at landing sites have been improved;

- capacity to analyse fish/fish product samples has improved;
- industry quality managers and fish inspectors have been trained;
- a collaborative approach in fish management has been sought.

By Commission Decision 1999/136/EC of 28 January 1999, Kenya was placed on Part II (Official Journal L.044 of 18 February 1999).

Mozambique
The government of Mozambique has (see also Box 5.4):

- legalized fish inspection, and provides inspection services/technical services to factories and vessels and training to fish inspectors at all levels;
- enhanced and defined the role of laboratories;
- adapted the HACCP system, an elaborate system which approves sanitary conditions and plans fishing vessels, among other things;
- established the Department of Fish Inspection as the competent authority within the Ministry of Fisheries;
- put in place a fisheries law which guarantees the safety of the fish export trade.

By Commission Decision 1999/136/EC of 28 January 1999, Mozambique was included on Part II (official journal L 044 of 18 February 1999).

Uganda
By the Commission Decision 98/419/EC of 30 June 1998 (190 of 4/7/98), Uganda was initially placed on Part II of the countries authorized to export fishery products to the EU. Subsequently, as a result of substantial investments in upgrading facilities at all levels of the fish production/marketing chain, Uganda was promoted to Part I in May 2001.

As a result of this positive development, namely resumption of fish exports to the EU, foreign exchange earnings increased, which in turn contributed to the foreign exchange rate stability. Factories are now operating at full capacity, implying increased direct employment in supporting services as well.

Although Uganda suffered loss of foreign exchange and reduced economic activities owing to the ban, some positive developments resulted from this experience, namely:

- the ban made authorities focus on the problems of the fish sub-sector, including sourcing of funds from donors – UNIDO;
- the fish inspection services have been streamlined and the capacity of the competent authority (DFR) strengthened;

BOX 5.4   MOZAMBIQUE: LEGISLATION AND
          INSPECTION CONCERNING
          FISHERIES[18]

In Mozambique the Ministry of Fisheries is responsible for
inspection and approval of licences for export and import, in
accordance with sanitary requirements. The Fisheries Law (3/90
of 26 September) has updated regulations and made them
compatible with the SPS Agreement. At the same time, the
Ministry ensures compliance with the European Union Council
Directive 98/83/EC of 3 November 1998 on the quality of water
intended for human consumption (which includes water used in
the food industry, unless it can be established that the use of
such water does not affect the wholesomeness of the finished
product).

The Fisheries Law also has provisions for:

- analysis and approval of projects to set up establishments
  for processing of fish products;
- approval of hygiene/sanitary conditions, and hygiene and
  quality control programmes of factories/vessels;
- certification of fishery products aimed for exports;
- laboratory control for the fish inspection programmes;
- organization of trading/extension programmes for the technical personnel of the fish inspection services and industry;
- promotion of research programmes.

In addition, the proposed 'Regulation of Inspection and Quality
Control of Fish Products' aims to:

- guide the development of the processing industry;
- update and modernize the national legislation in order to
  comply with the requirements of international markets;
- serve as the legal landmark for the responsibilities of the
  fish inspection service and the processing industry;
- serve, together with the 'Fisheries Master Plan', as an
  instrument for fisheries management and administration
  and as a landmark for the performance of the fish industry;
- be a sector instrument, but with implication from other
  sectors, such as health, customs and trade.

- a fisheries policy has been formulated, inspectors trained, equipment provided and fish inspection manuals developed;
- Uganda's fish gained access to the US market, which demanded a higher level of Hazard Analysis Critical Control Point (HACCP) systems from the fish factories than that demanded by the EU;
- internationally recognized laboratory services have been established locally, which will greatly facilitate export of other products and reduce costs;
- Ugandan consumers have benefited from the investment in better sanitary systems for fish harvesting and processing.

HORTICULTURE

Background

The horticultural sector is of key interest to several East African countries. In Kenya, for example, the area under horticulture in 1999 was estimated at 322 000 hectares of which 1600 hectares were under flowers, 189 000 hectares under vegetables and 131 000 hectares under fruits. The sector generated US$730 million locally and about US$200 million in foreign exchange earnings. Horticulture is currently the fastest growing industry in Kenya, contributing 26 per cent of the GDP and a third of the foreign exchange earned by the country.

The Kenya paper expresses concern about new European Union SPS measures for fruit, vegetables and other products, particularly the Commission Directive 2001/35/EC of 11 May 2001, which came into force in July 2001.[19] The directive fixes the maximum residue levels (MRLs) at 'analytical' zero, requiring that there be no trace of pesticide residue in fruits, vegetables and cut flowers intended for the EU market.

Structural Problems

Problems facing the horticulture sector are common in the three East African countries. Specifically, the sector has poor infrastructure, limited capital and financial resources, low investment, inadequate supporting services, lack of data information services, and weak and inappropriate legal framework, while experiencing high transport costs, especially air freighting. The sector is dominated by small-scale farmers. However, horticultural production plays an important role in Kenya, the United Republic of Tanzania and Uganda, not only in terms of foreign exchange earnings but also in employment and overall economic growth.

As mentioned earlier, Kenyan producers are concerned that, because of lack of experience and the difficulties they are likely to face when adapting to the new requirements, they may end up using wrong pesticides, which may result in production of low quality products.

The study on the United Republic of Tanzania notes that although a market for horticultural products exists, there are enormous constraints which include inadequate post harvest facilities, poor quality of the locally manufactured packing materials, inadequate access to financial instructions and high costs of energy.

The papers prepared for the Kampala workshop organized under this project note that it is too early to assess the impacts of the new EU requirement on exports of horticultural products. Yet, concern is expressed in both the Kenyan and the Ugandan papers that growth prospects of the industry are likely to be undermined by the new directive.

The paper on Kenya notes that the Kenyan government faces considerable resource constraints that limit its ability to respond to the EU requirements, particularly in the modernization of its basic infrastructure and facilities.

The paper on Mozambique notes that, while producers and exporters in other African countries have expressed great concern over meeting maximum residue levels (MRLs) for pesticides, none of those interviewed for the study in Mozambique had expressed concern about new MRL requirements in the European Union. The author attributes this to the low level of market knowledge.

Similarly, the paper on Uganda notes that, unlike Kenya, Uganda has not yet made sufficient adjustments to comply with the directive and is likely to suffer more. Although it is too early to assess the impact of the directive on Ugandan horticultural exports, small-scale producers and exporters are likely to close down owing to increased compliance costs in all aspects, as enumerated under the Kenya experience. Uganda, like Kenya, will need both technical and financial resources to support its horticultural industry if it is to continue exporting to the EU market. Training and sensitization of producers and government officials, upgrading of equipment and change-over costs have to be undertaken at a tremendous expense to the exporter.

CAPACITY BUILDING EFFORTS

All the papers point to the need for trade-related capacity building and include recommendations in this area. The Kenya paper, however, expresses concern that technical assistance often fails to address the fundamental day-to-day problems faced by developing countries, many of which relate to the overall level of their economic development. It argues that much of the technical assistance is reactive, in that it is provided once the problems of compliance to the SPS requirements have been identified rather than being proactive, that is, being part of a strategy aimed at general capacity building.

BOX 5.5　CAPACITY BUILDING EFFORTS OF ZIMBABWE

With regard to sanitary, phytosanitary and environmental–social issues Zimbabwe has adopted a proactive approach in order to remain competitive.

At the policy level, the government has explicitly included in its 1995–2020 agricultural policy framework the identification, adoption and implementation of internationally accredited phytosanitary inspection and quality control systems.

The government has been requiring growers and exporters to move towards integrated pest management and biological control. The Zimbabwean growers are being advised on the reforms of the EU regulations by their importers and the COLEACP (Comité de liaison Europe – Afrique/Caraïbes/Pacifique) through an EU-funded initiative. The reforms have also been incorporated in the national agricultural code of practice based on statutory and market requirements.

At the firm level, most importers' technical departments conduct regular audits of production, processing and handling systems with regard to chemical usage and environmental, workers' welfare and social issues.

The issue of concern for Zimbabwean horticultural producers is that the EU pesticide legislation on MRLs was set for most exotic crop/active ingredient combinations without consulting them.

Capacity building programmes cover assistance to developing countries to:

* implement their obligations under the SPS and TBT Agreements;
* participate in the work of international standards organizations;
* comply with national SPS measures and/or standards in major markets;
* comply with international standards;
* strengthen capacities to improve quality and compete in international markets.

The SPS and TBT Agreements contain provisions on technical assistance, especially in the first three areas. So far, technical cooperation and capacity building has focused largely on assisting developing countries in implementing their obligations under the SPS and TBT Agreements. However, the need to support the effective participation of developing countries has emerged as a key 'implementation issue' and has been emphasized in the Doha Ministerial Declaration. This is also emphasized in several country papers.

The papers also illustrate the need for technical assistance to comply with national SPS measures and/or standards in major markets, for example, in the fisheries sector. Such assistance can be provided on a multilateral or a bilateral basis. UNIDO, for example, has assisted Uganda in resolving problems in this sector and gaining 'Part I' status in the context of the European Union regulations concerning imports of fishery products. UNIDO announced further assistance to LDCs in the third UN Conference for the LDCs (Brussels, May 2001).

Bilateral assistance also plays a key role. In February 2002 the Commission of the European Union announced a new programme of more than €42 million to help African, Caribbean and Pacific (ACP) countries to overcome difficulties encountered in complying with consumer health standards in the fisheries sector.[20] The programme was launched in the framework of the ACP–EU partnership agreement and forms part of the European Union's overall strategy of trade-related technical assistance for developing countries.

The Commission recognized that

> Many ACP countries depend on the export of fishery products to provide both foreign exchange and employment in coastal regions. For over 60 ACP countries the EU is the major export market (the EU represented 76 per cent of total fisheries exports of these 60 countries). Maintaining access to the EU market is therefore of strategic importance but this access has been limited by the lack of ACP capacity to respond to sanitary requirements.

The programme will initially focus on the countries with the most acute needs and will cover key areas such as institutional capacity building, training and technical advice to the industry and the public sector, improvement of infrastructure, support for laboratories and training institutes and advice on export policy issues.

Institutions such as the ITC (WTO/UNCTAD) and bilateral donors assist developing countries in strengthening capacities to improve quality and compete in international markets.

The Joint Integrated Technical Assistance Programme (JITAP), through its cluster 15, Quality Management in the MTS, includes the following activities to promote 'export readiness' of beneficiary countries:[21]

- capacity of the national standards bodies, strengthened in MTS-related quality management and export packaging matters;

- advisory missions in export quality management and packaging in the MTS context, with particular reference to TBT and SPS Agreements;
- orientation tour for trainers in export quality management;
- operating the National Enquiry Points on TBT and SPS measures;
- database on international quality requirements in target markets for exportable products;
- database on national quality requirements (standards and regulations) in the countries covered.

Work under this cluster has focused on the preparation of the national standards and technical regulations. This is expected to help the National Enquiry Points in responding to enquiries.[22] The Tanzanian Bureau of Standards and the Ugandan National Bureau of Standards have prepared their national databases and receive comments from ITC and ARSO (the African Regional Standards Organization). Seven JITAP countries receive DIN GLOBAL regularly and also receive assistance for the preparation of the augmented database from ARSO. In the context of JITAP, needs were expressed to organize sensitization seminars on TBT/SPS, and on conformity assessment for exporters and importers in the JITAP countries. There is also a need to intensify the building of capacity in TBT/SPS and standardization in line with the JITAP approach, which requires the WTO to explain the rules, the UNCTAD to discuss the policy and development aspects, and the ITC to address the business aspects. The National Enquiry Points (NEPs) in all JITAP countries are preparing lists of the critical technical documents they need. The United Republic of Tanzania and Kenya have already submitted such lists.

There are a series of initiatives that deepen understanding and strengthen research capacities in the area of standards, identify the specific needs of the African countries and promote action plans to address issues in the area of standards and trade.

The World Bank (Development Economics Research Group and the World Bank Institute) has developed the Africa Trade and Investment Policy (ATRIP) Programme. The programme is supported by the United States Agency for International Development (USAID). The programme recognizes that a concrete and deeper understanding of the specific relationship between standards, technical regulations and trade performance in Sub-Saharan Africa is critical to the successful integration of these countries into the multilateral trade system. Moreover, innovative projects are needed. One example is the Africa Trade Standards Project (ATSP).[23] The World Bank and other institutions have recently created the Standards and Trade Development Facility (STDF). The programme 'Standards and Technical Barriers to Trade: Policy Research and Institution Building in Sub-Saharan Africa' has the following objectives:

- the development of five country-specific action plans to expand access to and use of international standards in Sub-Saharan Africa; this will be accomplished through assessments of the specific impacts of the standards and technical regulations on trade in the region;
- the identification of specific infrastructure and capacity needs in Sub-Saharan Africa, including public and private sector capabilities in meeting standards, to support the expansion of export opportunities and successful participation in the WTO;
- the designing of a pilot network in the region, based on the five action plans, to expand access to international standards and increase the region's ability to implement WTO obligations in the TBT and SPS Agreements.

The International Trade Centre (WTO/UNCTAD) and the Commonwealth Secretariat have also been promoting case studies on SPS measures and trade.[24]

The secretariat of the Organization for Economic Cooperation and Development (OECD) has been implementing a project on the 'Development Dimension on Trade and Environment', which focuses on identifying ways in which developed and developing countries can cooperate to strengthen the capacities of the latter to comply with environmental requirements of the former.[25]

UNCTAD and the Foundation for International Environmental Law and Development (FIELD) are initiating a new project on Building Capacity for Improved Policy Making and Negotiation on Key Trade and Environment Issues. This project will help beneficiary developing countries strengthen their capacities to respond to SPS and environmental measures and to participate in international standard-setting processes. UNCTAD and UNEP are cooperating in the UNEP–UNCTAD Capacity Building Task Force on Trade, Environment and Development (CBTF).

Work on standards is also relevant in the context of the UNCTAD programme on 'Technical assistance and capacity building for developing countries, especially LDCs, and economies in transition in support of their participation in the WTO post-Doha work programme' (UNCTAD/RMS/TCS/1). The programme contains a specific 'window' on environment and on environmental/SPS requirements and market access.

CONCLUSIONS

The papers highlight the economic and social effects of restrictions on exports, which may relate to genuine food safety concerns, on Eastern and Southern

African countries. The effects are manifest at both the macro- and microeconomic levels. The case studies on fisheries indicate that these effects are most pronounced in the export-oriented sectors that are highly dependent on specific developed country markets and for which the potential for trade diversion is limited. Governments and the private sector often perceive the SPS and environmental measures to be unjustified and the stringent threshold levels to lack a sound scientific basis. In many African developing countries there is a lack of awareness of SPS and food safety measures. However, governments and the private sector recognize that, in order to improve their export performance and the ability to compete in the domestic market, the only viable option is to build capacities to comply with standards in international markets. Technical cooperation, capacity building, and support for effective participation of African countries in WTO negotiations and the work of international standard-setting bodies are of key importance.

The key concerns expressed in the papers by African experts include the following:

- Exports can be subject to successive restrictions, as was the case for fishery products.
- Compliance with SPS measures and environmental requirements may be a 'moving target', because standards often become more stringent once producers achieve compliance. This, coupled with the fact that compliance often does not result in price premiums, implies a financial risk.
- Import restrictions may lack scientific justification (for example, the import ban on fishery products in the case of cholera).
- SPS measures in developed countries can be incompatible with the prevailing systems of production and marketing in developing countries, with insufficient account taken of local and/or regional needs and constraints.
- Insufficient use of standards results in lower prices in the international market.
- In most cases, technical assistance is provided only once problems of compliance with SPS requirements of the importing country have been identified, rather than being part of a strategy aimed at general trade-related capacity building.

RECOMMENDATIONS

Approaches

Despite the constraints faced by developing countries in Africa in meeting standards in developed countries and the perception that certain stringent SPS measures and environmental requirements may not be justified, the case studies point out proactive approaches to strengthening capacities to comply with food safety and environmental standards through actions at the national and regional[26] levels. It is clear, however, that substantive technical assistance and capacity building support is needed.

The study on Mozambique carried out under this project notes that the government and the business sector can adopt several policies and measures aimed at promoting standards and quality, with a view to enhancing competitiveness. These include establishing and/or improving supporting infrastructure (for example, appropriate testing, certification and accreditation facilities), dissemination of information, promoting cooperation between the government and the business community and between retailers/importers and producers/exporters and special measures in favour of SMEs. International organizations as well as bilateral and multilateral aid agencies can play important roles in establishing and upgrading national capacities in promoting quality, testing and certification.

The study further notes that increasing bilateral and/or multilateral cooperation must be emphasised to ensure the rapid transfer of technology and the provision of sufficient technical assistance, so that potential export products can become competitive, in the medium term, in regional and world markets. This implies that a process of innovation and enterprise development must be promoted, which in turn depends on improving credit facilities. The implementation of international standards domestically should be focused on those areas and crops destined for competition in the export market. Technical assistance can help in determining the costs of implementing various standards. There is also a need to lobby for the removal of any importing country standards that are 'unnecessary' or unduly burdensome.

The paper by Margaret J.Z. Ndaba (United Republic of Tanzania) notes that, as African countries aim to strengthen trade in the region and beyond, it is necessary to re-examine SPS and other measures so as to ensure that they do not continue to impose unnecessary trade barriers. In addition, measures should be taken by the East African Community (EAC) and the international community to strongly enhance the capacity of partner states to deal with the issues of SPS. Increasing awareness of the various standards in the export markets, as well as strengthening the infrastructure and capacity building, will eventually result in health-related standards in the EAC.

National and Regional Levels

The different papers produced under the project make several recommendations at the national and regional levels.

Kenya
The study on Kenya makes the following recommendations:

- increase human and institutional capacities to deal with SPS and food safety matters;
- sensitize the private sector on SPS requirements;
- improve information gathering and sharing;
- establish an information system that allows timely generation and dissemination of trade-related information to all stakeholders;
- strengthen national and regional capacities to conduct risk assessment and analysis;
- encourage joint ventures between foreign and local firms.
- provide technical and financial assistance to sectors that are sensitive to the liberalization process in order to enhance their competitiveness;
- improve the communication channels between the national SPS management systems;
- harmonize standards and regulations within the SADC region;
- devise a regional approach to plant and animal disease control and a coordinated system of surveillance, monitoring and risk assessment.

Mozambique
The study on Mozambique recommends the following actions:

- formulation of a national framework that can more effectively integrate national directives on SPS and food safety issues with technical assistance and capacity building efforts;
- improvements in information gathering and sharing (one of the first practical steps in this regard is the collection of information on existing national SPS measures and the difference in food safety standards among regional and international trading partners);
- establishment of an information system that allows for the timely generation and dissemination of trade-relevant information to all the stakeholders involved;
- increased scientific and technical capacity (currently Mozambique lacks the capacity to deal with specialized scientific processes and the technical equipment required for testing and verification processes);
- strengthening of national and regional capacity to conduct risk analysis (especially the Department of Plant Sanitation, to conduct phytosanitary inspections and issue certificates) through investment in staff recruitment, staff training, laboratory facilities and communication technology;

- devising a regional approach to plant and animal disease control, and a coordinated system of surveillance, monitoring and risk assessment;
- improvement in the communication channels between the national SPS management systems;
- sensitizing the private sector to relevant SPS requirements;
- assistance to the citrus sector (oranges, grapefruits and tangerines), whose lack of use of standards has, according to the Mozambique Institute for Export Promotion, resulted in lower prices in the international market;
- strengthening the capacity of the National Institute of Standards and Quality (INNOQ). Mozambique should have the capacity to certify its export products and not depend only on quality certifications by the South African Bureau of Standards.

United Republic of Tanzania

The study on the United Republic of Tanzania notes that, as the East African Community partners aim to strengthen trade in the region and beyond, it is necessary to ensure that issues such as SPS are re-examined so that SPS measures do not continue to impose unnecessary trade barriers. The study recommends the increasing of awareness of the various standards in the export markets and the strengthening of infrastructure and capacity to comply with health and environmental standards in international markets and in regional trade.

Uganda

The study on Uganda recommends that the experience in the fisheries sector be used to draw lessons for other sectors that have export potential but are sensitive to health and sanitary concerns. The study notes that Directive 96/23/EC of April 1996, which requires exporters to have a certified Residue Monitoring Plan in order to gain access to the EU market, could act as a trade barrier for products such as honey, fruits and vegetables. This study makes the following recommendations:

- Enquiry points for TBT and SPS at regional levels (COMESA, EAC, SADC) and development of region-wide standards should be pursued.
- At the national level, there is need to enhance trade promotion activities through dissemination of information on market opportunities and requirements, product development, import and export techniques and the development of trade support services. Human resource development is also essential through strengthening of national institutional capacities for foreign trade training.
- There is an urgent need to amend and upgrade the Fish and Crocodile Act to meet the present challenges of the fish industry.

Developed Countries and Multilateral Level

The studies, explicitly and/or implicitly, make several recommendations to authorities and other stakeholders in developed countries. These include the following:

- Use sound science in the development of standards.
- Promote technical assistance and assist developing countries in their participation in international standard-setting bodies in accordance with WTO obligations and commitments under the Doha Development Agenda.
- Technical assistance and capacity building should not be limited to merely helping developing countries in complying with standards imposed by donor countries, but should be an integral part of trade-related capacity building to support the participation of developing countries in Africa in world trade.
- Promote donor consistency. In many cases efforts by donors to promote export-oriented industries are undermined by obstacles to trade in the markets of developed countries. This may be the case for fishery products, horticulture and flowers. Chapter 6 points to similar problems in the case of organic coffee.

The study on Mozambique recommends the following actions at the multilateral level:

- Harmonization of standards and regulations within the SADC region, based on international formulations. Owing to the non-uniformity of standards, re-testing and re-certifying of products is common within the region. This results in large financial and economic losses to traders and national economies, including Mozambique.
- Conformity of SPS standards to international standards, based on scientific principles. SPS measures must be based on scientific principles in order to ensure that they do not become technical barriers that retard trade.

WTO

The country papers make several recommendations on the WTO issues. Some of these issues have been considered in WTO decisions on Implementation Issues and the Doha Ministerial Decision (see Annex I).

The Kenyan paper, for example, welcomes a review of the SPS Agreement so that it can meaningfully respond to the needs of developing countries.

Article 10 of the Agreement, which provides for developed countries to take into account the special needs of developing countries in the preparation for application of the SPS measures, should be reviewed in the light of the difficulties faced by developing countries. It is suggested that:

- Notification procedures should be simplified to assist developing countries to monitor and notify SPS measures promptly.
- Vague language in the agreement, such as reference to 'reasonable time', should be clarified.
- The quality of TA to developing countries should be improved and TA should be delivered at the time it is needed.
- Standards experts in developing countries should be supported so that the country can effectively participate in standard-setting work.

The SPS Agreement has provisions on special and differential (S&D) treatment[27] which provide, among other things, that developed countries take into account the special needs of developing countries in the preparation and application of SPS measures, encourage and facilitate the active participation of developing countries in the relevant international standard-setting organizations, and assist a developing country to fulfil the SPS requirement of an importing country. Therefore, there is need for:

- Technical assistance in implementing the SPS and TBT agreements, with a view to responding to special problems faced by developing countries in Africa. Such TA could include *inter alia* building up capacities in fields of accreditation, standards, metrology and certification.
- The effective participation of developing countries in Africa in international and regional standard-setting bodies through the provision of adequate financial resources.

Areas for Future Work

Further UNCTAD work, in cooperation with other institutions, particularly in Africa, and initiatives (including those outlined in this paper) on standards and trade in the African context could focus on:

- Promoting further studies, focusing on environmental requirements, such as issues included in Box 5.1.
- Assistance to developing countries in Africa in strengthening research capacities on the issues in standards and promoting policy dialogues aimed at identifying national and regional strategies to strengthen capacities to respond to SPS and environmental measures and take advantage

of new trading opportunities for environmentally preferable products. This could be done in the context of the UNCTAD–FIELD project and CBTF.

• Activities in the context of the UNCTAD programme on the 'Technical assistance and capacity building for developing countries, especially LDCs, and economies in transition in support of their participation in the WTO post-Doha work programme' (UNCTAD/RMS/TCS/1). The programme contains a specific 'window' on environment, including environmental/SPS requirements and market access.

Among market access factors, SPS measures create the greatest difficulties for exports of agricultural and food products from Africa. SPS measures are likely to become more comprehensive and stringent in the future. This has serious implications for the Eastern and Southern African efforts to increase exports of high value commodities, such as fishery and horticultural products.

The operation of SPS measures, for example in the fisheries sector, is also becoming more complex as a large part of the responsibility for enforcing such measures is shifted to the exporting country. Most developing countries in Africa, however, have poor technical capacity and cannot efficiently manage SPS and food safety matters.[28] Typically, essential facilities like laboratories are not adequately staffed, the scientific equipment is outdated for the requisite tests, and there is no systematic collection and storage of records. This situation is unlikely to improve in the short term, given the declining levels of public expenditure. There is a clear need for intervention to revamp most public testing facilities and also to incorporate the private sector in the national testing and regulatory systems.

In many developing countries in Africa there is a lack of awareness of SPS and food safety measures. There are also serious institutional constraints (see Box 5.6).

BOX 5.6   INSTITUTIONAL CONSTRAINTS FOR SPS COMPLIANCE IN THE SADC REGION[29]

It is generally accepted that appropriate and efficient institutional arrangements are a necessary condition to respond to SPS and environmental requirements and accelerate agricultural trade. In most developing countries in Africa, this condition is not adequately met owing to a variety of constraints. In a recent SADC workshop, participants identified a range of institutional constraints, most of which revolved around inadequate national capacity. These constraints were grouped into three broad categories:

Inadequate controls for SPS/food safety compliance: This presents a large hurdle for small-scale, cross-border traders, who, in fact, constitute the largest group of potential agricultural traders in the SADC region.

Sub-standard hardware infrastructure: Most African countries are not endowed with the necessary 'tools of the trade' to make scientific assessments of compliance. Key support services, such as laboratories, often do not have the technical or human capacity to undertake the requisite tests. In other cases, the laboratories do not have the capacity to efficiently provide nationwide coverage. Although there are a few accredited laboratories in the region, there is limited sharing of such resources within and between countries. This is partly due to the bureaucratic hurdles involved and partly due to a lack of awareness of the available capacity amongst the relevant actors. Strategies such as resource sharing can provide opportunities for increased networking and mutual recognition among (SADC) member states while minimizing the costs of duplication. In general, the cadre of officers who are competent in assessing risk and interpreting the requirements of the SPS/TBT Agreement is inadequate. While the agricultural trade arena is getting increasingly complex and highly technical, there is no corresponding investment in human or other resource capacity at the national or regional levels. The lack of capacity among member states is a result of inaction and/or muted responses from decision and policy makers responsible for agricultural trade.

Sub-optimal capacity for self-regulation: Most agricultural producers do not have adequate capacity for self-regulation. The reasons for this are varied but essentially entail inadequate incentives, especially at the trader level (except for those countries, like South Africa and Zimbabwe, with relatively large and organized commercial agricultural producers, processors and traders). There is merit in encouraging the private sector to take a leading role in designing guidelines for SPS-related policy formulation and law enforcement. There is also scope for the establishment or revamping of key non-governmental actors, such as national

> Standards Bureaus, to play a more active role in spearheading self-monitoring and regulation and also in enhancing general awareness and knowledge amongst the different stakeholders. In short, there is need to enhance the awareness of the benefits of quality in improving the attractiveness and competitiveness of agricultural produce in both regional and international markets.

The principal concerns expressed in the papers and the Kampala workshop in the area of standards and trade can be summarized as follows:

- Standards are, at times, perceived as moving targets, as they become more stringent once compliance is achieved. Thus, continued efforts are required to catch up with developments in the area of standards and to be able to export in the long run.
- Developed countries first impose stringent standards and then offer technical assistance to help developing countries overcome difficulties in complying with them, mostly so that they secure adequate supply. Technical assistance, however, is often not sufficient to make the investments needed to meet international requirements.
- Products often do not receive remunerative prices, among other reasons, because of standards. For sub-standard products, which are sold at low prices, transport costs become a large hurdle. Similarly, additional costs for testing, packaging and so on are difficult to absorb in the case of exports of low value-added products.
- Initiatives such as AGOA and EBA need to be accompanied by initiatives in the area of building supply capacities and meeting standards to allow developing countries in Africa to derive the full benefits.
- Certain measures do not seem to be fully justified when examined under sound science.

However, governments and the private sector recognize that, in order to improve export performance and the ability to compete in the domestic market, countries have no choice but to build capacities to comply with the standards in international markets.

NOTES

1. For details, see Chapter 1.
2. The countries that are covered in this chapter export largely to the European Union. Coupled with the fact that most exports from these countries enter the European Union duty free, this implies that changes in EU policies, especially with respect to standards, are crucial in the

discussion of improved market access to exports of interest to these and other Sub-Saharan African (SSA) countries. Apart from the EU and US markets, developments in other markets such as Japan are also important for diversification of SSA countries' export market. See T. Ademola Ovejide, E. Olawale Ogunkola and S. Abiodun Bankole, University of Ibadan, 'Quantifying the Trade Impact of Sanitary and Phytosanitary Standards: What is Known and Issues of Importance to Sub-Saharan Africa?', paper prepared for the workshop on 'Quantifying the Trade Effects of Standards and Regulatory Measures: Is it Possible?', Washington, 27 April 2000.

3. Methyl bromide is a highly toxic fumigant used in agriculture for crops such as tomatoes, strawberries and cut flowers. Its use also includes pest control in structures and stored commodities and for quarantine and pre-shipment treatment. Unfortunately, methyl bromide is also harmful to humans and a potent ozone-depleting chemical with a potential for destroying 60 times more ozone than each atom of chlorine from CFCs. Completing a methyl bromide phase-out is one of the remaining challenges for ozone layer protection and for improving the health of farmers. In 1997, the parties to the Montreal Protocol on Substances that Deplete the Ozone Layer agreed to a global methyl bromide phase-out schedule, requiring industrialized countries to phase out methyl bromide by 2005 and developing countries to freeze production and consumption by 2002 with a complete phase-out by 2015. Farmers who are dependent on methyl bromide will need to shift towards more environmentally sustainable agricultural practices. Such changes must come through sustained awareness-raising, training and capacity-building activities to provide farmers with the education and tools needed to successfully adopt alternatives. Fortunately, effective alternatives for most methyl bromide uses have been identified and many are already in use around the world. Sponsored by the Montreal Protocol's Multilateral Fund, the United Nations Industrial Development Organization (UNIDO) and UNEP have been assisting methyl bromide phase-out through demonstration projects in developing countries, including Kenya (Alternatives to the use of methyl bromide for soil fumigation in cut flowers at Kenya Agricultural Research Institute (KARI)) and Uganda (Phase-out of methyl bromide in cut flowers). (Taken from: http://www.uneptie.org/ozonaction/unido-harvest/)

4. Jabavu Clifford Nkomo, Benson Mutongi Zwizwai and Davison Gumbo, 'Trade and Environment in Zimbabwe', case study under the UNCTAD/UNDP project on Reconciling Trade and Environment Policies (1995), in Veena Jha, Anil Markandya and René Vossenaar, *Reconciling Trade and the Environment: Lessons from Case Studies in Developing Countries*, Edward Elgar Publishing, 1999.

5. Dr Halima Noor, EcoNews Africa, 'Sanitary and Phytosanitary Measures and their Impact on Kenya' (prepared under this project).

6. Cerina Mussa, 'Trade and Environment in Mozambique: Sanitary and Phytosanitary Measures' (prepared under this project).

7. Margaret J.Z. Ndaba, Economist, Ministry of Agriculture and Food Security, Dar es Salaam, Tanzania, 'Impact of SPS on Fish and Horticultural Products from East African Countries: The Case of Tanzania' (prepared under this project).

8. See Cerina Mussa 'Trade and Environment in Mozambique: Sanitary and Phytosanitary Measures'.

9. Spencer Henson, Ann-Marie Brouder and Winnie Mitullah (2000), 'Food safety requirements and food exports from developing countries: the case of fish exports from Kenya to the European Union', *American Journal of Agricultural Economics* **82** (5), 1159–69.

10. Cerina Mussa, op. cit.

11. Nimrod Waniala, Director, PSF/Trade Policy Capacity Building Project, 'Impact of SPS Measures on Uganda Fish Exports' (prepared under this project).

12. http://www.who.int/inf-pr-1998/en/pr98-24.html

13. Commission Decision 98/116/EC of 4 February 1998 also adopted special measures for the import of fruit and vegetables from Uganda, Kenya, Tanzania and Mozambique (Official Journal L 031 of 6 February 1998). The Commission argued that the infectious agent *Vibrio cholerae* survives on foodstuffs imported from these countries. As a preliminary precaution, the EU ruled that samples (covering at least ten per cent of consignments) of these foodstuffs should be subject to microbiological controls. However, since the World Health Organization

(WHO) advised that where the transport of fruit and vegetables from areas where cholera is present is in excess of ten days, the risk to health from these products is low, the measures applied mainly to products transported into the European Community by air. These measures were repealed by Commission Decision 98/719/EC of 8 December 1998 (Official Journal L 342 of 17 December 1998) *inter alia* because the Scientific Committee for Food expressed an opinion that the risk of human illness in non-cholera regions from exposure to *Vibrio cholerae* from imported fruit and vegetables from areas where cholera is at endemic or epidemic levels is low. In addition, sampling at the point of importation into the Community of 10 per cent of consignments of fruit and vegetables from Uganda, Kenya, the United Republic of Tanzania and Mozambique had revealed very low incidence of contamination with *Vibrio cholerae.*
14. Commission Decision 1999/253/EC.
15. Spencer Henson, Ann-Marie Brouder and Winnie Mitullah, *Food Safety Requirements and Food Exports from Developing Countries: The Case of Fish Exports from Kenya to the European Union, American Journal of Agricultural Economics* **82** (5) 1159–69. The assessment of the impact of the EU restrictions on the Kenyan fish supply chain was undertaken over the period June 1999 to May 2000. It had three main elements: (1) collection and analysis of secondary data, for example, volume and value of exports, mainly from published government sources; (2) interviews with government personnel, non-governmental organizations and other key informants; and (3) interviews with fish processors, fisher-folk and other members of the fishing communities on Lake Victoria.
16. Spencer Henson et al., op. cit.
17. Halima Noor, 'Sanitary and Phytosanitary Measures and their Impact on Kenya'.
18. Cerina Mussa, 'Trade and Environment in Mozambique: Sanitary and Phytosanitary Measures'.
19. Commission Directive 2001/35/EC amending the Annexes to Council Directive 90/642/EEC on the fixing of maximum levels for pesticide residues in and on certain products of plant origin, including fruit and vegetables, which came into force in July 2001 (Official Journal L 136, 18/05/2001 P. 0042–0048). See also Commission Directive 2002/5/EC of 30 January 2002.
20. 'Commission welcomes boost for trade-related technical assistance', press release, Brussels, 13 March 2002.
21. http://www.jitap.org/clust15.htm
22. JITAP Progress Report Nr. 2001/2.
23. The World Bank Group, International Trade and Development, Bridging the Standards Divide: Challenges for Improving Africa's International Market Access, www.worldbank.org.
24. See WTO document G/SPS/GEN/288.
25. The OECD project is envisaged in three sequential phases:

   * an analysis of the effects of environmental measures and regulations on developing country exports;
   * an outreach activity involving key stakeholders sharing experiences;
   * development of best-practice guidelines to address developing countries' difficulties in this area, including the goals of transparency and information sharing and dissemination.

26. In a recent SADC workshop, the establishment of a regional institution to address WTO and SPS/TBT issues was discussed. The overall consensus was that, while this would be ideal in the medium to long term, the priority must be the strengthening of capacity at the national and sub-national levels, if member countries are to maximize the potential returns of increased agricultural trade. The existing institutions within SADC could, however, be better utilized. It was suggested that these institutions could focus their activities on (1) more effective representation in key multilateral bodies, (2) better coordination between enquiry and contact points, and (3) improved information dissemination. Furthermore, these institutions could engage in highlighting emerging technical issues whose impact on trade could be better served if member states adopted a regional position.
27. The paper on the United Republic of Tanzania argues that the adoption of the WTO decisions and implementation of the Agreement on Agriculture has yet to contribute to an

improvement in the agricultural commodity trade of the United Republic of Tanzania. The basic commodities face constant price fluctuations or declines in their international market with damaging consequences for the export earnings and the terms of trade of the United Republic of Tanzania. Therefore S&D is essential.

28. With respect to the implementation of the SPS/TBT Agreements, the responsible national institutions are at different levels of evolution. In this context, unclear national notification authorities render the mechanisms for notification inefficient. Similarly, the information received from relevant international institutions, such as the IPPC and OIE, is frequently not transmitted to the critical operational levels, such as private traders and border post personnel. In some areas, such as food safety, there are no specific laws or other legal provisions to cover the standard requirements for trade. See SADC Consultative Forum on SPS/Food Safety, SADC SPS and Food Safety Issues: An Agenda for Action, *Proceedings of the Windhoek Workshop of SPS/Food Safety*, 20–22 November 2000.

29. SADC Consultative Forum on SPS/Food Safety, op. cit.

6. Organic Agriculture

René Vossenaar and Sophia Twarog

BACKGROUND

The UNCTAD secretariat, with the support of the International Development Research Centre (IDRC) in Canada, has been implementing a technical cooperation project to examine the linkages between environment- and health-related requirements in international markets and export opportunities of developing countries. One specific component of the project tries to identify policies that can be applied at the national and international levels to strengthen the capacities of developing countries to take advantage of emerging niche markets for organically produced products.

Such niche markets present promising opportunities for developing countries. However, in order to seize such opportunities developing countries must overcome a number of production and export constraints. Exporting organic products implies a number of challenges related to certification, import procedures and marketing strategies. This study examines some of these issues and seeks to identify policy responses that will support developing countries in their efforts to use market opportunities for organic agricultural products to promote their production and exports, and at the same time obtain environmental and developmental gains. It complements the analysis of possible trade barrier effects of environmental and health requirements presented in other scoping papers prepared under this project. In particular, the following issues are addressed:

- How can governments and the private sector in developing countries address production and export constraints?
- How can developed countries take into account the special conditions and needs of developing countries in their national organic standards and regulations and how can they facilitate import of organic products from developed countries?
- How can bilateral and multilateral aid agencies assist developing countries in promoting production and exports of organic agricultural products?
- What are the key trade issues in the area of trade rules?

The paper is largely based on the experiences of one developing country from each of the three regions covered by the project: Costa Rica,[1] India[2] and Uganda.[3] These experiences were discussed at the regional workshops organized under the project. This work also draws on conclusions and recommendations of recent meetings in which experts from Costa Rica, India and Uganda participated:

- the UNCTAD Expert Meeting on 'Ways to enhance the production and export capacities of developing countries of agriculture and food products, including niche products, such as environmentally preferable products', held in Geneva from 16 to 18 July 2001;[4]
- the Conference on *International Harmonization and Equivalence in Organic Agriculture*, organized by the International Federation for Organic Agricultural Movements (IFOAM), the Food and Agriculture Organization (FAO) and UNCTAD (Nuremberg, 18 and 19 February 2002);[5]
- the Policy Dialogue on Promoting Production and Trading Opportunities for Organic Agricultural Products under the UNEP–UNCTAD Capacity Building Task Force (CBTF) on Trade, Environment and Development (Brussels, 21 and 22 February 2002).[6]

KEY ISSUES

Opportunities

Increased demand for organic food, particularly as a result of heightened consumer concerns in the area of food safety and quality, generates trading opportunities for developing countries.[7] The demand is growing by approximately 10 to 20 per cent per year in several developed countries.

Markets, however, are still relatively small. In most developed countries the market share for organic agricultural products is not more than 1 to 2 per cent of the total demand for food products. The International Trade Centre (WTO/UNCTAD) estimates that organic markets in developed countries totalled close to US$20 billion in 2001. Forecasts for 2003 and 2005 are US$23–25 billion and US$29–31 billion respectively.[8] The forecasts are that markets for organic products in the United States and the European Union will amount to approximately US$11–13 billion and US$10–11 billion respectively in 2003. The estimated value of the Japanese market is much smaller, and has been downgraded to a value of around US$ 0.4 billion since the introduction of the Japanese Organic Standards (JAL). This chapter, therefore, focuses on the EU and US markets.

In developing countries, certified organic agricultural production is still very limited. However, significant shares of agricultural land are under traditional or 'alternative' production methods, with little or no use of agrochemicals. Such areas could be converted to certified organic agriculture provided that markets are available and certification costs can be kept low.

Constraints

In order to take advantage of niche markets for organic agricultural products, developing countries need to overcome a number of production and export constraints. Many of these constraints are common to agricultural production and trade in general. In addition to these general constraints, producers and exporters in developing countries face an array of specific constraints relating to production, government policies and infrastructure, transport and handling, market information, and certification.[9] They also need to compete in markets with stringent quality requirements, increasing pressure for subsidies, uncertain price premiums and preferences for locally produced food. One constraint for developing countries with a relatively large potential to increase organic production is the small size of international markets, especially for organic agricultural products from developing countries.

Production

The lack of technical know-how on organic production practices is often a constraint. Government agricultural extension services do not generally include organic agriculture per se. Another problem area is the lack of organic production inputs. Some countries have reported difficulties in acquiring the necessary organic composting materials, bio-pesticides and bio-fertilizers. Obtaining high quality seeds and planting materials has also been cited as a problem. There has been little research and development in developing countries on varieties and production methods best suited to organic agriculture. In some cases, securing the additional labour required for organic agriculture has also created certain difficulties. In addition, the required conversion period can pose greater challenges for developing country producers, particularly smallholders, as they often do not have the financial reserves to easily see them through a season or two of reduced yields. The Costa Rica and Uganda studies cite inability to capture economies of scale as another constraint.

Export

The constraints for increased exports of organic products from developing countries include high certification costs, lack of market information and marketing strategies, insufficient export facilitation, complex procedures in importing countries, and tariff and non-tariff protection in import markets.

Furthermore, traditional agriculture that has been practised for centuries often does not get appropriate recognition in developed country markets.

Certification and accreditation   Certification and accreditation issues play an important role. In most cases, developing country exporters depend on certification by international certification bodies to be able to market their products as organic in foreign markets. The costs of certification vary, but can be significant. Small developing countries, particularly LDCs, may find it difficult to set up national certification infrastructure. In fact, the case study on Uganda shows that exporters largely depend on aid agencies and transnational corporations to obtain certification. The case studies pay particular attention to certification costs for smallholders as well as possible ways to reduce such costs. Group certification, based on internal control systems, may be a solution.[10] IFOAM has provisions for group certification, but this mechanism may not be sufficiently recognized in importing countries.

Standards and import regulations   There is concern that the multiplicity of national and regional standards and import procedures in developed countries may create obstacles to imports of organic products originating in developing countries. The transaction costs resulting from the existence of multiple standards may be significant. In addition, under current circumstances, certification bodies in developing countries have to seek accreditation in different markets. Moreover, obtaining import permits may be time consuming.

Organic labels   Current rules concerning the use of official organic labels are sometimes discriminatory. For example, the use of official organic labels in the European Union is not open to non-EU producers. It is to be noted that, at present, such labels are not widely used even by the EU producers.

Risks   Certification is a necessary, but not sufficient, condition for entry into the international markets for organic products. Market dynamics may also pose certain risks to developing countries. The long-term implications of recent efforts to promote organic agricultural production, especially in Europe, for trading opportunities in organic products from developing countries are not clear. For example, the effects of the projected increases in organic production in developed countries (to a considerable extent induced by ambitious government plans and subsidies) on market prices and import levels are uncertain. Some have expressed concern that, if markets fail to expand at the same rate as production, there will be a downward pressure on prices, lower margins and incentives to keep out imports.

Market information and strategies   Limited market information and poor marketing channels can hamper exports of certified organic products from developing countries. The papers on India and Uganda indicate that certified products from developing countries are often sold as conventional products. The Uganda case study, for example, reports that organic farmers of cotton and sesame sold less than 20 per cent of their production as organic products during the 2000/2001 season. The India study shows similar results, for example, in the case of organic pepper.

Other factors   Some other factors may adversely affect the demand for products from developing countries. First, consumers of organic food are increasingly demanding locally produced food. Secondly, the eastward enlargement of the European Union will affect the organic food market in Western Europe. Several countries with economies in transition in Central and Eastern Europe are in the same position as developing countries, in the sense that an important number of farmers use little or no agro-chemicals. For example, a substantial share of the agricultural output in Poland is effectively produced by organic methods. If these countries join the European Union, their organic producers will be in a strong competitive position vis-à-vis producers from developing countries because of their proximity to the main consumer markets and their location within the EU market. This might imply that developing countries would run a marketing risk if they chose to substantially increase the output of temperate organic products to serve the EU market.

It follows that the commercial risks of embarking on a large-scale promotion programme for organic agriculture require careful attention, as building up standards and certification infrastructure that is credible in developed countries may be expensive.

Agricultural policies

Several developed countries, in the EU in particular, provide subsidies to assist farmers during the process of conversion to organic agriculture. Compensation is also extended to established organic farmers for their services to the environment. In some countries where these last subsidies were not available (such as in the UK), pressures were applied to increase post-conversion subsidies. The granting of subsidies in some countries may result in competitiveness concerns in other countries, including developed countries.[11] Other subsidies occur, for example, in the form of support for research and development. Generally, developing countries and some developed countries such as the USA, Canada, Australia and New Zealand do not provide subsidies.

Farm subsidies, in general, can lead to inefficient use of resources in organic agriculture, as in conventional agriculture. In other words, subsidies in one country, by affecting the price level and the quantity of production (number of farmers who can stay in business), affect farmers in other countries. This can distort the true picture of efficiency in resource use between organic farmers in different countries. The issue that may require attention is whether increased pressure for subsidies to promote organic agriculture could eventually adversely affect the competitiveness of products from developing countries.

Responses

The overriding objective of this project is to identify policy options to remove obstacles to the developing countries' exports and to strengthen their production and export capacities. In many cases, removing production and marketing constraints requires policies and measures at the local level. The case studies make a series of recommendations, including some with regard to institutional support and government policies towards organic agriculture. In addition, authorities and other stakeholders in the main importing countries could take measures to facilitate access to their organic markets. The studies also provide some insights on how bilateral and multilateral aid agencies can assist developing countries, particularly in promoting organic agricultural production, obtaining certification and identifying business partners in developed countries.

With regard to trade rules, organic agriculture and trade in organic food products have not yet been significant issues in the context of the WTO. The current emphasis on bringing about rapid increases in organic agriculture through a range of policy measures and growing international trade in organic food products may have implications for the discussions in the WTO. Organic food standards have been notified under the WTO Agreement on Technical Barriers to Trade (TBT). The possible trade policy issues include equivalence, subsidies, labelling, conformity assessment procedures and trade preferences.

IMPORTING INTO SELECTED DEVELOPED COUNTRIES[12]

As mentioned earlier, this scoping paper focuses on the markets of the European Union and the United States. Since the United States' organic programme is yet to be fully implemented, practical experience with official standards is largely limited to the European Union.

The European Union

The EU Council Regulation No. 2092/91 on organic production and labelling came into force on 22 July 1991.[13] The Regulation covers production, processing, labelling and inspection of agricultural products and foodstuffs from organic agricultural production. Council Regulation (EC) No. 1804/1999 amended it to also cover livestock production.

Article 11 of Regulation 2092/91/EEC, paragraph 1, opens the EU organic food market to products from third countries, based on the concept of equivalence. Altogether, there are basically two ways of exporting organic products to the European Union:

- Paragraph 1 establishes a 'third-country' list, indicating countries with which equivalence is established. However, only seven countries are on the list: Argentina, Australia, the Czech Republic,[14] Israel, Hungary, New Zealand and Switzerland. Costa Rica[15] and India have both asked to be included in this list.
- Paragraph 6: Organic products from countries which are not on the 'third-country' list can be marketed in the EU provided the importer submits documentation to confirm that the products are produced and certified according to rules equivalent to those of the EU. This provision, commonly referred to as the 'importer derogation', is scheduled to expire on 31 December 2005.
- Paragraph 7: An EU Member State assesses an inspection body in a third country and requests the Commission to approve it. The Commission can then add it to the 'third-country' list.

In order to be able to import under the provisions of Article 11, paragraph 6, the importer must provide the Member State with sufficient evidence to show that:[16]

- the imported product was produced according to organic rules equivalent to EU standards;
- the imported product was subject to inspection measures equivalent to the EU inspection requirements;
- the inspection measures are permanently and effectively implemented;
- the inspection body operates in compliance with ISO/IEC Guide 65.

Each importer must obtain a separate authorization for each consignment. Such authorization shall be valid only as long as these conditions are shown to be satisfied. Over 90 developing countries export in this framework to the EU, including the three developing countries covered in this paper.[17]

The European Commission Regulation (EC) No. 1788/2001 of 7 September 2001 defines detailed rules with regard to the certificate of inspection for imports from third countries under Article 11.[18] Since 1 July 2002 import procedures have been harmonized throughout the EU. For each consignment the approved authority or inspection body in the third country from where the goods are exported must produce an original 'certificate of inspection for import of products from organic production'. It must be submitted to and endorsed by the authority of the EU Member State where the product is imported, after which the product will be able to enter into free circulation within the EU.

Since July 1999, certification and inspection bodies must conform to the European standard EN 45011 or to ISO Guide 65. This disqualified a number of certifiers in developing countries that had been active in certifying exports to the EU. For non-EU and non-listed countries, the guarantee of conformity to EN 45011 must be provided by an official accreditation organization. Most developing countries do not have such an entity.

The United States

The Organic Foods Production Act (OFPA) of 1990 required the United States Department of Agriculture (USDA) to develop national standards for organically produced agricultural products and to establish an organic certification programme, based on recommendations of the National Organic Standards Board (NOSB). The National Organic Program (NOP) first proposed draft standards in December 1997. A revised proposal was issued in March 2000. The final regulation was adopted in December 2000, and implemented in October 2002.

Accreditation of goods imported from foreign countries can occur in three ways:

• Certifying agents operating in foreign countries may apply for USDA *accreditation*.
• The USDA determines, upon the request of a foreign government, that that country's authorities are able to assess and accredit certifying agents as meeting the requirements of the NOP.
• The USDA and a foreign government agree upon equivalency of standards and certification procedures, so that organic imports from this country are acceptable in the USA. There were 67 USDA Accredited Certifying Agents in late October 2002.[19]

Whereas the European Union sets extensive, detailed requirements for 'third world countries', including requirements for inspection bodies and operators in third world countries who seek to export organic products to the European Union, the United States organic regulation does not have such provision.[20]

CASE STUDIES FROM SELECTED DEVELOPING COUNTRIES

Costa Rica[21]

Background
Several papers examining the experience of Costa Rica indicate that the transition towards organic agriculture in Costa Rica over the last 15 years has been the result of several factors. These include initiatives of small agricultural producers motivated by the high cost of fertilizers, loss of efficiency of synthetic agro-chemicals, and the search for new markets, as well as health, environmental and biodiversity-related concerns. The area under organic production, or in the process of conversion, is approximately 9600 hectares, which represents 1.9 per cent of the total area under permanent cultivation. As much as 94 per cent of the certified organic farms are smaller than 5 hectares.

Small producers, therefore, play a key role in advancing organic agriculture. There are more that 4000 organic producers and approximately 135 organizations of organic producers. For the most part, small-scale organic producers are organized in groups according to regions and products; the largest group is made up of 1600 producers. Some provinces have local projects that group small producers, including indigenous communities, in sectors such as bananas, cocoa and coffee.

A large part of organic production in Costa Rica is exported to the European Union (mainly processed foods, such as banana purée, oranges, mango juice and coffee) and the United States (mainly coffee). The most important organic export products are coffee and bananas.

Production and export constraints
According to Felicia Echeverria Hermoso,[22] the main production and export constraints are that:

• the transition period and the certification process, which are usually expensive, discourage farmers from converting to organic agriculture;
• farmers lack appropriate support in research, technology transfer and financial resources (there is a need to re-educate extension workers and other agriculture related professionals);
• most small farmer organizations lack the knowledge and financial and/or administrative capacity to interpret and comply with market requirements;
• not having access to market information, many organic farmers who could potentially increase their production levels are reluctant to do so;

- organic farms are usually small and dispersed throughout the country, making it difficult to achieve economies of scale;
- organic markets are usually very demanding with regard to quality, packaging and certification;
- international markets usually demand large quantities of organic produce at rather short notice;
- many organic farmer associations able to access international markets need to pay for several certifications for different export markets.

As mentioned above, certification tends to be expensive. Many organic farmer organizations in Costa Rica have been able to access the international market, but most of the price premiums received have to be spent on several certifications, practically one for each importing country. The experience of a transnational corporation (TNC) based in Costa Rica illustrates this point.[23] The TNC processes and exports to the United States, France, Germany, Switzerland and Italy.[24] To be able to export to these markets, it needs multiple certifications. In particular, it uses the following certification bodies:

- for exporting to the United States: Oregon Tilt;
- for exporting to Switzerland: Bio Suisse;
- for exporting to the European Union: EcoCert.

The costs of certification are critical for small producers. In the same study, this is illustrated by the case of an organization of 70 small farmers who sell organic fruit to the TNC in question. The organization of small farmers has an internal control system (ICS). EcoLogica, a local certification body, carries out most of the inspections. EcoLogica has an agreement with EcoCert and Oregon Tilt. The organization of small farmers pays the following:

- to EcoLogica: a set fee (for inspection, reports and a certificate) plus 0.5 per cent of gross sales for the right to use the EcoLogica label (that is, certification costs);
- to EcoCert: a fee for certification and follow up costs (with regard to exports to Switzerland, Bio Suisse gives its approval through an agreement with EcoCert and charges the importers for the certificate).

Although certification continues to be a major constraint, the regional scoping paper for Central America (Chapter 4 in this volume) argues that in Costa Rica there has been a sizeable reduction in the costs of inspection and certification owing to the widening of the scope of action of the local certification and inspection agencies.

Institutional support

In the past, organic producers received most of their support directly from NGOs, cooperation agencies and some university projects. However, nowadays the public agricultural sector has become more actively involved in promoting this type of production. Organic agriculture is supported mainly by the National Production Council and the Ministry of Agriculture and Livestock (MAG). In 1995, Costa Rica established a National Programme for Organic Agriculture (NPOA) under the auspices of the MAG. These institutions work towards promoting and supporting organic production and commercialization of organic products. Some of the activities of the NPOA are:

- carrying out consumer-oriented promotion campaigns;
- promoting capacity-building programmes for organic agriculture;
- strengthening research in the field of organic agriculture;
- coordinating and unifying efforts between public and private organizations in support of organic agriculture.

Apart from the NPOA, institutional support is provided by 15 to 20 NGOs, church-based organizations, universities and the National Extension Direction of the Ministry of Agriculture and Livestock (with 85 agencies in 8 regions). The national research and technology transfer programme in organic agriculture (PITTA-P.O.) also plays an important role.

Certain financial resources are available, particularly through international aid agencies and NGOs, the Ministry of Foreign Trade and the Ministry of Agriculture and Livestock. Although not specifically aimed at organic farming, the 'Productive Re-conversion Fund' and other governmental trusts can be used. National banks are beginning to show some interest in organic agriculture, but the interest rates and requirements they apply to organic agricultural producers remain the same as those for conventional agricultural producers.

Institutions that promote national and international trade of organic products include NGOs (at national level). PROCOMER, of the Ministry of Foreign Trade, provides information and partial support to attend the BioFach Trade Fairs. The National Council of Production (CNP) supports organic agriculture in terms of marketing, product development, quality standards and market information.

National standards and certification[25]

In Costa Rica, the publication of the Environmental Law (No. 7574) in 1995 provided a legal basis for organic farming. This law establishes the general framework for organic production and certification, defining the role of the State in its promotion, research and control. The National Program of Organic

Agriculture was established in 1995 within the Ministry of Agriculture and Livestock (MAG). The 1997 Phytosanitary Law (No. 7664) further lays down requirements for the registration of operators, inspectors and inspection bodies, as well as the process for certification and approval of inspection bodies.

Organic certification   Inspection bodies are approved according to comprehensive legislation, in accordance with 4501/ISO 65 standards, and supervised by the competent authority. Certification agencies must be accredited by MAG in order to carry on their activities. The requirement that a product that is certified locally must also be certified in the country of destination forces them to establish alliances with other certification agencies in those countries. As may be expected, since the certification processes in the country are in the initial stages, there are very few certification agencies that have been registered and are accredited to provide these services in Costa Rica.

EcoLogica, the first local organic certification agency, is fully recognized by the MAG. It has certified close to 3000 producers, as well as 23 projects involving around 3500 producers. EcoLogica has established strategic alliances with foreign certifiers such as QAI (Quality Assurance International – USA), OTCO (Oregon Tilth Certified Organic – USA) and EcoCert (France). These alliances are being used as a mechanism to access foreign markets, as EcoLogica is not yet internationally recognized. Certification requirements have been established in accordance with the guidelines of the Oregon Tilth Certified Company, and have been adapted to the agro-ecological and socio-economic conditions present in Costa Rica.

EcoLogica provides services of inspection and certification of proceedings related to the production of all agricultural goods. It is also authorized to provide inspection services for QAI, Oregon Tilth and EcoCert.

Cost of certification   One of the constraints on organic farming in developing countries is the certification cost, which can be prohibitive for small producers. There is a clear consensus among producers that certification is necessary to be able to sell in international organic markets, but they are also concerned about the fact that in the absence of stable market conditions, certification can become an important economic barrier. The producer not only has to pay the fee for registering his productive unit as organic, but also has to pay a certification fee.

Certification is provided by private certification entities, both national and foreign. Its costs depend primarily on the size and location of the farm and on the quality of the information provided by the producer. Certification bodies may charge small producers less than they charge other producers. A local certification agency, EcoLogica, has the support of HIVOS in order to provide economic support for the producers.

To export organic products multiple certifications may be required. For example, production has to be certified with an accredited national certification agency and with another agency, depending on the country of destination.

Certification and associated costs may be a major problem for small producers. Different alternatives can be explored to address this problem. In the United States, for example, producers whose sales are less than $5000 per year can produce a sworn statement in which they assure that the organic certification requirements will be fulfilled, without being compelled to obtain the certification itself. Retailers and farmers who offer products with less than 70 per cent organic ingredients are also excluded from certification requirements.

Promoting group organization among small and medium scale farmers can help the transformation period by making it a more expeditious process and at the same time it can enhance mutual benefits such as lower certification costs.

Currently, each certification body has its own principles, requirements and guidelines for certification. In addition, governments are increasingly implementing regulations for organic production. Producers themselves believe that the main task is to define standards and organic agriculture certification schemes that secure product quality and the integrity of organic guarantee systems, at the same time ensuring that import procedures and certification/accreditation do not adversely affect either the producer or the consumer.

Inclusion in the EU 'equivalent third country' list (Article 11.1) European Union regulations stipulate that products can be imported as organic only if they have been produced in accordance with rules for organic production and are subject to inspection measures that are equivalent to EU organic regulations. Article 11 of Regulation 2092/91/EEC opens two ways to export organic products to the European Union. Paragraph 1 establishes a 'third-country' list, indicating countries with which equivalence is established. Paragraph 6 determines that organic products from countries which are not on the 'third-country' list can be marketed in the EU provided the importer submits documentation to confirm that the products are produced and certified according to rules equivalent to those of the EU. Such authorization shall be valid only as long as these conditions are shown to be satisfied. Commission Regulation (EC) No. 1788/2001 of 7 September 2001 defines detailed rules with regard to the certificate of inspection for imports from third countries under Article 11.6. For each consignment, the approved authority or inspection body in the third country from where the goods are exported must produce an original 'certificate of inspection for the import of products from organic production'.

To export organic produce to the EU market, paragraph 11.1 clearly offers much easier conditions than paragraph 11.6. However, currently only seven countries (among them Argentina) are on the 'third-country' list. Over 90 developing countries, including Central American countries, export under Article 11.6.

Costa Rica has taken steps to be included in the 'third-country' list. This would bring important advantages in terms of predictability and costs of exporting organic agricultural products.

In this connection, an EU inspection team visited Costa Rica in 2000. Some key findings were:

- The minimum requirements for organic farming laid down in Costa Rican legislation are, in general, equivalent to Council Regulation (EEC) No. 2092/91.
- The structure of the organic farming inspection and supervision system in Costa Rica is well developed, in spite of being rather recent. It is supported by comprehensive legislation.
- The inspection bodies are approved according to EN 4501/ISO 65 standards and supervised by the competent authority.
- Most of the producers are organized in groups.
- The global control of the organic system still shows some weaknesses and lack of consistency, partially due to the short accumulated experience.
- Parallel production is allowed in Costa Rica, unlike in the EU.

The EU team recommended the following:

- The Costa Rican authorities should take appropriate measures to address certain inadequacies of the inspection system, especially concerning parallel production, the national list of registered producers and processors and the competent authority's monitoring and supervision of organic production and exports.
- The Costa Rican authorities should make sure that inspection bodies set appropriate rules for group inspection and certification, and should verify their application, in order to guarantee the reliability and effectiveness of the control system.
- The European Commission should include Costa Rica in the 'equivalent third-country' list under Article 11(1) of Council Regulation (EEC) No. 2092/91, provided that the recommendations have been adequately followed and the Costa Rican authorities inform the Commission of the action taken.

Harmonization of organic food regulations   Trade in organic food and the growth in organic agricultural production are hampered by the lack of harmonized regulations among potential trading partners. The adoption of international guidelines is an important first step in providing a harmonized approach to regulations in the organic food sector, thus facilitating trade in organic food, but further efforts are needed. Arrangements for mutual recognition of national guarantee systems will reduce uncertainty regarding standards and the use of labels for imported organic products, protect the interests of consumers and producers, and facilitate international trade.

The NPOA has established general procedures related to accreditation of certification agencies, as well as rules and regulations for the inspection of organic agriculture. Specific laws and regulations set a legal framework for organic agricultural production. The competent authority dealing with issues related to the inspection of organic agriculture in Costa Rica is the Direction of Phytosanitary Protection Services of the Ministry of Agriculture. Within this Direction, the Department on Accreditation and Registration of Organic Agriculture is authorized to carry out the following tasks: implementing legislation concerning organic agriculture, creating a registry of producers and approving and supervising different private and public inspection bodies.

Costa Rica has good certification and accreditation infrastructure. There are three authorized inspection bodies, two of which have the authority to both inspect and certify. The two national certification agencies that have been accredited in Costa Rica are the EcoLogica agency and the AIMCOPOP agency. The German agency BCS has offices in Costa Rica and has also been accredited by the national authorities. This agency has its base in the European Union (EU). It undertakes inspection duties in Costa Rica, but certification takes place in the EU.

It is expected that Costa Rica will soon be included in the EU 'third-country list' under Regulation 2092/91 (Article 11.1).[26]

Recommendations

In the light of lessons learned so far, the NPOA has identified the following priorities:

- strengthening alliances with media and consumers (to deepen awareness and knowledge of institutions and farmers and promote domestic consumption);
- providing training for extension workers;
- developing incentives (to support farmers in transition to organic agriculture, create favourable credit conditions and provide low-cost certification alternatives);
- building a national strategy through a participatory process (to develop long-term concerted policies and consolidate the National Organic Agriculture Movement and build private–public sector alliances).

India[27]

Background

India has traditionally practised organic agriculture, but the process of modernization, particularly the Green Revolution, has led to increased use of chemicals.[28] In recent years, however, limitations of agriculture based on chemical use and intensive irrigation have become apparent and there has been a resurgence of interest in organic agriculture. Renewed emphasis on organic agriculture originates from two concerns: (a) falling agricultural yield in certain areas, as a result of, *inter alia*, excessive use of chemical inputs and decreased soil fertility, and (b) environmental concerns. Exports also play a role, but perhaps less than in other countries.

Several movements, such as LEISA (low external input sustainable agriculture) have been promoted in India. However, the scope of such programmes has been relatively limited. Policies towards organic farming are still in the making and information is scarce. Farmers and NGOs are almost the only source of information on the current nature and extent of organic farming in India and very limited information is available from government agencies or certification bodies. Primary information has been collected under UNCTAD projects. Case studies carried out under different UNCTAD projects cover Darjeeling tea, spices and coffee. A survey of 28 organic spice growers was conducted in the Idukki District. A survey of two groups of coffee growers was also conducted.

Production and export constraints
An important constraint on the conversion to organic agriculture is the lack of assured markets and price premiums. Certification costs, and technical standards (applicable to all products), may pose obstacles to exports of organic food products from developing countries. Furthermore, rapidly growing organic vegetable and fruit markets in developed countries tend to rely largely on locally produced food. In so far as this is not a situation of competitive advantage but part of a concerted campaign to consume locally and protect local producers, comprehensive policies need to be put in place to promote imports of organic food from developing countries. This includes, in particular, measures in the area of trade policy.

The Indian government created a National Steering Committee to develop National Guidelines for Organic Production. The National Programme for Organic Production (NPOP) provides an institutional mechanism for production and export of organic food products, taking into account the requirement of international markets. The declared objectives of the NPOP were:

- to declare standards for organic production;
- to recognize specific bodies for preparing approved packages of practices for specified products and approving certification programmes;
- to allow the recognized bodies to accredit agencies to inspect and certify that products are the result of following the prescribed practices;
- to seek recognition from and accord reciprocal recognition to standards of other nations and trading blocks;

- to institute a logo and prescribe its award by accrediting bodies to products that qualify to bear the Indian organic label.

Under the NPOP, National Standards were published in March 2000. The Standards are based on the Basic Standards of Organic Agriculture and Food Processing of IFOAM with suitable modifications taking into account the agricultural and climatic conditions prevailing in India.

The National Steering Committee has designated the Tea Board, the Coffee Board, the Spices Board and the Agricultural and Processed Food Products Export Development Authority (APEDA) as accreditation agencies for the products under their responsibility.

Lack of market information and marketing strategies is a major constraint to market development. For example, export channels for organic coffee from India are not fully established. Marketing policies to promote the use of brand names and other mechanisms, including electronic commerce, to move organic products out of the commodities markets and auctions are needed to increase premiums or simply to find markets.

Small markets for organic pepper nevertheless constitute a constraint and three quarters of certified organic black pepper has been sold in markets for conventional products.

Price premiums

The case studies indicate that price premiums for growers are uncertain and difficult to secure. This is partly due to the fact that marketing chains tend to be complex.[29] Thus, even in cases where the consumers and retailers are willing to pay a price premium, such premiums do not seem to have benefited the producers.

In the case of pepper, it was difficult to obtain price premiums. In fact, since prices of conventional pepper steadily rose from 1997, the organic prices agreed upon earlier turned out to be less of a bonus than originally thought.

In the case of Darjeeling Tea, one major reason for tea gardens to turn organic was that yields were decreasing (although not merely owing to excessive usage of chemicals). In addition, in the early 1990s, tea gardens had to substantially reduce the usage of pesticides and chemicals because of restrictions on chemical residues in the export markets. Thus, moving all the way to organic tea was not seen as a big, extra step. Finally, in the early 1990s, a market premium of over 80 per cent prompted many growers to export organic tea. Twenty of the 87 tea gardens in Darjeeling, most of them 100 per cent export oriented, converted to organic tea production. However, only ten gardens, exporting directly to buyers in Germany, Japan and the United States, experienced increased profit margins. In order to benefit from organic tea farming, market diversification into other products such as herbal tea, green tea and eco-tourism may be required.

Most of the profitable enterprises had invested a substantial portion of their profits in marketing tea in their main markets.

Institutional support

Initially, local IFOAM members and associates, farmer organizations and other stakeholders led the organic agriculture movement in India. Currently, the Spices Board, an organization of the Indian government, and NGOs, such as the Peermade Development Society (PDS) actively support organic production. The Spices Board, for example, has elaborated guidelines for organic production, offers training in organic farming practices and has institutionalized a scheme for meeting 50 per cent of the cost of inspection and certification by accredited certification agencies. Other commodity-specific boards, such as the Tea Board and the Coffee Board, also support organic production. Recently, the government has initiated some programmes in support of organic agriculture, but it does not provide significant subsidies.

The basic infrastructure for regulating the growth of organic agriculture in India has thus been established. However, much remains to be done, such as obtaining recognition of the Indian standards by the international standards organizations as well as the standards organizations in important markets, involvement of producers to ensure that the standards adequately reflect field situations and accrediting credible certification agencies.

Recommendations

Organic agriculture in India helps maintain and improve soil fertility over long periods of time and this translates into sustainability. In such cases, organic agriculture can increase productivity, improve and protect the environment, protect human health and ensure sustainable development. Methods of organic and biodynamic cultivation can also significantly increase yields in traditional agriculture. The study[30] makes the following recommendations:

- review traditional agricultural practices to document useful techniques and resources, including rare and precious species and varieties, specialty varieties, cultivation practices including sowing and planting, soil preparation and protection and organic fertilizers used by farmers for thousands of years;
- explore and apply local traditional varieties in adapting organic agriculture to various niches of the ecological and socio-economic conditions of each locality;
- develop microbiological technologies, combining modern technologies and indigenous knowledge and practices;

- combine in the most effective way the use of crop varieties with integrated pesticide management (IPM) and integrated nitrogen fertilizer management (INFM), thereby promoting the use of locally available resources including alluvial soil, alluvial water, green biomass and legumes.
- select and breed crops for pest and disease resistance and for tolerance to adverse agro-ecological conditions, and promote high quality products to meet export requirements;
- select and protect areas with ecologically-safe conditions (no pollution, little soil degradation), so that certified organic agriculture can be practised there.

Uganda[31]

Background
A study by the lead researcher for the African project component argues that Uganda is well placed to adopt organic agriculture, thanks to the abundance of land and the lack of generalized use of chemical products. Conversion could easily be done among small-scale producers, a main characteristic of agricultural production in Uganda.

The paper shows that experiences, in particular with regard to production and market access, vary across products. Some products have already been exported for some years and have benefited from external support in terms of know-how and certification. Such is the case of cotton and sesame, promoted by a collaboration launched in 1994 between the Swedish International Development Agency (SIDA), the Uganda government and some private companies. The experience of other products, such as organic coffee, is more recent.

Production and export constraints
The study discusses constraints facing organic agriculture in Uganda, related to (a) production, (b) market access and marketing, and (c) institutional and policy-related issues. Production constraints include:

- the cost of certification and the need to maintain high quality standards: the small size of the organic sector makes it difficult to achieve economies of scale; the fact that small producers are dispersed over a large area increases inspection costs;
- the lack of price premiums in the domestic market;
- the lack of know-how and insufficient training and extension facilities;
- uncertainties about land ownership: farmers have to be sure that they will be able to benefit from investing, for example, in improved soil fertility;

- insufficient financial support and credit facilities;
- overproduction in some areas.

The major marketing constraints include:

- a lack of information on organic markets;
- difficulties in penetrating external markets. As a result, most producers sell through transnational corporations rather than exporting directly to distributors;
- absence of an organized national market and distribution system;
- poor infrastructure (including a poor road network in rural areas and limited airport handling facilities);
- uncertainty concerning demand and price premiums, which provide insufficient incentives to farmers to make the additional efforts needed for organic production;
- difficulties in generating sufficient volumes for export, partly because small-scale producers are located in different areas.

The main institutional and policy constraints may be summarized as follows:

- absence of a clear government policy on promotion of organic products or financial or other support available to entrepreneurs;
- lack of a national body to support organic agriculture through national coordination and international negotiations;
- lack of locally based certifying bodies.

The Uganda paper has not addressed the extent to which import procedures or other issues related to conformity assessment have been an obstacle to exports of organic products. Other studies, however, indicate that marketing of Robusta coffee from a successful EPOPA project in Bushenyi, Uganda, has been hampered by delays in obtaining import permits for the German market.[32]

Price premiums
The study reports that during the 2000/2001 seasons organic farmers could sell less than 20 per cent of their organic cotton and organic sesame as organic products. The rest had to be sold as conventional products. However, where organic farmers do receive price premiums, these tend to be significant. In the case of coffee, a 20 per cent premium over the conventional price is offered. Organic cotton farmers receive a price premium of 25 per cent. Organically produced horticultural products fetched price premiums of 120 per cent and

African Organics paid its growers of pineapple, apple, banana, passion fruit and ginger a price premium in the range of 40 to 80 per cent.

A case study on cotton and sesame in the Lira district in Northern Uganda shows that the production costs of organic and conventional coffee and sesame are very similar. Whereas yields and unit cost of production are not very different, the profits are higher for organic farmers as a result of price premiums.

Recommendations
Organic agriculture offers an avenue for farmers to improve on farm efficiency and profitability to a level higher than that under traditional management and the majority of the small-scale producers can afford to make this change. The opportunity for Uganda to become a relevant exporter of organic products depends mainly on its certification capacity. It currently lacks a locally based certification body. A national institution that would actively support organic agriculture in Uganda and facilitate the creation of a local certifying body is needed to lower certification costs and to provide incentives. It would also be necessary to ensure permanent supervision of the crops and to demonstrate the significance of the potential market for organic products in order to avoid overproduction, as has occurred in the past.

The study makes the recommendation that the government should develop a clear policy on organic agriculture and play a proactive role in designing supportive policies. Areas of support could include:

* creation of awareness, and promotion of a local market for organic products;
* if producer subsidies are deemed to be advisable, credit programmes for organic agriculture would be possible and the establishment of local standards and certification schemes could also be subsidized;
* identification of markets;
* provision of information on prices and possible market saturation.

National bodies such as the Uganda Export Promotion Board (UEPB) could also undertake these activities. In addition, these exporters could gainfully focus their out-grower initiatives in areas where they can easily realize a critical mass and accordingly reduce costs of supervision and marketing.

International assistance could be channelled into:

* assisting with certification costs, at least initially;
* assisting exporters in obtaining direct contacts with buyers in Europe (to obtain higher price premiums). This is especially important in immature markets where traders may receive monopoly rents.

CONCLUSIONS

All three papers emphasize the important potential economic, social and environmental benefits of organic agriculture in developing countries. Similarly, it is argued that organic agriculture can increase productivity, improve and protect the environment, protect human health and ensure sustainable development. Yield levels under organic management may be lower than those where fertilizers have been applied, but they tend to be higher than under traditional management practices. Thus, organic agriculture offers an opportunity, affordable to small-scale farmers, to improve farm efficiency and profitability above levels achieved under traditional management.

While many farmers in developing countries have practised organic methods of production for centuries, experience with certified organic agriculture is relatively new. This poses great challenges to governments and farmer communities. The experiences from Costa Rica, India and Uganda show that there is considerable interest in these countries in exploring opportunities for organic agricultural production and exports. In all three countries, small producers play a key role in organic agricultural production. NGOs and rural organizations have been instrumental in promoting organic agriculture, in particular in Costa Rica and India, whereas aid agencies play a relatively large role in Uganda. In all three countries, the government institutions have gradually taken a more active role in promoting production and exports. Costa Rica and India have relatively well established certification infrastructures, whereas in Uganda exports largely rely on aid agencies and transnational corporations to obtain certification. Both Costa Rica and India have taken steps to have their certification and inspection systems recognized by the EU in order to be included in the EU 'third-country' list to gain easier access to the EU market.

Yet, the case studies indicate that producers in developing countries interested in taking advantage of market opportunities for environmentally preferable products, such as organic agricultural products, in many respects face problems similar to those of producers struggling with stringent SPS and/or environmental requirements. These include the need to comply with standards set by the importing country, certification costs and transaction costs resulting from multiple standards. In some cases, authorities or even certification bodies and/or supermarket chains deliberately favour locally or regionally produced food products over imports.[33] It follows that comprehensive policies at the national and international levels are required, including in the areas of trade policy and capacity building. The next section summarizes key recommendations.

RECOMMENDATIONS

Strengthening DCs' Capacities to Address Production and Export Constraints

Raising awareness and promoting policy dialogues[34]
All the papers recognize the need to raise awareness of trading opportunities for organic products as well as the environmental, economic and social benefits of organic production. The institutions that can lead such a process are already in place, such as the National Programme of Organic Agriculture in Costa Rica, APEDA in India and UEPB in Uganda. NGOs also play a key role, for example the National Organic Agricultural Movement of Uganda.

Research and development, training
The studies also recommend further research and development to promote organic farming in developing countries. Examples can be found in the India case study. Training for organic production, certification and marketing also needs to be provided.

Development of national legislation and standards
The studies on Costa Rica and India emphasize that the development of domestic standards is essential for the promotion of organic production and for the creation of domestic certification infrastructure. National standards can also contribute to the creation of domestic niche markets. The Uganda case study is silent on this issue, but recommends the establishment of a certification body located in Uganda. Costa Rica and India have already established national standards.[35]

Addressing certification costs
In most cases, developing country exporters depend on certification by international certification bodies to be able to market their products as organic goods in foreign markets. Small countries, in particular the least developed countries (LDCs) such as Uganda, often have significant problems in establishing national certification infrastructure. Apart from recommending the establishment of a certification body located in Uganda, the case study calls on the international community to assist exporters in meeting certification costs.

Several steps can be taken to reduce certification costs in developing countries while maintaining the integrity of the organic system and the credibility of the certification. This issue is examined in Box 6.1.

BOX 6.1   HOW CAN CERTIFICATION COSTS IN DEVELOPING COUNTRIES BE REDUCED?[36]

A certification body should:

- be able to certify to various public and private standards
- be accredited ISO guide 65
- maintain a high quality and professional work
- assure the certified product an access to all markets
- provide the applicant with the update standards
- be willing to cooperate with the local staff, train and use domestic inspectors and work with local domestic certification bodies.

Certification includes the following cost elements:

- inspection on site
- report
- evaluation of the report
- decision of certification
- establishment of certificate
- follow-up – Transaction – Export – Import – Documents.

The factors influencing the cost of certification include:

- inspection fees
- certification fees
- travel costs
- inspection plan – frequency of the inspection
- analysis.

How can a balance be established between certification cost and credibility of the certification?

- inspection done by local staff
- adequate fees – local fees
- low travel costs
- provisions for smallholder group certification
- certification based on internal control system (ICS)
- risk assessment. Approach for external control.

What can be done to achieve this balance?

- develop programmes to train organic farmers and small-holder groups
- adapt certification and inspection plans to the local situation
- ensure that the farmers get the right price for their production.

Developing a domestic market
The study on Costa Rica recommends that the development of a domestic market be promoted. Because of its size, India could also benefit from this.

Market strategies
The case studies seem to indicate that price premiums for growers are uncertain and difficult to secure. This is due, in part, to the fact that marketing chains tend to be complex. Thus, even where consumers and retailers are willing to pay a price premium, such premiums do not always seem to have benefited the producers.

The country studies, especially those on India and Uganda, highlight the need to develop market strategies and to identify possible partners, including exporters, foreign buyers, distributors and consumers, in order to establish appropriate marketing strategies

Appropriate government support
Lack of clear government policies and appropriate government support has been identified as an important constraint in all case studies. The governments of Costa Rica and India have recently adopted a more active role. Uganda has also made some progress in providing institutional support.

Facilitating Imports of Organic Products into Developed Countries

Authorities and other stakeholders in main importing countries can implement several measures to facilitate access to their organic markets for products from developing countries, particularly by:

- seeking to reflect the needs of developing countries in meeting organic standards and import procedures; for example, organic standards should provide for group certification with adequate use of internal control systems;
- promoting harmonization and mutual recognition of organic standards, including between public and private standards, based on equivalence;

- ensuring transparent and understandable requirements and procedures for imported products, especially from developing countries;
- providing information on organic standards and regulations, market opportunities and other factors relevant to exporters from developing countries;
- promoting consumption of organic agricultural products, including from developing countries; for example, by providing consumer information;
- exploring trade preferences for organic agricultural products from developing countries.

The India paper proposes to explore trade preferences for organic agricultural products. Proposals have been made, for example in the United States, to use tariff rate quotas (TRQs) to promote specific categories of organic products.[37]

The Role of Bilateral and Multilateral Aid Agencies

Multilateral and bilateral donors, as well as import promotion agencies, can provide technical assistance to help promote organic agricultural production, obtain certification and identify business partners. For example, the Swedish International Development Agency (SIDA) started the EPOPA (Export Promotion of Organic Products from Africa) Programme in 1995 to help African countries to export organic products from Africa.[38] EPOPA is now active in Uganda and the United Republic of Tanzania and projects are under way in other countries. Similarly, CBI, an import promotion agency from the Netherlands, together with the Uganda Exports Promotion Board (UEPB), assists Ugandan farmers to produce and export organic foods and spices.

Bilateral and multilateral aid agencies play an important role not only in promoting production of organic agriculture, but also in assisting developing countries in marketing organic products. EPOPA, for example, requires a close working relationship between the exporters and the importers.[39] CBI promotes organic products from Uganda in European markets.

Issues in the Area of Trade Rules

The India case study includes some recommendations in the area of trade policy and trade rules, focusing on trade preferences for organic agriculture, the use of subsidies, technical assistance and special measures for small producers in developing countries. The following issues are of particular concern:

- the implications, if any, for developing countries of the subsidies in developed countries that assist their farmers in converting to organic production;

- the identification of ways to facilitate imports of organic products through enhanced transparency and practical application of the concept of equivalence, taking into account the WTO Agreement on Technical Barriers to Trade;
- key trade issues related to international, national and regional organic standards;
- the need for transparent and non-discriminatory labelling;
- possibilities of granting special and differential (S&D) treatment, including trade preferences, to organic products originating in developing countries.

In the post-Doha process, a number of issues could be considered. These include an examination of the extent to which mandated negotiations aimed at reducing or eliminating tariff and non-tariff barriers to environmental goods and services (Doha Ministerial Declaration, paragraph 31) could benefit developing countries' exports of organic agricultural products.

Possible Follow-up

Working closely with IFOAM, FAO, ITC and other relevant institutions, the following follow-up activities could be considered. Some of these activities could also be carried out in the context of an UNCTAD/FIELD project on trade and environment and/or the UNEP–UNCTAD CBTF. Assisting interested developing countries in designing and implementing appropriate government support for organic agricultural production could be achieved by:

- promoting studies focusing on:
  - the identification – at the product level – of yields, costs and profitability of organic production as compared to conventional agricultural production;
  - the identification of promising products;
  - the identification of ways to reduce certification costs for organic producers in developing countries;
  - the identification of production, marketing and institutional constraints;
  - the identification of options for overcoming these constraints.
- Policy dialogues, which could focus on:
  - creating an awareness of the potential commercial and environmental benefits of organic agriculture;
  - promoting multi-stakeholder committees.
- In cooperation with IFOAM, FAO and other relevant institutions:

- exploring mechanisms for recognition of guarantee systems of developing countries;
- promoting unilateral and mutual recognition;
- examining ways to promote the practical application of the concept of equivalence;
- promoting dialogues with relevant authorities in developed countries;
- promoting a framework of harmonization;
- examining trade rule aspects.
- In cooperation with ITC, IFOAM and relevant authorities in developed and developing countries:
  - ensuring transparent and simple rules governing imports of organic products, including through the application of the concept of equivalence;
  - exploring trade preferences for organic products;
  - examining market strategies;
  - disseminating results of market research to interested developing countries;
  - promoting studies and training in interested developing countries;
  - examining possibilities to use e-commerce to promote exports of organic products from developing countries;
  - facilitating and promoting partnerships with donors and fair-trade organizations;
  - facilitating and promoting partnerships between developing country exporters and institutional buyers in importing countries.

ANNEX: RESEARCH QUESTIONS

1. In your country, what are the major constraints on production and exports of organic agricultural production?
2. What policies have been adopted by the government (and the private sector) of your country towards organic agriculture?
3. What are the major experiences with regard to exports (where relevant and possible, exports to the EU and US markets should be examined separately), in particular with regard to
   a. how certification is obtained
   b. difficulties, if any, in complying with import requirements
   c. whether price premiums have been obtained?
4. How should the government and the private sector in your country address production and export constraints?

5. In your view, how can developed countries facilitate imports of organic products from developing countries?
6. How can bilateral and multilateral aid agencies assist developing countries in promoting production and exports of organic agricultural products?
7. What are the key trade issues in the area of trade rules?

NOTES

1. Roxana Salazar, 'Barriers to organic agriculture: the case of Costa Rica', July 2001.
2. Veena Jha, 'Production and trade in organic agricultural products: India and Viet Nam', study carried out under UNCTAD/UNDP projects IND/99/965 and VIE/98/036, and presented at a workshop in Havana, May/June 2000.
3. Nimrod Waniala, 'Production and trading opportunities and constraints for organic agriculture in Uganda', study carried out under project INT/98/A61. Mr Waniala is Director, Private Sector Foundation (PSF), Trade Policy Capacity Building Project, Kampala, Uganda.
4. UNCTAD, *Ways to Enhance the Production and Export Capacities of Developing Countries of Agriculture and Food Products, Including Niche Products, such as Environmentally Preferable Products: Background note by the UNCTAD secretariat*, Geneva, 2001. The outcome of the expert meeting is contained in document TD/B/COM.1/41 and TD/B/COM.1/EM.15/3.
5. http://www.ifoam.org/press/harmonisation_conference.html
6. The report of the meeting can be found on http://www.unctad.org/trade_env/test1/meetings/brussels/finalreport.doc. See also http://www.unctad.org/trade_env for papers submitted to the meeting and PowerPoint presentations.
7. René Vossenaar and Veena Jha, UNCTAD, 'Trading opportunities for organic food products from developing countries', paper prepared under the UNCTAD/FIELD project on 'Strengthening Research and Policy-Making Capacity on Trade and Environment in Developing Countries', presented at the project workshop in Dar es Salaam, April 2001.
8. http://www.intracen.org/mds/ and R. Kortlech-Olesen, ITC, personal communication, December 2002.
9. Sophia Twarog and René Vossenaar, 'Obstacles Facing Developing Country Exports of Organic Products to Developed Country Markets', IFOAM Conference on Organic Guarantee Systems, 17–19 February, Nuremberg, Germany, in cooperation with FAO and UNCTAD.
10. In developing countries, where many farmers are poor and cultivate small plots of land, inspection and certification is excessively expensive per unit of output. Most, therefore, practise group certification based on Internal Control Systems. Group certification is possible only when there are sufficiently large numbers of farmers growing the same crops by the same methods and under similar conditions.
11. Luanne Lohr argues that agri-environmental support payments to European organic farmers give them a competitive advantage in capturing the global organic market. Since these payments promote environmental protection, rather than providing direct production support, they are not subject to challenge under WTO rules. Lohr argues that organic farmers in the United States are at a disadvantage owing to lack of similar government support. The Conservation Security Act could level the playing field by providing farmers with financial support for practices that protect the environment – including organic production. See Lohr, L. (2001), *The Importance of the Conservation Security Act to U.S. Competitiveness in Global Organic Markets*, Faculty Series 01-19, Dept of Agricultural and Applied Economics, University of Georgia.

12. Taken from UNCTAD (2003), 'Trading opportunities for organic food products from developing countries', Geneva.
13. European Commission, Directorate-General for Agriculture. Organic Agriculture, *Guide to Community Rules*.
14. It took the Czech Republic (which at the time of application to the EU already had a substantial organic sector) six to seven years to get approval to be placed on the EU third-country list. See Gunnar Rundgren, 'Is there a need for a regulatory framework?', *Organic Standard*, © Grolink AB, Issue 11, March 2002.
15. Costa Rica submitted an application in February 2000. An EU mission visited Costa Rica in November 2000. In its Final Report, the mission recommended to include Costa Rica in the third-country list, provided that the Costa Rican authorities inform the Commission that action has been taken to implement certain recommendations within 6 months. See European Commission, 'Organic Farming in Costa Rica', DG(SANCO)/1252/2000 – MR Final.
16. Commins, K. and Kung Wai, O. (2002), *Regulation of Imports into Major Markets*, in IFOAM Conference on Organic Guarantee Systems, 'International Harmonisation and Equivalence on Organic Agriculture', February, in cooperation with FAO and UNCTAD.
17. According to a recent ITC/FAO study, 'In practice, the duration of the process to obtain an import permit can vary considerably. Some importers reported that it is a matter of weeks in some countries (e.g. the Netherlands), while it can take up to several months in other member states. In France, for example, some trade sources said that in the past it used to take up to six months to obtain an import permit. However, they said that there has been considerable progress recently, leading to a more reasonable time frame (generally not exceeding two months).'
18. This Regulation defines detailed rules with regard to the certificate of inspection required pursuant to Article 11(1)(b) and (3) of Regulation (EEC) No. 2092/91 and with regard to the submission of such certificate for imports undertaken in accordance with the provisions of Article 11(6) of the same Regulation.
19. See http://www.ams.usda.gov/nop/CertifyingAgents/Accredited.html
20. Riddle, J. and Coody, L. (2002), 'Comparison of the EU and US Organic Regulations', in IFOAM Conference on Organic Guarantee Systems, 'International Harmonisation and Equivalence on Organic Agriculture', February, in cooperation with FAO and UNCTAD.
21. Based on R.Salazar, 'Barriers to Organic Agriculture: The Case of Costa Rica', July 2001; papers by the Ministry of Foreign Trade; and Felicia Echeverria Hermoso (National Organic Agriculture Programme of Costa Rica), 'Desarrollo de Politicas y Acciones Institucionales para Apoyar la Produccion y Comercializacion de Productos Organicos en Costa Rica, paper presented at the UNCTAD Expert Meeting on Ways to Enhance the Production and Export Capacities of Developing Countries of Agriculture and Food Products, Including Niche Products, Such as Environmentally Preferable Products, Geneva, 16–18 July 2001.
22. Felicia Echeverria Hermoso (2001), op. cit.
23. Felicia Echeverria Hermoso, presentation at the CBTF Policy Dialogue on Promoting Production and Trading Opportunities for Organic Agricultural Products, Brussels, 21–22 February 2002.
24. The case study lists the following basic information: CIF price for the conventional product: US$450 per tonne; the CIF price for the organic product: US$1200 per tonne; the cost to the corporation for a tonne of processed organic product: US$348.
25. Taken from a paper by E. Gitli and M. Perez-Esteve, presented at the Workshop on Standards and Trade, UNCTAD, Geneva, 16–17 May 2002.
26. Costa Rica submitted an application in February 2000. A European Union mission visited Costa Rica in November 2000. In its Final Report, the mission recommended to include Costa Rica in the third-country list, provided that the Costa Rican authorities inform the Commission that action has been taken to implement certain recommendations within 6 months. See European Commission, 'Organic Farming in Costa Rica', DG(SANCO)/1252/2000 – MR Final.
27. Veena Jha, 'Production and Trade in Organic Agricultural Products: India and Viet Nam', paper presented at the workshop in Havana, May/June 2000.

28. Veena Jha (2000), op. cit.
29. Marketing of organic products is a major problem for Indian farmers. There is no critical mass of producers in many sectors to enable economies of scale for processing, servicing, research and market development.
30. Veena Jha (2000) op. cit.
31. This section is based on Nimrod Waniala, 'Production and Trading Opportunities and Constraints for Organic Agriculture in Uganda'.
32. http://antenna.nl/agroeco/projects/projects.htm
33. Pressures to reduce 'food miles', invoking environmental concerns, may also have adverse implications for certain categories of organic products from developing countries (report of the CBTF Policy Dialogue).
34. The CBTF Policy Dialogue in Brussels concluded that multi-stakeholder dialogues in developing countries can play a key role in raising awareness and in designing holistic policies towards organic agriculture, as well as generating government support. Multi-stakeholder processes for developing fair and effective national policies and certification programmes should also be encouraged. CBTF, in cooperation with IFOAM, ITC and FAO, can play a positive role in facilitating national and regional processes to be set in motion, including regarding standards and certification (in particular on group certification) at the regional level, as well as in promoting pilot studies aimed at identifying how to reduce certification costs (see report of the Policy Dialogue).
35. In the CBTF Policy Dialogue in Brussels several experts stressed the need to develop national legislation, standards and certification infrastructure to encourage the development of the organic sector in developing countries. Others felt that this was not necessarily the first priority in developing countries with a very small organic sector and that government intervention should prioritize extension service research and inclusion of organic agriculture in government policies and plans. Government support is one option for making certification affordable to small producers. (See report of the Policy Dialogue.) On this issue also see Gunnar Rundgren, 'Is there a need for a regulatory framework?'
36. Based on a presentation by Michel Reynaud (EcoCert) in the CBTF Policy Dialogue on Promoting Production and Trading Opportunities for Organic Agricultural Products, Brussels, February 2002.
37. In the USA, imports of sugar are subject to TRQs. The quota sugar usually pays no or a very low duty, whereas over-quota sugar pays a high duty. Organic sugar falls into the category of specialty sugar, a subset of the refined sugar quota. In 1999/2000 the US Department of Agriculture raised the specialty sugar quota, in large part to accommodate the growth in organic sugar demand in the United States. In the light of projected high growth in organic sugar demand, interested parties approached the US government to seek application for an additional quota line in the HTSUS that would specifically accommodate organic sugar. See Peter J. Buzzanell (Executive Director, Peter Buzzanell & Associates, Inc.) 'Organic Sugar: Short Term Fad or Long Term Growth Opportunity?', presented for the International Sugar Organization, 9th International Seminar, 'Hot Issues for Sugar', London, UK, 21 November 2000.
38. EPOPA is a sub-programme of SIDA's Private Sector Development. Its execution has been commissioned to Agro Eco Consultancy in the Netherlands. Projects can be initiated in all countries in Africa where Sweden is engaged in private sector development. http://www.sida.se/Sida/jsp/Crosslink.jsp?d=293.
39. When African exporters offer products, the local coordinator (country manager) and Agro Eco will help in finding importers. Support is available for sending samples, testing residue, exchanging product specifications and some other services. EPOPA provides assistance in project organization, research and marketing. The feasibility study can be financed, as well as consultancy, training and initial certification.

7. Summary and Conclusions

Veena Jha

EFFECTS OF ENVIRONMENTAL AND HEALTH MEASURES ON TRADE

Environmental requirements are different from other factors, such as product quality or fashion, which may also affect developing countries' exports. For example, environmental requirements, especially those related to process and production methods (PPMs), are more likely to be based on specific values than other requirements. Pressure groups may be especially vocal on issues of environmental protection, even outside their own countries. In addition, importers may want their foreign suppliers to comply with certain PPM-related requirements. One element, which is particularly relevant in the case of health and SPS measures, is the possible use of the precautionary approach as opposed to strict scientific evidence. It is important to note that, depending upon the purpose of the measure that is applied vis-à-vis imports, each measure will have different legal consequences under the WTO. But this should not, in any way, prevent WTO Members from pursuing what they believe are legitimate policy objectives, whether related to environment, food safety or plant and animal health.

The importance of SPS measures in the global context is growing because of the increased trade in food products. First, the growth in trade in food products is responsible for the increase in the international transmission of pests. Secondly, production chains are becoming more complex and new food-borne diseases are being detected. Additionally, GATT tariff bindings diminished the possibilities of national industry protection, providing ample room for non-tariff barriers. Finally, consumer interests in certain markets demand that standards should focus on environmental concerns and not just on issues of quality or innocuousness. Obviously, if the number of standards increases, direct or indirect conformity assessment procedures to determine that relevant requirements in technical regulations are fulfilled will also multiply. According to a study carried out in the United States, the activities of testing laboratories which carry out conformity assessment evaluation have been expanding by 13.5 per cent a year.[1]

Food safety and environment standards will be very difficult to distinguish in the future. The Doha declaration links environment and health and safety standards together when talking of environment standards (paragraph 6). In fact, the EU agriculture commissioner in his post-Doha statements spoke about the importance of such measures in the European Union.[2] The EU White Paper on Food Safety also talks about the link between environment and health standards and the need for measures based on precaution. Analysis of measures over the past five years shows that such measures are increasing and will become important in the post-Doha context.

General Effects

Most researchers in this project were of the view that the potential gains that could have been obtained through tariff reductions have not been fully realized and in some cases have been eroded because of problems involved in meeting SPS standards.[3] Guatemalan producers of poultry have complained that SPS regulations keep their competitive products out of developed country markets. They are, therefore, reluctant to open their own markets to products from developed countries.[4]

Plant health regulations for fruits and vegetables present numerous difficulties for Latin American and Caribbean exports such as Mexican avocados and Brazilian apples, grapes and mangoes.

> To avoid the use of health measures as covert restrictions to trade is actually more of an aspiration than a reality, due to the protectionist attitude assumed by some first world countries, who use their high scientific and technologic level in poultry health to establish health measures that turn into non-tariff restrictive barriers to market access. Thus, it is not strange that when a partially exporting country reaches a certain level, close to the established norm, the norm is modified to make compliance with it more difficult. (Búcaro, 1998: 40).[5]

Problems faced by exporters include lack of timely and accurate information, the simultaneous application of multiple standards and regulations, the costs and difficulties of testing and verification procedures, the perceived lack of scientific data for specific thresholds or limit values and the uncertainty arising from rapidly changing requirements in overseas markets. Phytosanitary regulations and food standards also create market access problems on account of differing national standards, lack of transparency and inconsistent application of procedures.

Main types of SPS- and environment-related problems
According to the *List of Detentions* published regularly by the United States Food and Drug Administration (USFDA) the characteristics of detentions vary according to the geographical region. The major cause of detention for products

from South Asia is filth, followed by microbiological contamination, low acid canned food and labelling problems.[6] The major reason for detentions from Latin America was found to be exceeding MRLs and the major reason from Africa was rotting. Notwithstanding these broad categories of reasons, there were specific issues raised in each of the studies that deserve attention.

Impact of environmental and health measures on specific products[7]
This chapter compares the similarities and differences in the experiences of different countries and different regions in coping with SPS standards for the same product. Often the standard itself is the same, for example the European Union regulations on fisheries. The purpose of this section is to test the general propositions outlined in the first chapter and to come up with a list of problems which are common to all countries. This will help in developing strategies for compliance with environmental and health standards.

Fisheries and Shrimps

Stringent hygiene and sanitary requirements in developed countries in particular provisions concerning the use of HACCP (Hazard Analysis Critical Control Point), have affected marine exports from several South Asian and African countries. Failure to comply with such requirements has resulted in products not qualifying for export to the European Union and the United States, or products incurring 'automatic detention' in the United States.[8] In addition, the European Union banned imports of fishery products originating in Bangladesh (1997), India (1997), Mozambique (1997), Uganda (1997 and 1999), Kenya (1997 and 1999) and the United Republic of Tanzania (1997 and 1999). These bans have subsequently been lifted, but may have long-term effects on the countries concerned. Particular attention is paid to the difficulties in complying with such requirements, compliance costs and their trade effects.

Compliance costs
The need to comply with the EU norms significantly increases the cost of production and entry into the EU markets. Prior to EU norms, exports from South Asia were mainly in bulk form; the equipment required was plate freezers, refrigeration equipment for freezing, processing and cold storage. The EU requirement involves heavy investment in infrastructure and equipment, apart from higher running cost. For example, it is now necessary for each factory to have a potable water system, continuous power (standby generators), effluent treatment plants, flake ice machines, chill rooms and a laboratory. It is estimated that such upgrading involves an expenditure of about US$250 000 to US$500 000 per unit as fixed cost.[9]

The Seafood Exporters Association of India claims to have spent US$25 million on upgrading of its facilities to meet the regulations. Appropriate training of the personnel involved in various stages of production and processing are not included in this cost estimate.

In Bangladesh it was estimated that the total cost of upgrading the facilities and equipment and training the staff and workers to achieve acceptable sanitary and technical standards was about US$18.0 million. The annual cost of maintaining the HACCP programme was estimated to be US$2.4 million.[10] Costa Rican processing plants have generally adapted well to HACCP necessities.[11] This is partly a result of heavy investment in infrastructure. During 1999 and 2000 the tuna processing companies invested US$15 million in refurbishing, expansion and, of course, sanitary controls. Apart from this, all of the exporting plants have designed an HACCP plan that, according to the best of their abilities, minimizes the occurrence of the hazards associated with fish. When the requirement was introduced in 1997, some plants brought US HACCP experts to assess and help them draft their HACCP plans in the FDA format. There has been no clear strategy for the expansion of HACCP to the boats. INCOPESCA and CANNEP are in the process of drafting a project to address this problem. They will identify which ships feed processing plants that export to the European Union. Thereafter, they will look for national and international funds (probably Canadian) to implement an HACCP plan on those vessels. The initial investment may have to be done only on a few vessels. Nevertheless, it is expected that soon the USA will follow this line. In that event, the whole fleet will have to be refurbished, but there is no real economic possibility of this happening.

Opportunity costs

The loss to Uganda in terms of reduced returns as a result of a continued ban was estimated at US$36.9 million. The loss to the fishermen on account of reduced prices and lower fishing activity was estimated at US$1.0 million per month. What was considered even more damaging was the fact that the Nile perch, which had been regarded as a proper substitute for cod in low season in Europe before the ban, took a long time to regain its popularity. A marketing drive, which may prove very costly, is required to restore it to the former level of acceptance.[12]

In Kenya a ban on fishery exports to Spain and Italy (in November 1996) resulted in a drop in foreign exchange earnings of 13.1 per cent, while exports to the European Union fell by 33 per cent and to Spain by 86 per cent from 1996 to 1997. To date, fish exports have not regained the pre-ban levels. In December 1997, an EU ban was imposed on imports of fresh fish from three Eastern African countries and Mozambique because of a cholera outbreak. Kenya considered this ban unfortunate, as it had already put in place curative and preventive measures before the imposition of the ban. The impact on Nile perch was even more significant, as the exports from Kenya to the EU dropped by 66 per cent with a decrease of 32 per cent in the value. A third ban on the import of fish products from Lake Victoria came into effect in April 1999, and this ban was lifted only in November 2000. The ban on fish exports from Uganda and Tanzania was lifted earlier, which Kenya found strange as the three countries share the same Lake Victoria.[13]

Paradoxically, the trade effect of the ban on the import of shrimps caught by fishing boats that did not use TEDs was positive for Costa Rica. Costa Rican exports filled market spaces left open in the USA by countries like Thailand. Costa Rica's market share increased from 10.2 per cent in 1995 to 11.8 per cent in 1996. Nevertheless, since then Central American exports have stagnated, probably owing to natural production limits and incipient aquaculture development.[14] This example, however, demonstrates that there will be winners and losers even among the developing countries.

Impacts on industry structure
The total effect of the EU standards is very difficult to gauge at this point in time. What appears likely is that small firms will become suppliers to large firms, which will then export their products. Thus, the market premium that the small producers were able to obtain before the EU ban would fall drastically. Large firms may break even in five to seven years, but small firms may go out of business. Larger establishments will be more likely to survive than smaller ones, not only because of economies of scale but also because of the infrastructure facilities and the space facilities that complying with such standards requires.

In all the countries studied in Africa, as well as in Costa Rica, most of the fishermen were artisan fishermen. This made investments as well as training difficult. Implementing the HACCP standard along the production chain has proved to be very difficult. In most countries surveyed, large firms were able to install HACCP standards whereas small firms had to enter into subcontracting relationships with large firms.

Around 80 per cent of the Costa Rican fishing fleet is categorized as 'crafty'. Many vessels are just light barges with no space for refrigerating or sewage facilities on board. Even if installations were possible from an engineering point of view, economically they are simply not feasible for most small fishermen. It is the same with collecting centres on the ports.[15] In 1995 there were 258 collecting centres. Presently, most of them do not have an HACCP plan and there is no possibility of applying one, owing to poor infrastructure.

Apart from this, testing facilities and procedures constitute an important shortcoming for the private sector. Presently, the national facilities for testing of heavy metals have equipment problems.[16] Tests for HACCP would cost US$52 000 a year for histamine tests alone, compared with the current US$500 a year – 14 times higher. This does not completely prevent product rejection at the US borders. In these kinds of cases, US authorities refused entry to fish lots. According to the import personnel, sampling and testing detected histamine presence. The Costa Rican company re-imported the container to Costa Rica where it underwent testing at private and public laboratories. Both results indicated no problem at all. This may have to do with the handling of the samples by US authorities. Sometimes samples are sent by mail systems to testing facilities. This mailing could be done under inappropriate temperature conditions, resulting in decay of a sample not representative of the whole lot quality.[17]

Policy responses to the standards
The Government of India, in an attempt to meet EU standards, issued an Order dated 21 August 1995, specifying elaborate process standards, arguing that 'it is necessary to maintain the highest quality standards as per the health requirements of the importing countries that would encompass the standards of directive No. 91/493/EEC'.

Following the EU ban on Indian fishery products, certain seafood processing plants and freezer vessels have been re-inspected and approved for exporting to the EU countries. Bangladesh, with technical assistance from the EU, has substantially upgraded its facilities and now has HACCP approval for a number of its plants.

Most African countries examined in this study have created a competent authority for fish inspection and the need to implement quality controls based on self-control systems, such as the HACCP, in the industry has resulted in the following, which will be positive for the economies in the long run:

- legalization of the activity of fish inspection;
- training and administrative organization at central and regional levels of the fish inspection services;
- establishment of laboratories;
- adaptation plans and development of quality based criteria for licensing.

Similarly, the study on Uganda points to a shift in the focus of the authorities as a result of the EU ban; the government solicited for support from UNIDO. The fish inspection services have been streamlined and the capacity of the competent authority strengthened. A fishery policy has been formulated and the inspectors trained. Fully equipped microbiological laboratories have been set up, as have monitoring programmes, and Ugandan consumers have benefited from a better sanitary system for fish harvesting and processing. All the other countries surveyed also pointed to these positive effects.

On the other hand, Costa Rican producers believe that they should comply with SPS regulations. They see no gain in opposing the SPS measures. Perhaps, rooted in this conviction is the fact that the Costa Rican strategy in all these cases has been non-confrontational.[18] Costa Rica did not even submit any claim as an interested third party in the WTO litigation process. Instead, the country embarked on a series of negotiation processes defined by:

- engagement in international negotiations with the issuing country, leading either to international agreements or to certifications programmes;
- enactment of national legislation;
- seeking approval by showing commitment to internationally accepted norms (for instance, the recent adoption of the FAO Code);
- seeking recognition of differing national circumstances that render US regulations inapplicable, by issuing scientific reports on the issues concerned (substantial equivalence).

Horticultural Products

Even though India is the largest mango producer with the largest number of varieties in the world, exports of mangoes and mango pulp have not really been significant. India is also very competitive in terms of the cost of production of mangoes; the major handicaps are the SPS measures.[19]

Kenyan fresh produce exporters are hit by the new European Union regulations on pesticide application, which should have come into force in July 2000 but were postponed for a year. By fixing the maximum residue levels at 'analytical' zero, the regulations require that there be no trace of pesticide residue on fruits, vegetables and cut flowers intended for the European markets.

Kenya's tropical climate demands the frequent application of pesticides that have, over the years, proved to be effective; but the European Union wants these to be discontinued. Kenyan producers fear that, owing to lack of experience and other factors, there may be wrong pesticide application by farmers, resulting in low quality crops. Unless Kenyan horticultural producers and exporters adapt rapidly to the new measures, forgo the use of certain banned pesticides and provide information about the pesticide used on the fresh produce that is being exported, they will lose their market share built up over the years.

Kenya is at a distinct disadvantage, for not only does it lack the technical, scientific and financial resources to challenge measures grounded on risk, but it is also a hostage to the measures imposed by its export markets for having complied with current measures at great cost. It may find itself incurring further capital expenditure and loss of trade because of the imposition of new measures based on different risk assessments.

Quality–price problems
In India the exporters of mango pulp have had fixed buyers for years. The buyers of Indian mango pulp have helped to sort out quality and other potential problems in the import markets, but at the same time have allegedly used quality requirements as an excuse to offer lower prices. The exporters claim that the quality issue becomes a major hurdle when buyers have excess stock or the prices of the goods have fallen below the agreed/contracted price in the international market. In such cases, sometimes the exporters have to accept price discounts, especially because of the perishable nature of the goods. The African exporters (e.g. Kenyan) of horticultural products claim that though there have been few rejections of products, they are often forced to accept unprofitable prices at the ports on account of problems with the quality of the goods. As these are perishable products, rather than risk a return of the goods, the producers feel compelled to accept price discounts.

Cost of compliance
Indian exporters also claim that vapour heat treatment of mangoes is very expensive. A lack of vapour heat treatment plants was a major constraint in exporting fresh mangoes to the European Union and the United States. Several facilities do not have the necessary infrastructure for this treatment and thus exports to the United States have not grown. The cost of labelling the product could be as high as 10 per cent of the total value added. The total testing costs could also be as high as 10–15 per cent of the total costs. The relative cost of inputs varies according to the harvest, being low in a year of good harvest and high in the case of a bad harvest. These cost differentials, which could be as high as 50 per cent, cannot be passed on to the consumer. The processing formalities after the shipment arrives at the ports are often long, leading to demurrage and loss.

The technology costs are high: the cost of an imported gas chromatograph for evaluating pesticide residues may be as much as 50 per cent of one consignment; the running costs may be an additional 2 per cent per consignment.

Some Indian exporters claim that there is a lack of clarity in the specification of SPS measures for mangoes. A major problem with respect to fruit exports is the lack of clarity in standards. For example, exports to Jordan require a certificate stating that the product (a) is not radioactive, (b) does not contain dioxins and (c) does not contain certain pesticide residues. However, buyers often do not provide detailed specifications about the pesticides that have to be checked for. Each pesticide may require a different testing method, which may be expensive to conduct; even documentation may cost as much as 1.5 per cent of the total value of the cargo.

For the horticultural industry in Kenya adherence to the new MRL requirements is the main concern. Compliance costs are high. European markets have favoured large producers and exporters, who are able to control their production practices, especially the interval between pesticide spraying and picking. Small firms, which are unable to access financial resources for the required changes to be made, risk closure of their operations. Small producers are also handicapped by the high cost of transportation, limited access to credit and technical information and lack of adequate agricultural policy. Despite SPS and environmental requirements, however, Kenya has become a large exporter of flowers to the European Union.

In Kenya the capital cost of the changeover from one type of pesticide already in use to another type, which may prove less effective or require more frequent application, or may prove in later years to be as toxic to the consumer, the operator or the environment, is an expense which only the large-scale producers will be able to incur. Inevitably, many producers unable to access additional resources will go out of business.

Additionally, farmers already face a particular problem reported widely in Kenya. Logistics, in particular airfreight for perishable products, can represent a major barrier to goods which might have met all necessary SPS measures relating to production but, through lack of resources, still might not comply with the required measures at all levels of the marketing chain.

While Kenya supports the overall objectives of the SPS measures and recognizes that they have long-term benefits, there is concern that the cost of compliance during the transitional period will be prohibitive.

Knowledge of SPS issues, both within the relevant government departments and in the horticultural supply chain, with few exceptions, is limited. Education and training, which are expensive, will have to be undertaken to ensure that all those involved, from the relevant minister down to the individual producers, 60 000 of whom are small-scale farmers in high-potential areas, are familiar with the SPS requirements of the importing countries and adhere to them to the letter, if wastage is to be avoided.

Policy responses

The responsibility for administering different Acts of Parliament governing the agricultural sector was fragmented in the past. In order to consolidate regulatory Acts and strengthen their enforcement mechanisms, the Kenya Plant Health Inspectorate Service (KEPHIS) was established. The KEPHIS monitors the government, business sector, scientists and farmers in all matters relating to quality control of agricultural inputs, produce and plant health. Institution building of this kind has often come in the wake of standards in the developing countries.

Another positive development has been the establishment of certification and testing agencies, often as a response to the fact that foreign certifiers are very expensive and eat up a sizeable proportion of the value added.

Tropical Beverages

This section explores the SPS problems faced by exporters of tropical beverages. In Sri Lanka problems in complying with SPS standards have been reported by the coffee growers, and the export of coffee has been steadily declining as the quality of the coffee is far below the required SPS standards in Europe, especially with respect to MRL. It is speculated that lack of quality production is the main reason for the declining trend. The prices obtained for Sri Lankan coffee are 41 per cent less than the average world market price for coffee, and the cocoa prices are 34 per cent lower.[20]

Cost of compliance

Coffee from Cuba has also been reported to contain over 3 ppb of toxic material. The EU is still in the process of formulating these standards but, when they come into force, they will affect more than 50 per cent of coffee exports from Cuba. The cost of sample analysis will be in the range of US$10 000 per sample of 5000 tonnes, plus there will be additional losses if the product is devalued owing to the detection of toxic matter in any of the lots going to the EU. Coping with these standards will entail very high costs for the economy.

In recent years, there have been growing reports of pesticide residues in Indian tea affecting its market access. For example, Germany complained about high residue levels of ethion in Darjeeling teas. There is only one institute, the Pesticide Residue Laboratory, which can test commercial samples of tea in India. Another problem is the cost factor. It is reported that the test required for clearing a consignment for Germany costs roughly US$234 per analysis. This is unaffordable, at least for the bulk tea exporters, who get a much lower price than specialized tea producers.

Positive effects and policy responses

The Tea Research Association of India now monitors pesticide residues. Exporters apply the ISO 3720 standard, which was developed by India and recognized by the ISO. The Indian standards are even more stringent than the ISO standards and the domestic standards of all other countries except Japan. The best tea is supplied to the UK and Japan, while lower quality tea goes to countries like Russia, Poland and Iran. The stricter EC standards apply to exports to the UK, while for Japan it is enough to get an EIC inspection done. Thus, this is one case where the standard-taker role was changed to a more proactive one of standard-setter.

Conclusions

Meeting SPS standards demands acquisition of technology, heavy investment, training of personnel and better management from the level of procurement of raw materials to packaging and selling. A few processing/manufacturing units follow good manufacturing practices (GMP) and a few are accredited to ISO 9000 and 14000 series.

The infrastructure for testing and certification available in the countries studied by this project is insufficient to meet their needs. Apart from the laboratories of the Directorate of Marketing and Inspection, the Export Inspection Agency and the Commodity Boards/Export Promotion Councils, there are only a few laboratories in the private sector which can undertake analytical work, including risk assessments. Some manufacturing/processing units have developed their own in-house laboratories for quality evaluation. The cost of certification, especially inspection and testing, is beyond the reach of small and medium enterprises. Almost all producers have also reported a lower price realization, primarily due to poor standards. Capacity problems, especially the lack of technology and finance, have been found to be important bottlenecks.

Lack of clarity and transparency in the implementation of standards has been found to be a major problem. What is most distressing to producers is that compliance with SPS standards does not ensure better price realization. In fact, since the markets are commodity markets, they are driven by supply and demand factors rather than quality. Thus, meeting SPS and environmental requirements is a minimum condition for market access, but not a sufficient condition for earning higher prices.

ARE ENVIRONMENTAL AND HEALTH STANDARDS PROTECTIONIST?

In the studies conducted by this project the view has frequently been expressed that certain SPS standards may be protectionist. This chapter examines the views and the evidence, as well as the arguments, expressed by the consultants in examining these standards. It looks at the various product groups which have been examined by this project, as cross comparison of countries with varied experiences in the same product groups can yield valuable results.

Marine Products

According to the Costa Rican study on the US ban on import of shrimps harvested without the use of TEDs,

[s]ome might argue that this is a case of 'green protectionism' (that is, using an environmental measure to protect a domestic industry). However, given the fact that this measure left imports of shrimps from aquaculture, non-sea turtle areas and non-trawler areas unimpeded, the US shrimp fishing industry still faced ample competition. Thus, the claim that this is a case of 'green protectionism' is probably erroneous.[21]

According to the Costa Rican study, this statement is not completely accurate. It is true that aquaculture shrimp, non-sea turtle areas and non-trawler areas were unrestrained. It is also true that some big exporters like Ecuador (19 per cent of the US market in 1995) produced shrimps mostly through aquaculture techniques.[22] Nonetheless, at the time it was estimated that as much as 30 per cent of US shrimp imports were going to be affected by the restriction.[23] If one takes into account that US fishing vessels only supply a third of the shrimp consumed in that country,[24] a potential 30 per cent reduction in import competition is not negligible. Hundreds of millions of dollars' worth of imported shrimps were denied market access, and were replaced by shrimps farmed by US trawlers, which would in effect have been more destructive for the environment.[25]

It is also felt that inflexible compliance procedures may seek to protect the domestic certification industry. Obviously, if standards increase, direct or indirect conformity assessment procedures to determine that relevant requirements are fulfilled will also multiply. According to a study carried out in the United States, the activities of testing laboratories that carry out conformity assessment evaluation in that country have been expanding by 13.5 per cent a year.[26] The study claims that standards are often tied to specific conformity assessment procedures for this very reason, and their effectiveness in achieving the relevant objectives, environmental or otherwise, may be of questionable value.

The African countries also claimed that a European Union ban on fishery products, following the outbreak of cholera in some African countries, was continued despite insufficient scientific evidence. The WHO intervened to have the ban (1998) lifted. The WHO explained that, despite the fact that 50 countries had been affected by cholera since 1961, there had been no documentation of any outbreak of cholera from commercially imported food.[27] Similarly, the FAO noted that cholera bacteria do not survive proper cooking and drying, and thus cooked, dried or canned products are safe and do not transmit cholera.[28]

The countries further claim that, at this point in time, an amendment to the health certification was the only mandatory requirement of the EU. This could have been put in place within days after the EU raised the cholera scare. It would have been less onerous than the ban.

In the case of horticulture, the Commission Decision 98/116/EC of 4 February 1998 adopted special measures for the import of fruit and vegetables from Uganda, Kenya, the United Republic of Tanzania and Mozambique. The Commission argued that the infectious agent, *Vibrio cholerae,* survives on foodstuffs imported from these countries. As a preliminary precaution, the European Union ruled that samples of these foodstuffs (covering at least ten per cent of the consignments) should be subject to microbiological controls. However, the World Health Organization (WHO) advised that, where the time taken to transport fruits and vegetables from areas where cholera is present is in excess of ten days, the risk to health from these products is low, and so the measures applied mainly to products transported into the European Community by air. These measures were repealed by the Commission Decision 98/719/EC of 8 December 1998, *inter alia*, because the Scientific Committee for Food opined that humans who live in non-cholera regions face a very low risk of developing the disease from exposure to *Vibrio cholerae* present in fruit and vegetables imported from areas where cholera is at endemic or epidemic levels. In addition, sampling of 10 per cent of the consignments of fruit and vegetables from Uganda, Kenya, the United Republic of Tanzania and Mozambique at the point of entry into the Community had revealed very low incidence of contamination with *Vibrio cholerae.*

Aflatoxin Contamination

Indian producers have perceived the stringency of aflatoxin standards, as well as prescribed testing methods (known as the Dutch code), as unjustified. This raises questions about the appropriate use of risk management. The main objections raised are:

- Standards set are hypothetical and unreal, as they are not backed by supporting scientific evidence (to save two in a billion).
- Lack of mutual recognition of inspections and standards and lack of involvement of developing countries in the standard-setting process.
- No rationality of the sampling size and testing procedures/methods adopted. The lower the sample size, the greater is the risk of rejection of good lots.
- Lack of financial and technical resources to implement stringent require- ments is the biggest obstacle for India.

India has, on an experimental basis and with the help of UNDP, produced aflatoxin-free peanuts. However, it does not get even a five per cent premium at the producer end as buyers prefer to buy aflatoxin-containing peanuts and process them in Europe for sale at much higher prices. As substantial amounts of aflatoxin can be removed through processing, the standards for raw products are much lower than those for table-ready products. The exporters have complained that these standards, therefore, prevent them from obtaining higher value and are purely protectionist, intended to protect the processing industry in the EU. The intent is to pay as low prices as possible for raw products on account of quality standards and not pay higher prices for higher quality products.

In the case of rice as well, Indian producers have complained that aflatoxin standards serve protectionist purposes. In the first six months of 2000, roughly 22 consignments of basmati and non-basmati rice to the United States were rejected on the grounds that they were filthy and contained 'foreign' matter. Pesticide residues are a major problem for exports to the EU and Japan, and some problems relating to aflatoxins in rice have also been reported.

Basmati or premium grade rice faced more severe problems than non-basmati rice.[29] Exporters believed that the USFDA standards and the relative stringency of the basmati rice standards were primarily on account of protection provided to domestic producers in the United States.

Producers also reported that just removing foreign matter as well as pesticide residues would increase costs by 8–10 per cent, which would be unacceptable to the US and EU markets. There is an average of three to six months' delay in clearing rice consignments, which would thus incur very high interest costs. The price reduction after this delay may be about 5 per cent of the total consignment. Thus, the incentive to export rice to the United States is very low.

Perceived Lack of Coherence Between Standards

There is a significant difference between international standards and domestic standards in some countries within the same region. For example, the standard for tea, which is an infusion, and spices, which are consumed in minuscule quantities, tend to have the same MRL. Given that the intake per dish or per serving is unlikely to be the same, many researchers interviewed in the course of this project have deemed such standards inappropriate.

The standard-setting processes also differ between the EU countries. The British standards for tea are not the same as those applicable in Germany and vice versa. British familiarity with the production conditions of tea has led to a standard-setting process which is different from that of Germany. Often this is also interpreted as being protectionist, as there may be little justification for the divergence of standards between countries.

POTENTIAL PROBLEMS RELATED TO STANDARD SETTING AND IMPLEMENTATION

Lack of Transparency

The lack of transparency in implementing SPS measures has affected exports of spices from India. For instance, Spain detained some consignments of chilli exported from India without specifying the exact limit value for determining contamination by aflatoxin. There is no common regulation in the EU laying down uniform standards and codes of practice for imports. Consequently, there is no fixed permitted level of aflatoxin or pesticide residues. This wide variation in the standards adversely affects the export of spices from India. Another case in point is the export of meat to the EU. Although India has been free from rinderpest since 1995, the EU has its reservations. Similarly, despite India being the largest producer of milk, exports of milk to the EU are not permitted, as Indian cows are not mechanically milked. Exports of shrimp to the EU by India were also thwarted on the grounds of SPS standards not being met. Interestingly, shrimps continued to be exported to the United States throughout the ban imposed by the European Union.[30]

Checking on standards may be further complicated because there is no focal point from where information on the standards can be obtained. Sources from the MAG in Costa Rica indicated that the protocols on HACCP for the poultry sector were submitted to the US authorities in 1998, while others said that they were sent in the first months of the year 2000. In the end, it was found that official communication of the remittance was sent from Costa Rica on 18 December 2000, and that the first protocol was submitted on 16 June 2000.[31] Delays in accreditation of Costa Rica for HACCP could have been due to the time that it took the importing countries' authorities to submit the protocols. But Costa Rican producers and national authorities insist that the problem arose because each time they complied with a requirement a new one came up, and delays came from new requests for information and criteria for inspections that were not contemplated before.

Good quality products from a national processing company were rejected. According to import personnel, sampling and testing detected histamine presence. The Costa Rican company re-imported the container to Costa Rica, where it underwent testing at private and public laboratories. Both results indicated no problem at all. This may have to do with the handling of the samples by the US authorities. Sometimes samples are sent by mail systems to testing facilities. This mailing could be done under inappropriate temperature conditions, resulting in decay of a sample, which is not representative of the quality of the entire consignment.

Furthermore, there might be different testing procedures. The EU calls for national analysis protocols equivalent to those mandated by the EC directives. Of course, this presupposes knowledge by Costa Rican authorities of the current procedures used in the EU. In that case, they could assess whether the national protocols comply with the EU level of protection. On their visits, the EU inspectors have offered exchange opportunities for Costa Rican laboratory technicians so that they can get acquainted with the procedures in European laboratories. Yet it is alleged that this offer never crystallizes into concrete actions.

The transparency of the standard is impossible when standards are ill defined, the requirements associated with them have yet to be clarified, and the goalposts shift continually. For example, in Kenya smallholders suffer from limited access to technical information that is often tied to contracts with particular exporters or embodied in costly, often expatriate, consultants. The majority of small producers only learn of the standards through a process of trial and error.

Complexity of SPS Standards

Almost all the countries examined by this project found certain regulations unnecessarily complex, irrelevant to the production conditions of the exporting countries and excessively expensive to implement. The African countries studied by this project claimed that certain measures were initiated by Spain and Italy in the first instance and then extended at their insistence to the rest of Europe. As Spain and Italy are large fish producers, the African countries studied by this project did claim that the measures were perhaps used to protect Spanish and Italian fish markets.[32]

In response to the EC requirements, the African countries studied by this project said that setting up a competent authority to guarantee the effective implementation of the relevant legislation and its subsequent inspection by the EC took over two years for most of them, leading to a substantial loss of export income and even changes in tastes for a particular kind of fish. Recovering lost markets has taken a long time and the pre-ban level of exports has yet to be reached in most African countries.

The case of aflatoxin standards illustrates the increasing stringency of SPS measures and the complexity of testing methods.[33] In the aflatoxin case, slight differences in sampling methods cause a disproportionate risk of rejection, as illustrated in the case of Indian peanuts. Similarly, in the case of honey, the measurement of standards on the MRL in Cuba has proved an impossible task, owing to the complexity of the technology and testing methods.[34] Risk assessment methodologies are also getting increasingly complicated and cases of conflict of scientific data have yet to be resolved by WTO panels or otherwise.

Another issue that demonstrates the complexity of health standards is a kind of 'standards escalation' (similar to tariff escalation), which can be observed in some cases. The standards for raw peanuts tend to be less stringent than the standards for table-ready peanuts.[35]

The procedural requirements often added to difficulties in implementing standards. These requirements could discourage countries from selling to OECD markets. Many countries may prefer neighbouring and less stringent markets. For example, one of the fundamental requirements necessary to export poultry products to the USA, for example, is for a country to be declared Newcastle disease-free.[36] It took Costa Rica five years to be declared Newcastle disease-free. The process involved a series of joint and individual efforts among representatives from the entrepreneurial sectors and from the corresponding governmental institutions, the Ministry of Agriculture and Livestock (MAG) in Costa Rica and the United States Department of Agriculture (USDA) through its Animal and Plant Health Inspection Service (APHIS). The declaration enabled Costa Rica to enter the list of countries eligible to export live birds, poultry meat and by-products to the USA.[37]

Threshold Limits

Consumer movements, environment protection agencies and food safety enforcement agencies are prescribing increasingly strict standards for macro-cleanliness, microbial loads, aflatoxin and pesticide residues. Many exporters have questioned the threshold limits. For instance, Japan insists on a DDT residue level of 0.4 ppm on non-manufactured tobacco, while the international standard is as high as 6 ppm. Indian tobacco has a DDT residue level of 1–2 ppm, which is within the limits prescribed by the international standards, but Japan does not allow the import of non-manufactured tobacco on phytosanitary grounds because India cannot meet the standard.

Another example is that of spices. The issue of the permissible average daily intake of certain chemicals and chemical compounds is before the Pesticide Residue Committee of the Codex Alimentarius Commission. The argument is that spices constitute a very minuscule portion of dishes/servings of food and therefore the maximum residue limits fixed for directly consumed agricultural products cannot be applied to spices. The same is true of other sectors, too, and this logic has already been applied in the case of Indian tea. However, the standards set by the Codex have not changed.

Similarly, Kenya reports that producers of fresh products have to comply with a new law on the MRL. By fixing the MRL at 'analytical' zero, the new regulations require that there be no trace of pesticide residue on fruits, vegetables and cut flowers intended for European markets. Kenya's tropical climate demands the use of frequent applications of pesticides. Thus, compliance with this standard may be difficult in Kenya.[38]

Other studies besides those conducted under this project have shown similar results. Another study from Cuba (conducted under a DFID project) showed that the MRL limits for honey were so low that it was impossible for the instruments in Havana to check them. The testing of these limits was carried out in Germany and the cost involved was very high. However, Cuba does not have the resources for installing such sophisticated equipment in the near future and fears that it may have to continue to send its honey to Germany for testing.

The US standard on TEDs prescribed the specific size of the TED acceptable to the US authorities. As specified earlier, this did not suit Costa Rican fishing conditions:

> [I]n the white shrimp fisheries of Costa Rica the amount of logs and debris inhibit proper TED function and may cause significant shrimp and fish loss up to 37.73 and 43 per cent respectively. Bottom shooting 8 inch Seymour TEDs with enlarged escape holes apparently improve performance recording losses between 4 and 12 per cent in shrimp catch. The continuation of research into performance of Super Shooter and Seymour TEDs with 6 and 8 inch bar spacing is necessary to advise the Costa Rican shrimping industry on models and modifications that suit the industry best, without endangering the sea turtles.[39]

Standard-takers instead of Standard-setters

In fact, developing countries tend to be 'standard-takers' rather than 'standard-setters'.[40] This situation is explained by variables that tend to influence the pattern of standard development in different economic sectors:

* industry size and concentration;
* dominance of specific suppliers or buyers;
* level and speed of technological advancement;
* public interest in safety, health and environmental protection.

One of the problems of developing countries in participating in international standard-setting mechanisms is the cost involved, as well as the lack of technical expertise, in developing basic information and studies to support their arguments in international bodies.

Participating in international standard-setting processes requires a better understanding of the role of the Codex Alimentarius Commission (CAC), upgrading of production and post-harvest technologies and keeping in mind the food safety standards that prevail at the global level. This requires not only large investments, but also education among producers, processors and exporters, and it will be a long-drawn-out effort for South Asia. Technically, South Asian countries may ask for a longer period for implementation, but this is unlikely to yield trade benefits. A better option would be to build capacity and ask for technologies at concessional rates to help achieve these standards as soon as possible.

Case studies conducted in Brazil, Indonesia and Germany by other organizations for similar products have also shown that standards are not easily transferable from one country to another, given the differences in terms of climate and population density, as well as differences in the degree of scarcity of environmental goods. This is especially true for standards referring to buildings (number of windows in the broiler house, explosion control in oilseed processing, and so on) or to the use of certain pesticides (different effects in tropical or non-tropical environments).[41]

The study of poultry in Costa Rica illustrates a particular problem which arises from this phenomenon. Costa Rican consumers of poultry have a distinct preference for chicken legs, whereas consumers in the USA have a distinct preference for chicken breasts. While Costa Rica is competitive in the production of the whole chicken, it cannot compete with American prices for chicken legs. Given the comparative advantage structure, it would make sense for Costa Rica to import chicken legs and export chicken breasts. However, while US imports would be permitted into Costa Rica, the export of Costa Rican chicken breasts to the United States would be extremely difficult because of the stringent SPS measures. Thus, distortions in comparative advantage would result, because Costa Rica is a standard-taker instead of a standard-setter.

The different bargaining positions of the standard-takers and the standard-setters is clearly highlighted in the case of Darjeeling tea. When faced with onerous standards of the MRL in German markets, the industry, which controls roughly 30 per cent of the tea markets, united to set an SPS standard, which was recognized under the ISO. This standard gave it a strong bargaining position for a long time and fostered the ability of the industry to sell directly to the buyers.

An extreme case of being on the receiving end as a standard-taker can be seen in the case of mango pulp exporters from India and Pakistan. In years of excess stocks, standards have been found to be more stringent than when stocks are low.

In most cases, African producers have found that their products have not been rejected on account of lower standards. However, they have been subjected to different price discounts on the grounds that their products do not meet standards. This is perhaps the most common experience of the countries examined by this project, owing to the fact that these countries are standard-takers rather than standard-setters.

Relevance of the Standards to the Production Conditions of the Exporting Countries

Standards may be inappropriate to the production conditions of the exporting countries; for example, the legislation regarding the ban on shrimps that had been harvested by trawlers which did not use the turtle excluder device. On 25 November 1996 the CIT clarified that shrimp harvested by manual methods that did not harm sea turtles, by aquaculture and in cold water, could continue to be imported from non-certified countries.[42] The 1996 guidelines provided that certification could be granted by 1 May 1996, and annually thereafter, to harvesting countries other than those where turtles do not occur or that exclusively use means that do not pose a threat to sea turtles

> only if the government of [each of those countries] has provided documentary evidence of the adoption of a regulatory program governing the incidental taking of sea turtles in the course of commercial shrimp trawl harvesting that is comparable to that of the United States and if the average take rate of that incidental taking by vessels of the harvesting nation is comparable to the average rate of incidental taking of sea turtles by United States vessels in the course of such harvesting.

Thus, while the regulation allowed enough leeway for the adoption of suitable regulatory programmes, in practice it meant the implementation of the US government guideline that TEDs had to be used.

The size of the TED specified by the United States was inappropriate for Costa Rica (p. 193). After protracted negotiations the United States agreed to make changes in its size.[43] The fishermen were reluctant to use the TEDs, which made enforcement even more difficult. On the basis of their experience in the Gulf of Mexico, the United States set the bar spacing at 10 centimetres as the prescribed width of the TED. As opposed to the Gulf of Mexico, the Costa Rican shoreline receives water from short but highly torrential rivers. Therefore, there is an enormous amount of organic material carried by the rivers to the shoreline where shrimp fishing takes place. This is especially true in the rainy season (two thirds of the year). Accordingly there are considerable amounts of organic waste in the seabed. This is not the case in the Gulf of Mexico, North Carolina, Texas or the Gulf of Maine, the areas where shrimp fishing is normally done in the United States.

Imported from the USA at a cost of $300 each,[44] 4-inch (10-cm) TEDs were constantly obstructed by organic waste. Hence, the TEDs provoked economic losses and did not help the turtles, which could not escape since the escape gate got blocked. This resulted in economic losses. First of all, jammed TEDs required more engine power in trawling, which translated into increased fuel costs. But, most important, it was estimated that of the total catch 70 per cent was waste and only 30 per cent was shrimp.[45] This made shrimp fishers unwilling to use the TEDs.

Similarly, the EU standard on fisheries stipulated the number and size of toilets, and required that floors and ceilings of the facilities be washed with potable water. In the district of Cochin in the state of Kerala, this was considered excessive in view of water shortages and the fact that a large percentage of the population did not get enough potable water to drink.

Domestic Regulatory Problems

South Asian countries particularly identified domestic regulatory problems as an important constraint in improving standards. Quarantine regulations have indirectly constrained Sri Lanka's potential exports. It is unable to access improved varieties of seeds and plants, resulting in the inability to meet international market requirements. This has particularly inhibited the development of Sri Lanka's ornamental flower export industry.

Even if there are domestic regulations, they are difficult to enforce. For example, a 1948 law prohibits the killing of turtles and commercial sale of their eggs in Costa Rica.[46] It is also a signatory of international conventions dealing with this species, for instance, the 1973 Convention on International Trade in Endangered Species of Wild Fauna and Flora (CITES).[47] The CITES recognizes all seven species of marine turtles as threatened with extinction and lists these species in Appendix I.

The local regulatory body in Costa Rica, INCOPESCA, however, has admitted major enforcement problems due to lack of resources and low pay scales of the inspection personnel. The number of inspections has currently declined because of the lack of appropriate boats.

The current legal framework, especially that of land tenure, and the taxation policy do not enable Tanzanians to fully exploit the production and marketing opportunities created by the emerging free market environment. They are particularly regressive for agricultural investment. Moreover, liberalization, according to the study, has reduced the bargaining power of farmers who earlier belonged to cooperatives.

The enforcement of SPS measures requires a mix of instruments such as conformity certificates, inspections, quarantine requirements and import bans. The United Republic of Tanzania developed an Act in 1997, which is based on the standards developed under the International Plant Protection Convention. The IPPC has now been modified to suit the WTO Agreement. However, the United Republic of Tanzania still needs assistance to develop sanitary policy and legislation and capacity building to enforce this legislation.

Other Capacity Problems

There are several infrastructure and resource related problems in South Asia which have inhibited compliance with SPS and environmental standards. For example, even though India accounts for almost 60 per cent of the global mango production, it cannot export mangoes to the United States, as this country demands vaporized heat treatment of mangoes, facilities for which did not exist in India until recently. Its grape exports were often rejected owing to high pesticide residues. Even egg powder exports suffer because of pesticide residues, which are supposed to have travelled through maize feed. Peanut exports in 1999 are said to have suffered immensely, compared with 1998, primarily owing to high degrees of aflatoxin (Gulati, 2001).[48] All these problems could have been eliminated with better testing equipment and facilities.

Similarly Uganda's competent authority notified the EU in April 1999 that it could not guarantee the safety of the fish. The EU demanded a comprehensive monitoring programme, which would determine levels of organochlorine pesticides, organophosphate pesticides and sediments from the lake. Uganda lacked such testing facilities and the Government Chemist and Makerere University laboratories were unequipped to test for pesticides and heavy metals in fish, water and sediments. It took about one and a half years for Uganda to install all the necessary authorities as well as graduate to Part I, which qualifies it to export as a third country to the EU.

In the case of Nepal, adherence to SPS measures is complicated by problems of inadequacy of human resources, insufficient laboratories and inspection services, lack of expertise in risk analysis and lack of harmonization of the legislative framework. This is further compounded by a preponderance of small and scattered food enterprises, insufficient supply of quality inputs such as fertilizers and chemicals, and lack of financial resources to effectively participate in Codex meetings.[49]

Pakistan's exports of vegetables and fruits have suffered because of the country's limited ability to enforce the SPS standards. Import of fruits and vegetables by European countries, North America, Japan and China had remained low, both in the pre- and post-Uruguay Round period. It was anticipated that the complete integration of agriculture into the WTO would open avenues for exports, but stringent standards of human, animal and plant health safety and strict methods of inspection have been major handicaps to expanding exports.[50] Financial as well as technical constraints are viewed as the most important handicaps in implementing the SPS standards.

In the United Republic of Tanzania, poor rural roads limit farmers' access to markets for inputs and produce. They also increase the time between harvesting and sale, thus leading to a further deterioration in the quality of the produce. Post-harvest losses are estimated at between 30 and 40 per cent of the produce. The absence of communications in rural areas is a serious constraint on the dissemination of knowledge and market information, both of which are vital to the survival of farmers in a free market economy. Lack of infrastructure also means that only four per cent of the available fruits and vegetables are processed. Weak research-extension–farmer linkages have limited the diffusion of research results and restricted the researchers' ability to diagnose and respond to the farmers' real problems. The main capacity problems highlighted by Tanzania are the following:

- inadequate post-harvest facilities;
- poor quality of the locally manufactured packing materials;
- inadequate access to financial institutions;
- high tariff charges for power, which make it difficult to use several calibration instruments.

In Mozambique, 90 per cent of fishery products for export are accounted for by only three large companies with foreign capital and experience of fishery management, including quality control and compliance with the regulatory requirements of the international markets, in particular the application of the HACCP system. Even these companies, however, face certain problems in complying with all the requirements.[51] Smaller companies face even greater problems. In 1997, after the Marine Fishery Regulation came into force, all the vessels had to apply for approval of their sanitary conditions and their hygiene plans to be able to operate. Of the approximately fifty establishments used for exports, only six had rehabilitation plans for setting up a system of self-control for quality and only those have been approved to export to the European Union.[52]

The burden of translating the standards-related documents into local languages and spreading information on what exactly the standard would entail falls on the poorly funded agriculture extension services of developing countries. For example, in Tanzania, though agricultural exports contribute about 56.3 per cent of the total export earnings, their share of the total expenditure by the government is less than 3 per cent.

CONCLUSION

To conclude, almost all the countries and the regions examined by the project have indicated that standards were not implemented transparently, were complex in nature and that their own capacity problems made it difficult for them to implement SPS and environmental standards.

In most cases, producers are suspicious of stringent SPS standards, especially as they cause trade disruptions and may make their products uncompetitive. In their view, protection of markets does not take place merely for goods which are produced domestically in the developed countries. Protectionism is also manifested in the fact that importing countries may discourage value addition in the exporting countries through the use of the SPS standards. This helps them to protect their jobs and enterprises. Producers also feel that stringent standards are a way of protecting retail margins while bidding down producer prices.

In fact, the studies show that despite trade preferences under the ACP and now the EBA, East African countries encounter substantial market access problems on account of SPS standards. Thus they feel that this is a new form of protectionism.

NOTES

1. See generally National Research Council, *Standards, Conformity Assessment, and Trade*, Washington DC, National Academy Press, 1995.
2. See Jha, V., *Economic Times*, November 2001.
3. Ashok Jha, Proceedings of the Conference on 'South Asia Workshop on Agriculture, SPS and the Environment: Capturing the Benefits for South Asia', New Delhi, 11–13 January 2001.
4. Gitli, Eduardo, 'Costa Rican and Central American Capacity to Respond to Health, Sanitary and Environmental Requirements', paper prepared for this project.
5. Búcaro, Jorge Mario (1998), *La Avicultura Centroamericana: Desarrollo y Modernidad*, Federación de Centroamerica y del Caribe (FEDAVICAC), Guatemala, November.
6. Karki, Tika, 'Issues on SPS and Food Standards for Nepal', paper presented at the UNCTAD/World Bank workshop on 'A New WTO Round – Agriculture, SPS and the Environment – Capturing the Benefits for South Asia', 11–13 January 2001, New Delhi.
7. The study on marine products draws upon an exhaustive survey done by Atul Kaushik and Mohammed Saqib for UNCTAD under project IND/97/955.
8. India's marine exports attract automatic detention in the United States. Automatic detention means the product must be sampled and tested before it gains entry into the country, which means delays, storage costs and maybe a substantial part of the United States rate. According to some estimates at present the value of detained fishery products in the USA is valued at US$14 million (or 15 per cent) out of total exports of US$108.2 million to the country in 1996–97 (Chemonics–ACE Project, 1998, ibid.).
9. Seafood Association of India.
10. EU Ban on Shrimp Imports from Bangladesh: A Case Study on Market Access Problems Faced by the LDCs', by Professor Mustafijur Rahman, presented at the CUTS Seminar on SPS Standards and Trade, April 2001.
11. As of 16 June 2001, there were 33 processing facilities with permission to export to the EU and the USA.
12. Nimrod Waniala, 'Impact of SPS Measures on Uganda Fish Exports', paper prepared for the project.
13. Halima Noor, 'Sanitary and Phytosanitary Measures and their Impact on Kenya', paper prepared under this project.
14. Valverde, Max, 'SPS and Environmental Barriers to Trade in Fisheries from Central America', paper prepared for the project.
15. These centres buy and collect fish from fishers for later commercialization to processing plants.
16. 20 June 2001 interview with Silvia Murillo, Laboratory Technician of the Official Fish Testing Facility, Ministry of Agriculture.

17. Valverde, Max, op.cit.
18. This is not a general rule in Costa Rican trade policy. For instance, in 1996 Costa Rica was the first WTO member to request the establishment of a panel to demand the removal of a US safeguard measure conditioning access of cotton underwear manufactured in the country. The panel ruled that the US quotas breached the Agreement on Textiles. See Costa Rica, *Examen de las Políticas Comerciales, Informe del Gobierno*, World Trade Organization, 9 April 2000.
19. Primary research with questionnaires was carried out for 30 mango pulp exporting firms in the context of this project. The author is grateful for the research assistance provided by Ms Shilpi Kapoor for this survey.
20. Herath, A., *A Study of Compliance of Sanitary and Phytosanitary Requirements in Beverages and Spices in Sri Lanka*, Economics Research Unit, Department of Export Agriculture, Sri Lanka, 2000.
21. See http://www.foei.org/activist_guide/tradeweb/turtle.htm, Friends of the Earth.
22. Aquaculture provides 90 per cent of Ecuadorian shrimp exports. See Skou, Lene, 'Rules to protect sea turtles could block shrimp imports', *Journal of Commerce*, 30 April 1996, p. 4.
23. Ibid.
24. See Samocha, Tzachi, 'More seafood, please', *Journal of the American Society of Agricultural Engineers Review*, **6** (4), April 1999, pp. 11–12.
25. See Skou, Lene, op. cit., p. 4.
26. See generally National Research Council, *Standards, Conformity Assessment, and Trade*, Washington DC, National Academy Press, 1995.
27. Noor, Halima, 'Sanitary and Phytosanitary Measures and their Impact on Kenya', http://r0unctad.org/trade_env/test1/meetings/standards/kenya3doc.
28. Press release 98/21, www.fao.org
29. Primary information was collected from approximately 20–25 rice-exporting firms. The author gratefully acknowledges the research assistance provided by Mr Chandrasekhar for this survey.
30. Paper presented by Mr Ashok Jha at the Workshop on 'A New WTO Round – Agriculture, SPS and the Environment – Capturing the Benefits for South Asia', New Delhi, 11–13 January 2001.
31. Specifically, on 18 December, the following formularies were submitted: *Regulations for Meat and Poultry Products Inspection, Slaughter/Processing, Compulsoriness Questionnaire, Health Questionnaire, Animal Disease Questionnaire*. In turn, the questionnaire *Criteria for Assessing the Adequacy of the Residue Control Program* was submitted on 16 June 2000.
32. Noor, Halima, 'Sanitary and Phytosanitary measures and their impact on Kenya', paper presented at the African Workshop on Standards and Trade, 13 September 2001, http://r0.unctad.org/trade_env/test1/meetings/standards/kenya3.doc.
33. See Tsunehiro Otsukti et al. See also *Saving Two in a Billion*. Veena Jha, paper presented in the second workshop organized under the project Strengthening Research and Policy Capacities in Trade and Environment in Developing Countries, Havana, May 2000. Also see below the case of peanuts in Chapter 3.
34. Study presented by Cuba to the DFID project.
35. Basu, 'Issues on SPS and Environmental Standards for India – the case of aflatoxin in peanuts', paper presented at the South Asian workshop.
36. The Newcastle Commission was created (Executive Decree 2005-MAG) on 2 July 1991. However, until 6 April 1996, Costa Rica was not officially declared Newcastle disease-free. However, according to personal communications from the Costa Rican Chamber of Poultry Producers, the process actually lasted for 8 years, starting from the moment when national endeavours began, requiring a lengthy preparation stage before the Newcastle Commission was legally established.
37. By the year 2000, the countries declared Newcastle disease-free by the USDA were Australia, Canada, Chile, Costa Rica, Denmark, Fiji, Finland, France, Great Britain (England, the Isle of Man, Scotland and Wales), Greece, Ireland, Luxembourg, New Zealand, Spain, Sweden and Switzerland (Code of Federal Regulations 9CFR94.6).

38. Noor, Halima, op.cit.
39. Ibid.
40. CTE report
41. Grote, Ulrike, ZEF, Bonn, 2001, 'Analysis of Cost Implications of Environmental Standards in Brazil, Indonesia and Germany', unpublished paper.
42. See *Earth Island Institute* v *Warren Christopher*, 948 Fed. Supp. 1062 (CIT 1996).
43. Study on fisheries.
44. 20 June 2001 phone interview with Javier Catón, Puntarenas Fishermen Chamber President. TEDs imported from the USA are aluminium made. Yet Mr. Catón mentions that they have little durability, so some fishermen are building their own TEDs with galvanized iron, in which case the cost decreases. However, see Chapter 4, note 32
45. Ibid.
46. See Article 28 of the Fish and Marine Hunting Law No. 190, 1948.
47. Adopted on 3 March 1973 and entered into force on 1 July 1975, with 152 parties as of 15 May 2001. Appendix I includes all species threatened with extinction which are or may be affected by trade. Trade in these species is subject to strict regulation through both import and export permits. See www.cites.org.
48. Gulati, A., paper prepared for the World Bank–UNCTAD Seminar, 11–13 January 2001.
49. Karki, Tika, 2001, 'Issues on SPS and Food Standards for Nepal'.
50. Qureshi, S., paper presented on Pakistan at the workshop on 'A New WTO Round – Agriculture, SPS and the Environment – Capturing the Benefits for South Asia', New Delhi, 11–13 January 2001.
51. Fish Inspection Department, 'Mozambique HACCP Experience', submitted to the workshop in Kampala.
52. Ibid.

8. Ways Forward[1]

Veena Jha

To address the constraints described in the earlier chapters, and on the basis of the findings of the project on Capacity Building for Diversification and Commodity-based Development, a number of policy initiatives can be formulated and implemented. The main challenges that have emerged at the national and regional levels deal with capacity constraints. At the multilateral level, several questions have been raised about standard-setting processes and trade rules. This chapter, therefore, first examines policy responses to capacity problems at the national and regional levels and the initiatives required to deal with the standard-setting processes at the multilateral level. The Doha Declaration, recognizing the importance of complying with these standards, has repeatedly emphasized the technical assistance required in meeting them.

NATIONAL LEVEL

At the national level, a lot of effort has already gone into building infrastructure and disseminating information to improve the safety of specific food sectors in all countries. Export development organizations have already started working towards evolving standards for the quality of foods which are necessary for trade promotion in the export market.[2] However, national awareness of the necessity of food safety is yet to be developed in every area of the food growing and processing chain.

Awareness Raising

- An awareness programme on food, covering all sectors of food and food-related industries, should be implemented nationally.[3]
- Growers' awareness of methods of lowering costs and raising quality should be increased.[4]
- State assistance should be provided at central collection and processing points to maintain the homogeneity of quality. Governments should establish National Enquiry Points facilitating the flow of timely and reliable information on SPS.

- Developing countries should take advantage of private options such as the actions of the Centre for the Promotion of Exports from Developing Countries, located in major developed countries.[5]

Training

- National training programmes, benefiting technical personnel working in different laboratories, both private and government, need to be established, mainly to educate them on various analytical methods and the use of new equipment. This is possible with the establishment of national training centres.
- R&D for better use of solar energy in drying agricultural products, for example, needs to be stepped up. This would avoid the use of harmful chemicals which leave traces in the process of drying. South–south cooperation on R&D would be particularly beneficial, as it would provide useful opportunities to exchange information on methods that help in meeting SPS standards in tropical conditions.
- Regional training programmes could also provide multiple benefits. Regional cooperation offers better understanding of the problems in ensuring food safety and can provide solutions that need not always be based on complete science but can rely on traditional methods.

National and Regional Standard-setting

National

- A comprehensive food safety rule should be formulated that will cover all food and food related activities.
- The establishment of special task forces for specific sectors could be contemplated.
- National standards, based on the recommendation of the National Codex Committee, must be developed.
- Provisions may be given in the rule for periodic revision of standards based on changes in the business environment and overall concerns about food safety.
- Countries foreseeing the enactment of technical standards should rapidly adapt their national legislation to the requirements of the external markets, if such standards are considered reasonable. Regulatory completeness is important.

Regional cooperation agreements

Regional trade and regional economic cooperation agreements should also find a way of dealing with the harmonization of standards. The harmonization of standards and the organization of inspection services would help all countries in the region to move towards higher standards in a cost effective manner. It may also provide a useful avenue for challenging standards which may be considered unreasonable.

Technology, Innovation and Enterprise Development

Innovation can be in the form of new methods for processing and packaging, with greater emphasis given to environment-friendly inputs. The very use of new products or processes can cut cost and make the product more competitive in the market.

Funds for this could come from an active search for development funds for such purposes, or from alliances between public and private universities in the case of testing facilities. If this is not possible, private enforcing schemes could be sought as an alternative. What is more important is close cooperation between producers and national public agencies. This is absolutely necessary not only when seeking compliance with international standards, but also when fighting against unfair interpretations and practices.

Often branding and gaining brand recognition can prevent onerous checks at the border. Developing countries should strive for this as a strategy for alleviating trade problems arising from SPS measures.

Small and Medium Enterprises

SMEs are unable to implement comprehensive SPS measures, such as getting their units accredited under the ISO 9000 series or the HACCP. They need specific measures such as technological support, support for investment in improving infrastructure and support for accreditation under ISO 9000/HACCP and other umbrella certification schemes.

It is also possible to explore the feasibility of umbrella certification for units which produce the same kind of food products and maintain the same level of food safety standards. This will reduce the cost of certification, since it only involves the periodic inspection of standards or procedures adopted by the firms. These are helpful in enhancing food safety, both in domestic and export markets.

Institutional Changes

Responding to environment- and health-related requirements, including SPS measures, requires institutional changes, such as:

- A national agency can be set up to coordinate studies, for example, on pesticide residue monitoring.

- A regional network of national laboratories can be established so that products which cannot be tested in one laboratory can be tested in another country in the same region.
- There can be effective and regular participation in the Codex Committee meetings of experts drawn from different areas of work.
- The Ministry of Agriculture should collect information on good agricultural practice (GAP) and submit it to the Codex and implement it to comply with HACCP at the farm level.
- Programmes may be formulated and implemented for the wider use of IPM/IDM technologies, especially in crops where excessive use of pesticides and chemicals has been prohibited.

MULTILATERAL LEVEL

More Transparent and Participatory Preparation of Standards

A participatory approach in the preparation of standards would benefit both importers and exporters. Forums like the Codex Alimentarius Commission, the International Office of Epizootics and the Secretariat of the International Plant Protection Convention are engaged in the preparation of universal standards, sampling and analytical methods, the levels of permitted contamination and so on.

Specific recommendations for this area are:

- Ensure that all members are up to date in the fulfilment of notifications.
- All comments on standards should be taken into account in the process of their formulation. Members should specifically respond to the countries which have raised objections to the standards.
- Develop a database of SPS rules and regulations that can have major impacts on trade.
- Notify the detailed methodology and risk assessment factors taken into account in determining standards.

Noting the problems, the Doha Declaration asserts that action should be taken on the basis of the following to increase the transparency of the measure:

- Where the appropriate level of SPS protection does not leave scope for the phased introduction of a new measure, but specific problems are identified by a Member applying the measure, they shall, upon request, enter into consultations with the importing country to find a mutually satisfactory solution to the problem, while continuing to achieve the desired level of protection;

- Subject to the conditions specified in paragraph 2 of Annex B to the Agreement on the Application of SPS Measures, the phrase 'reasonable interval' shall be understood to mean normally a period of not less than 6 months. It is understood that time frames for specific measures have to be considered in the context of the particular circumstances in which the measure is being applied and the actions necessary to implement it. The entry into force of measures that contribute to the liberalization of trade should not be unnecessarily delayed.

When the first report on these initiatives was presented, the three sisters, that is, the Codex Alimentarius Commission, the OIE and the IPPC, informed members that more and more developing countries were participating in the process, though their number was still small. One of the problems was that the work of the organizations was not relevant to developing countries. Their participation is still below the representative level. According to the Codex, infrastructural constraints at the national level for the evaluation of draft standards, as well as the cost of travel, inhibited the proactive participation of developing countries. Effective TA programmes are required to remove these constraints. These measures would be really successful if developing countries moved from being standard-takers to standard-setters.

Trade Rules and International Standard-Setting Processes

In addition, as far as Articles 3.1 and 12.4 are concerned, there is need to better define international standards:

- The SPS Committee should be encouraged to develop a set of rules that the relevant international body should adhere to in keeping with Article 3 of the Agreement.
- If the participation of developing countries is inadequate, the Codex Commission should conduct a clinical study in developing countries before establishing standards, especially with respect to contaminants, pesticides, animal diseases and so on. The SPS committee must also evaluate what steps have been taken to ensure the effective participation of developing country members.
- The ISO and the Codex follow different standard-formulation processes and the SPS committee should study this. In both cases, standards should take into account the prevailing level of technological and socio-economic development and trade.
- Only consensus based decisions should be adopted.

- Efforts should be made to minimize the increasing politicization of standards and the pressure of lobbies by ensuring a more broad based participation in standard-setting.[6]

Technical Assistance under Trade Rules

Special and differential provisions under Article 10 should be implemented by making them more specific and mandatory. An examination of the steps taken by developed country members in providing technical assistance is called for. Studies, such as this one, on identifying market access barriers arising from such measures should also be fed into the technical assistance mechanisms.

The provisions of Article 9 should be translated into specific measures and guidelines that can be easily implemented. Measures for transferring technology on preferential and non-commercial terms for preparing and adopting standards should be explored. Article 9 should, therefore, make reference to the upgrading of personnel and equipment of laboratories, certification bodies and accreditation institutions and to strengthening the ability of developing countries to deal with scientific issues, especially those related to risk assessment and to the recognition of pest- or disease-free areas and areas of low pest or low disease prevalence.[7]

The provisions of Article 9 of the SPS Agreement, that is, technical assistance for developing countries, need to be codified for utilization by developing countries. Technical assistance must be extended on the science of measures and not merely to educate developing countries on the measures. The connection should be made between credits, donations and grants and the ability of developing countries to establish necessary infrastructure facilities.

The Doha Ministerial Declaration urged the Director General of the WTO:

- to coordinate with financial institutions in identifying SPS-related technical assistance needs and how best to address them;
- to continue his cooperative efforts, including with a view to according priority to the effective participation of least developed countries and facilitating the provision of technical and financial assistance for this purpose.

Equivalence under Trade Rules

Article 4.1 should clearly spell out equivalency. In this context, the setting up of internationally financed regional and sub-regional laboratories and certification bodies and accreditation institutions in developing countries should be included in this Article. These institutions would function under the supervision of the Codex, the OIE and the IPPC. Moreover, mutual recognition of conformity assessment and certification procedures should be pursued to avoid conflicting interpretations with respect to standards. Some of these concerns about equivalence have been reflected in the Doha Ministerial Declaration. In particular, the declaration

> takes note of the Decision of the Committee on Sanitary and Phytosanitary Measures (G/SPS/19) regarding equivalence, and instructs the Committee to develop expeditiously the specific programme to further the implementation of Article 4 of the Agreement on the Application of Sanitary and Phytosanitary Measures.

Special Measures for LDCs

For LDCs, such as Bangladesh, Nepal, Uganda, the United Republic of Tanzania and Mozambique, special measures are necessary. Full implementation of SPS measures should be sensitive to the trade-disruptive and the trade-restrictive nature of such measures for exports from the LDCs; adequate preparatory measures must be ensured in the exporting countries prior to the imposition of any penalty on their exports; adequate financial and technical assistance should be given to the LDCs to facilitate conformity with SPS requirements; the nexus between trade and aid should be strengthened; programmes under the Integrated Framework Initiative, which envisages technical assistance for trade-related capacity building in the LDCs, should be adequately funded and supported.

In this context, the Doha Declaration urged Members:

- to provide, to the extent possible, the financial and technical assistance necessary to enable least developed countries to respond adequately to the introduction of any new SPS measures which may have significant negative effects on their trade;
- to ensure that technical assistance is provided to least developed countries with a view to responding to the special problems faced by them in implementing the Agreement on the Application of Sanitary and Phytosanitary Measures.

RECOMMENDATIONS FOR FURTHER WORK

Recommendation for further work include the following:

- The UNDP offices in several South Asian countries have shown keen interest in collaborating with UNCTAD on the issue of SPS and environmental measures. The results of this report could be used to formulate useful strategies to meet SPS standards in different regions.

- The IDRC could use the results of this project in its national and regional offices, especially to pursue further work on regional and national strategies to meet the SPS standards.
- The results of the project could also be submitted to the Committee on SPS and TBT.
- International and national standard-setting bodies, as well as international organizations such as the FAO and UNIDO, could further develop work programmes on the basis of some of the recommendations outlined by this project.
- Further studies, focusing on environmental requirements, could be undertaken.
- Assistance could be given to developing countries to strengthen their capacities for research on issues of standards and the promotion of policy dialogues. This would, in turn, identify national and regional strategies to strengthen capacities to respond to SPS and environmental measures and take advantage of new trading opportunities for environmentally preferable products. This could be done in the context of the UNCTAD-FIELD project and the CBTF.
- Activities could be undertaken in the context of the UNCTAD programme on 'Technical assistance and capacity building for developing countries, especially LDCs, and economies in transition in support of their participation in the WTO post-Doha work programme' (UNCTAD/RMS/TCS/1). The programme contains a specific 'window' on environment, including on environmental/SPS requirements and market access for developing countries, particularly LDCs.

ANNEX 1: ENVIRONMENTAL MEASURES

Technical standards (which are voluntary) and regulations (which are mandatory), as well as SPS measures, are the most frequent forms of non-tariff barriers to trade. Environmental standards and regulations refer, for example, to:

- product content (limit values for certain substances)
- banned substances
- recycled content
- emissions
- energy efficiency
- recyclability, degradability and/or other product characteristics.

Labelling requirements are also increasingly used for environmental purposes. Labelling requirements can be mandatory or voluntary (for example, eco-labelling).

Import licences and quantitative restrictions are normally used to implement measures pursuant to multilateral environmental agreements, in particular the CITES, the Basel Convention and the Montreal Protocol. Import bans have also been implemented pursuant to recommendations by the International Commission for the Conservation of Atlantic Tunas (ICCAT).

Product taxes and charges can be based on some characteristic of the product (such as on the sulphur content in mineral oil) or on the product itself (for example, mineral oil). Product charges may be imposed with two aims: (a) to raise revenues and/or (b) to discourage the production and consumption of products on which the tax is levied.

Packaging regulations can include any of the measures mentioned above. The case studies make some reference to packaging requirements concerning fishery products and tea.

Informal (non-government) requirements can play an important role. These include, for example, buyers' requirements, including supply-chain management by transnational corporations (TNCs) and supermarket chains, as well as NGO actions.

The WTO Environmental Database

Useful information on environment-related measures or provisions can be found in the WTO Environmental Database (EDB).[8] This database constitutes a list of environment-related measures or provisions that were notified under the WTO agreements.

It should, nevertheless, be noted that notifications give only a limited picture of environmental measures with a potential impact on developing countries' exports, for the following reasons:

- measures based on international standards do not need to be notified to the WTO;
- notifications only cover *new* measures and provisions or *changes* in existing ones, not the stock of existing measures and provisions;
- certain environmental measures may not be notified to the WTO; for example, voluntary measures are subject to less stringent notification provisions than mandatory measures.

This section draws on the most recent WTO report (WT/CTE/W/195), which lists notifications in 2000 as well as environment-related measures, provisions or programmes in the Trade Policy Reviews carried out in 2000.[9] The report shows six categories of border trade measures, that is, measures notified under the Agreements on the TBT, the SPS, Import Licensing and the Safeguards and Customs Valuation (see Table 8.1). Most of these notifications have been issued under the TBT and SPS Agreements.[10]

Table 8.1   Notifications on environment-related border trade measures (2000)

	Notifications related to the environment	Total number of notifications	Share of environment-related notifications (%)
TBT	97	639	15.2
SPS	27	468	5.8
Import licensing	14	70	20.0
Quantitative restrictions	5		
Safeguards	1	87	1.1
Customs valuation	3	36	8.3

With regard to notifications under the SPS Agreement, the WTO secretariat recognizes that it is a matter of judgement whether or not to treat certain SPS measures as environment-related measures. In 2000, 468 notifications were issued under the SPS Agreement. Measures taken for the safety and protection of human, animal and plant health have not been included in the environmental database. The WTO included 27 SPS notifications, considered to be directly related to the environment, in the database.

Among the 651 notifications circulated pursuant to the TBT Agreement in 2000, environment was mentioned as the main objective or one of the objectives of 97 notifications. The share of environment-related notifications was 15.6 per cent of the total notifications in 2000. Environment-related notifications have been steadily increasing over the years, as illustrated in Table 8.2.[11]

With regard to import licensing requirements for environmental purposes, 14 out of 17 notifications submitted under the Agreement on Import Licensing Procedures (ILP) referred to measures in accordance with multilateral environmental agreements, such as the Basel Convention, the Montreal Protocol on Ozone-Depleting Substances and the Convention on International Trade in Endangered Species (CITES).

Safeguard measures invoking environmental objectives are rare. The database on environment-related notifications issued in 2000 nevertheless contains one notification under the Agreement on Safeguards.

Among the notifications pursuant to the Decision on Notification Procedures for Quantitative Restrictions (QRs), five pertained to the environment. These notifications listed import prohibitions, quantitative restrictions

Table 8.2   Notifications to the TBT Agreement (2000)

Year	Number of environment-related notifications	Total number of notifications	Percentage of environment-related notifications
1980–1990	211	2687	7.8
1991–2000	610	5322	11.5
1980–2000	821	8009	10.2
1991	35	358	9.7
1992	36	394	9.1
1993	42	487	8.6
1994	35	508	6.9
1995	41	365	10.6
1996	53	460	11.5
1997	89	794	11.2
1998	98	648	15.1
1999	84	669	12.5
2000	97	639	15.2

or non-automatic licensing for ozone depleting substances, endangered plants and animals and used vehicles under Article XX of the GATT.

Among the 36 notifications made under Article 22.2 of the Agreement on Implementation of Article VII of the GATT 1994 (Customs Valuation) in 2000, three notifications pertained to the environment.

ANNEX 2: ORGANIC PRODUCTS

Characteristics of the Sector

Regional studies estimate that in Central America there were approximately 42 thousand hectares under, or in the process of shifting to, organic production in the year 2000. The largest area was in Guatemala (35 per cent), followed by Costa Rica and Nicaragua (*El Financiero*, 17 June 2001). The organic movement is widely supported by aid agencies and NGOs, but until recently did not receive significant support from governments. At times, organic agriculture is supported in the context of 'fair-trade' initiatives. Some fair-trade organizations claim that up to 80 per cent of the products (for example, coffee) they buy from poor farmers is organic certified.[12]

Since small producers have developed organic agriculture in an unsystematic manner, there is no strategy to promote a major agrarian reconversion process. Governmental actions have been limited to isolated efforts by some departments or officials. Thus, there has been a shortage of mechanisms to support producers in areas such as research, access to specific markets, financing, training, choice of better techniques and certification and verification mechanisms, which could permit consolidation of organic agriculture as a fully viable option. Support has come primarily from NGOs[13] such as HIVOS (Humanistisch Institue voor Ontwikkelingssamenwerking), OXFAM and Pan Para El Mundo, through the promotion of partnerships as well as other forms of cooperation with small-scale farmers, financial assistance for certification and support for legislation in the different Central American countries.

Costa Rica has taken a lead in the development of organic agriculture, although the sector is not yet fully consolidated.[14] The area under organic production or in the process of conversion is approximately 9600 hectares or 1.9 per cent of the total area under permanent cultivation. As much as 94 per cent of the certified farms are less than 5 hectares in area. There are more than 4000 organic producers and approximately 135 organizations of organic producers. Small producers, therefore, play a key role in advancing organic agriculture.

Recently, the government and other stakeholders have become more actively involved in promoting organic production and exports.

National Organic Standards and Regulations

In Costa Rica, the publication of the Environmental Law (No. 7574) in 1995 provided a legal basis for organic farming. This law establishes the general framework for organic production and certification, defining the role of the State in its promotion, research and control. The National Program of Organic Agriculture was established in 1995 within the Ministry of Agriculture and Livestock (MAG). The 1997 Phytosanitary Law (No. 7664) further lays down the requirements for the registration of operators, inspectors and inspection bodies, as well as the process for certification and approval of inspection bodies.

Organic Certification

Inspection bodies are approved according to comprehensive legislation, in accordance with 4501/ISO 65 standards and supervised by the competent authority. Certification agencies must be accredited by the MAG in order to carry on their activities. The requirement that a product that is certified locally must be also certified in the country of destination forces them to establish alliances with other certification agencies in those countries. Since they are in the initial stages of certification processes in the country, there are only very few certification agencies that have been registered and are accredited to provide these services in Costa Rica.

Eco-Logica, the first local organic certification agency, is fully recognized by the MAG. It has certified close to 3000 producers, as well as 23 projects involving around 3500 producers. Eco-Logica has established strategic alliances with foreign certifiers such as QAI (Quality Assurance International–USA), OTCO (Oregon Tilth Certified Organic–USA) and EcoCert (France). These alliances are being used as a mechanism to access foreign markets, as Eco-Logica is not yet internationally recognized. Certification requirements have been established in accordance with the guidelines of the Oregon Tilth Certified Company and have been adapted to the agro-ecological and socio-economic conditions present in Costa Rica.

Eco-Logica provides services of inspection and certification of proceedings related to the production of all agricultural goods. It is also authorized to provide inspection services for QAI, Oregon Tilth and EcoCert.

Cost of Certification

One of the major constraints on organic farming in developing countries is the certification cost, which can be prohibitive for small producers. There is a clear consciousness among producers that certification is necessary to be able to sell in international organic markets, but they are also concerned that in the absence of stable market conditions, certification can become an important economic barrier.[15] The producer not only has to pay the fee for registering his productive unit as organic, but also has to pay a certification fee.[16]

Certification is provided by private certification entities, both national and foreign. Its costs depend primarily on the size and location of the farm, and on the quality of the information provided by the producer.[17] Certification bodies may charge small producers less than they charge bigger ones. A local certification agency, Eco-Logica, has the support of HIVOS in order to provide economic support for the producers.[18]

To export organic products multiple certifications may be required. For example, production has to be certified with an accredited national certification agency and with another agency, depending on the country of destination.

Certification and associated costs may be a major problem for small producers. Different alternatives can be explored to address this problem. In the United States, for example, producers whose sales amount to less than $5000 per year can produce a sworn statement in which they assure the fulfilment of organic certification requirements, without being compelled to obtain the certification itself. Retailers and farmers who offer a product with less than 70 per cent organic ingredients are also excluded from certification requirements.

Promoting the organization of groups among small and medium scale farmers can help to make the transformation period more expeditious and at the same time it can enhance mutual benefits, such as lower certification costs.

Currently, each certification body has its own principles, requirements and guidelines for certification. In addition, governments are increasingly implementing regulations for organic production. Producers themselves believe that the main task is to define standards and organic agriculture certification schemes that secure product quality and the integrity of organic guarantee systems, at the same time ensuring that import procedures and certification/accreditation do not adversely affect either the producer or the consumer.[19]

Efforts to be Included in the EU 'equivalent third country' List (Article 11.1)

European Union regulations stipulate that imported products can be deemed organic only if they have been produced in accordance with the rules for organic production and are subject to inspection measures that are equivalent to the EU organic regulations. Article 11 of Regulation 2092/91/EEC opens two ways to export organic products to the European Union. Paragraph 1 establishes a 'third-country' list, indicating countries with which equivalence is established. Paragraph 6 determines that organic products from countries which are not on the 'third-country' list can be marketed in the EU provided the importer submits documentation to confirm that the products are produced and certified according to rules equivalent to those of the EU. Such authorization shall be valid only as long as these conditions are shown to be satisfied. Commission Regulation (EC) No. 1788/2001 of 7 September 2001 defines detailed rules regarding the certificate of inspection for imports from third countries under Article 11.6. For each consignment the approved authority or inspection body in the third country from where the goods are exported must produce an original 'certificate of inspection for import of products from organic production'.

To export organic products to the EU market, paragraph 11.1 clearly offers much easier conditions than paragraph 11.6. However, currently only six countries (among them Argentina) are on the 'third-country' list. Over 70 developing countries, including Central American countries, export under Article 11.6.

Costa Rica has taken steps to be included in the 'third-country' list. This would bring important advantages in terms of predictability and costs of exporting organic agricultural products.

In this connection, an EU inspection team visited Costa Rica in 2000. Some key findings were:[20]

- The minimum requirements for organic farming laid down in Costa Rican legislation are, in general, equivalent to Council Regulation (EEC) No. 2092/91.
- The structure of the organic farming inspection and supervision system in Costa Rica is well developed, in spite of being rather recent. It is supported by comprehensive legislation.
- The inspection bodies are approved according to EN 4501/ISO 65 standards and supervised by the competent authority.
- Most of the producers are organized in groups.
- The global control of the organic system still shows some weaknesses and lack of consistency, partially due to the short accumulated experience.
- Parallel production is allowed in Costa Rica, unlike in the EU.

The EU team recommended the following:

- The Costa Rican authorities should take appropriate measures to address certain inadequacies of the inspection system, in particular those concerning parallel production, the national list of registered producers and processors and the competent authority's monitoring and supervision of organic production and exports.
- The Costa Rican authorities should make sure that inspection bodies set appropriate rules for group inspection and certification and should verify their application in order to guarantee the reliability and effectiveness of the control system.
- The European Commission should include Costa Rica in the equivalent third-country list under Article 11(1) of Council Regulation (EEC) No. 2092/91, provided that the Costa Rican authorities inform the Commission of the action taken and that the recommendations have been adequately followed.

Harmonization of Organic Food Regulations

Trade in organic food and the growth in organic agricultural production are hampered by the lack of harmonized regulations among potential trading partners. The adoption of international guidelines is an important first step in providing a harmonized approach to regulations in the organic food sector, thus facilitating trade in organic food,[21] but further efforts are needed. Arrangements for mutual recognition of national guarantee systems will reduce uncertainty regarding standards and the use of labels for imported organic products, protect the interests of consumers and producers and facilitate international trade.

Conclusions

It has been proposed that the Central American countries redefine and update the operational methods of the agricultural business, aiming to substitute the already obsolete 'poor agriculture' scheme by a 'new agriculture' approach that focuses on markets, information, innovation, differentiation and productivity.[22] Further incorporation of environmental considerations into production and marketing can improve the competitive edge and increase the agricultural sector's potential as a generator of sustainable economic development.[23]

However, for organic agriculture to become a viable alternative to agricultural production there is a need to develop a proper support system. Since there are no direct financial support strategies for organic farming, technological transfer, access to markets, training, access to financial sources, a proper legal framework, adequate certification mechanisms and appropriate political direction need to be developed.

Costa Rica does not have state-supported mechanisms in place that may benefit organic over conventional production. Conventional agriculture has an advantage over organic: there are benefits granted for the importation of some agrochemicals for agriculture.[24] Organic producers, on the other hand, must incur additional expenses to sell their products, such as registration, certification, and increased control and administration costs, for which they receive little or no compensation. The national regulations on organic agriculture do not mention economic incentive mechanisms. Consequently, the cost of the certification process becomes a significant burden for organic producers. The irony of this is that the cost of certification acts as a tax that must be paid by anyone who decides to change his production to organic.

As a result of a national non-traditional export promotion drive in the 1980s, agricultural production diversified into new products, but with the same old philosophy of the green revolution, using more and more synthetic agrochemical inputs. This transition was strongly subsidized for 15 years, but only to promote exports. The renewed demand for safe and healthy food, as well as for safer working conditions in the agricultural sector, provides opportunities for organic agriculture. But most organic producers in Central America are small farmers with little knowledge of the exporting process and with no price premiums in the domestic market. There is an urgent need to develop policies in this connection, especially regarding subsidies or incentives to promote the transition to organic agriculture. The farmers need favourable credit conditions, support in the transition period and low cost certification alternatives. In addition, Costa Rica has to develop a national commitment to develop long-term policies in order to consolidate organic production. Government action is often taken only when a severe problem arises (such as the restructuring of loans in sectors severely affected by low international prices or lack of competitiveness in the domestic market). With the growth of the organic sector in quantitative and qualitative terms, a national strategy is expected to bring about some improvements in national priorities and policies.

NOTES

1. This chapter is based on the recommendations in all the studies covered by the project.
2. See scoping papers for South Asia, Central America and Africa in Chapters 3–5.
3. Case study on spices in South Asia, [pp. 108–17].
4. Case study on horticultural products in Kenya, [pp. 188–93].
5. Case study on fisheries in Central America, [pp. 144–65].
6. See ICTSD, *Bridges between Trade and Sustainable Development*, first issue, 2000.
7. Ibid.
8. The EDB was established in 1998 (see WT/CTE/3) in fulfilment of the recommendation in the 1996 Report of the CTE to the Singapore Ministerial Conference (WT/CTE/1) for the Secretariat to compile and update annually all environment-related notifications to the WTO.
9. WTO, Environmental Database for 2000, note by the Secretariat, WT/CTE/W/195, 20 June 2001.
10. Environment-related notifications were also issued in 2000, under the agreements on subsidies (32), agriculture (40) and TRIPS (5). Most of the notifications on regional trade agreements (RTAs) also included provisions relating to environment. However, these notifications did not refer to border measures and are therefore less relevant in the context of this paper. No environment-related measures or provisions were found in notifications under the WTO agreements on anti-dumping, state trading, GATS, balance of payments, textiles and clothing, preshipment inspection, rules of origin, government procurement or information technology.
11. These include notifications on organic agriculture.
12. See the case of TransFair in www.transfairusa.org
13. Amador, Manuel, *Comercialización de productos orgánicos en la región centroamericana*, research done for IICA, 2001.
14. Manuel, Amador (Interview, July 2001) recognizes that the region lacks sufficient legislation and regulations that may help consolidate the organic sector and that there is a general shortage of basic information regarding production systems, certification and its importance. Local markets are practically non-existent.
15. Ibid. Also interview with Pedro Cussianovich.
16. According to people from APROCAM, an organic blackberry company, they have paid between $3000 and $10 000 yearly for the certification.
17. Geovanny Delgado, general manager of Eco-Logica, (interviewed on 23 July 2001) stated that the fixed cost is $175 annual, plus $100 for each day in the field and a percentage of 0.5% on annual sales. The daily cost is increased by travel, lodging and other expenditures. In general terms, the basic cost for the producer may be $425. If done in groups, as proposed, the cost could be less. In some cases the buyer pays the certification costs.
18. Delgado, Geovanny, ibid.
19. Solano, Carlos, *Memoria: Simposio Nacional de Agricultores (as) Orgánicos y Opciones para el Desarrollo Alternativo*. VECO-COSTA RICA-PNUD – CEDECO-COPROALDE-MNC-PAN PARA EL MUNDO. 1st ed. San José, 2001.

20. European Commission, Health and Consumer Protection Directorate-General, Final Report on a mission carried out in Costa Rica from 6 to 10 November 2000, in the field of Organic Farming in Costa Rica.
21. International Federation of Organic Agriculture Movements (IFOAM) Basic Standards provide a framework for certification bodies and standardizing organizations worldwide to develop their own certification standards. The Codex Alimentarius Commission has developed guidelines for the production, processing, labelling and marketing of organically produced goods. See Codex Alimentarius, 'Guidelines for the Production, Processing, Labeling and Marketing of Organically Produced Foods', GL 32 – 1999. See also http://www.fao.org/es/esn/codex/STANDARD/standard.htm
22. INCAE.HARVARD (1999), Centroamérica en el Siglo XXI, Bases para la discusión sobre et futuro de la region, una agenda para la competitividad y el desarrollo sostenible.
23. Ibid.
24. In Costa Rica pesticides have been subject to negligible import duties. There is a significant amount of product expressly exonerated from duties. The Agricultural Production Act No. 7064 has a specific chapter dedicated to incentives for conventional agricultural producers. See the Regulations of the General Sales Tax Law, no. 14082-H. According to Chapter 3 (Exemptions), agricultural inputs, including pesticides, are exempted from the tax.

Index